STEVEN J. STEINBERG ■ SHEILA L. STEINBERG
Humboldt State University   Humboldt State University

GIS

GEOGRAPHIC INFORMATION SYSTEMS FOR THE SOCIAL SCIENCES
Investigating Space and Place

SAGE Publications
Thousand Oaks ■ London ■ New Delhi

For information:

Sage Publications, Inc.
2455 Teller Road
Thousand Oaks, California 91320
E-mail: order@sagepub.com

SAGE Publications Ltd
1 Oliver's Yard
55 City Road
London EC1Y 1SP
United Kingdom

Sage Publications India Pvt. Ltd.
B-42, Panchsheel Enclave
Post Box 4109
New Delhi 110 017 India

Printed in the United States of America

Library of Congress Cataloging-in-Publication Data

Steinberg, Steven J.
Geographic information systems for the social sciences : investigating space and place / Steven J. Steinberg and Sheila L. Steinberg.
      p. cm.
Includes bibliographical references and index.
ISBN 0-7619-2872-3 (cloth) — ISBN 0-7619-2873-1 (pbk.)
   1. Social sciences—Research—Methodology. 2. Geographic information systems.
3. Spatial analysis (Statistics) I. Steinberg, Sheila L. II. Title.
H62.S7542 2006
300′.285—dc22

                                                    2005007114

This book is printed on acid-free paper.

05   06   07   08   09   10   9   8   7   6   5   4   3   2   1

Acquisitions Editor:	Lisa Cuevas Shaw
Editorial Assistants:	Margo Crouppen and Karen Gia Wong
Production Editor:	Kristen Gibson
Copy Editor:	Cheryl Duksta
Typesetter:	C&M Digitals (P) Ltd.
Cover Designer:	Edgar Abarca

GIS

GEOGRAPHIC INFORMATION
SYSTEMS FOR THE SOCIAL SCIENCES

To our son, Joshua

Contents_____

List of Boxes, Figures, and Tables _____

Preface _____

This book introduces the application of geographic information systems
(GIS) as an analytical tool for the social sciences. Although GIS technology is not new to the social sciences, it is only recently that it has gained
wider recognition as a valuable tool for the practitioner as well as the
researcher in these fields. GIS software has become both more affordable
and easier to use, which has led to wider acceptance of the technology, not
only in traditional areas such as geography and demography but also in
areas as wide ranging as anthropology, social services, public heath, community and regional planning, sociology, and various other social science
disciplines. It is a technology that is becoming increasingly more popular in
local, regional, and state planning efforts related to community planning,
social services, and public health, among others. In fact, the value of GIS and
spatial analysis techniques in almost any social science discipline is limited
only by the creativity of the people interested in its application to their own
work.

As we write this book, GIS training and coursework continue to become
more widely available at a variety of levels, including high schools, universities, and community colleges, as well as in GIS users groups. Although this
book introduces the underlying theory and application, it is not intended as
a manual for GIS software. It is a companion to assist you in understanding
the capabilities of GIS and approaches to using GIS in your own social science applications. It is a book to help the non-GIS expert to conceptually
understand how to use GIS. An additional, unique aspect of this book is that
we focus specifically on how to integrate GIS into qualitative research. This
book does not focus on the command details of a specific GIS software package. Instead, it presents the wide array of analytical design and analysis
methods that can be used with the GIS software you choose. We allow readers flexibility in their choice of GIS software, ranging from free GIS applications to commercially available products.

It is important to realize that because GIS is an ever-evolving technology
and because there are dozens of companies producing GIS software, there is
no way we can even begin to cover all possible operations, commands, and

capabilities of the technology in a text of this nature. Instead, our goal is to provide readers an introduction to many of the basic concepts and steps necessary in completing a GIS analysis for social science. You should not consider this a comprehensive text of everything possible with GIS: There are more concepts and commands available in a high-powered GIS system than any one person could possibly hope to master. Rather, most GIS professionals tend to focus on those aspects of GIS most applicable to the work they do, typically using only a small fraction of the power of the software system at any one time.

We encourage you to use this text as a springboard into your exploration of GIS and how it can be used to perform the types of analysis that interest you. We discuss the basic considerations necessary in planning and carrying out your own GIS analysis. Because GIS is an ever-changing technology, it is not unusual for many of the specific commands, menus, and tools available in any particular software to change, improve, and be modified as new versions of the GIS software are released. This typically results in multiple possible approaches to accomplish any given task.

We hope you find this book a valuable addition to your exploration of GIS applications in the social sciences and welcome your feedback and suggestions. We encourage you to visit our Web site (http://www.socialsciencegis. org) to become part of a growing online community of social science GIS practitioners. As a companion to the book, our Web site provides a forum for communication and exchange, analysis examples, sample data sets, and links to other relevant Web sites. The site also provides visitors a place to share their own ideas, suggestions, and examples as they incorporate GIS tools in their work.

Organization of This Book

This text is organized into 10 chapters, each beginning with a brief description followed by lists of primary chapter objectives and outcomes. At the ends of several chapters, we include Web sites and reading suggestions as appropriate to the topics in that chapter. The presentation sequence of topics is appropriate to readers with little or no experience with GIS and related map analysis concepts and research design. However, readers with more experience may wish to skip some chapters or approach them in a different sequence. Each chapter is written to stand largely independent of the others. In those places where knowledge of material elsewhere in the book is important, we provide a reference to the relevant chapter or section.

Key terms that may be new or less familiar to readers are included in a glossary at the end of the book. An index to major topics is also provided for readers seeking information about specific items.

Chapter Summaries

A brief summary of each chapter follows.

Introduction

This section sets the stage for GIS in the social sciences. It includes social science examples to assist readers new to GIS in understanding the value of spatial analysis in addressing social science questions.

Chapter 1: Introduction to GIS

This chapter introduces, defines, and explains three primary components and associated concepts common to any GIS, including appropriate examples relevant to social science research methods. The chapter serves as a foundation for later sections of the text. We illustrate the versatility and wide-ranging applicability of GIS.

Chapter 2: GIS Basics

This is a chapter on fundamental GIS theory and concepts. It also covers the essential material regarding the use of GIS for analysis. The chapter begins with an example of spatial data analysis to give readers an understanding of how GIS applies to areas of research they may be engaged in. The chapter then provides guidance in developing questions one might examine using GIS and how to begin formulating those questions. This is followed by a discussion of the common GIS data models. The chapter concludes with a discussion of geographic and mapping concepts essential to proper data analysis and presentation of results in GIS.

Chapter 3: Topics for Sociospatial Research

In this chapter, we explore how incorporating a spatial context into your investigation can enhance your analysis by providing additional insights and information not previously considered. We first explore approaches for defining goals of a project and, in doing so, determining if GIS analysis techniques will enhance the outcome. The chapter includes sections on developing project goals and approaches, including relevant examples that explore the potential of spatial analysis as a part of social science research. We also include suggestions for the application of these approaches when locating or collecting data for your own research. These examples illustrate how common data types can be tied to the spatial realm of the GIS.

Chapter 4: Research Design

This chapter explores the primary steps in narrowing the purpose of your sociospatial analysis and the approach to be taken. We begin with a discussion of important factors related to developing a research design and analysis, including key stages of the research process and examples using the spatial perspective provided by GIS. We also examine different approaches to operationalization and consider several common pitfalls of research design. The chapter concludes with a section on research ethics and approaches to ensuring confidentiality and accuracy when using spatially linked data in GIS.

Chapter 5: Qualitative Research Methods and GIS

This chapter offers a discussion of how GIS can be integrated with various forms of qualitative research. Some of the specific forms of qualitative research that are addressed include grounded theory, participant observation, ethnography, and oral histories. This chapter provides a concrete discussion of sociospatial grounded theory research, including seven specific steps for the integration of GIS into one's research. Coding and analysis of spatial qualitative data are also discussed.

Chapter 6: GIS Data Collection and Development (Sources, Input, and Output)

This is a chapter on GIS data sources, including data from existing sources, including the Internet, as well as one's own data. We also discuss integration of other data types, including those not explicitly formatted for a GIS. We introduce fundamental concepts related to locating and organizing data for use in a GIS. A section on database fundamentals and organization is provided to assist readers who are not familiar with these concepts as they relate to GIS. Because GIS may be used for data development and storage and as an analysis tool, it will often be used in conjunction with other familiar tools, techniques, and software packages. A discussion of formatting and transferring data between sources is included. Finally, a section discussing the various outputs GIS offers is provided in the context of visual, variable, and statistical data outputs that are relevant to the analysis.

Chapter 7: Measurement

This chapter explores issues of data collection that may influence the selection of data variables for an analysis, including methods for the collection of both social and geographic parameters within the context of their appropriateness for analysis in a GIS. The chapter also examines data selection and level of measurement as they relate to the GIS database. Sampling approaches and the unit of analysis in data development and analysis are also discussed in the context of the selection of appropriate variables to best work within a spatial analysis. When choosing variables in a GIS, the social scientist must always be cognizant of the geographical links between spatial and social variables.

Chapter 8: Data Documentation and Model Development

This chapter provides a discussion of the ethical and practical reasons to ground truth data, an important research practice of checking the relevance and accuracy of data that are created, analyzed, or output from a GIS to minimize error. An introduction to data documentation standards (metadata) is also included here. Approaches to planning a GIS analysis and techniques for doing so (phases of abstraction) are included, using realistic examples that benefit via the addition of a spatial component. Examples are provided showing how researchers might enhance their view of data as having a valuable geographic element.

Chapter 9: Analysis, Interpretation, and Application

The focus of this chapter is the analysis of social science data using GIS, including the computer program to be used and the level of analysis. Approaches to carrying out the GIS analysis, and techniques for doing so, are included, using realistic examples that benefit via the addition of a spatial component. Examples are provided showing how researchers might enhance their view of data as having a valuable geographic element. We introduce numerous forms of analysis, including those that most commonly apply to analysis situations researchers are most likely encounter as they begin to use GIS technology. Major topics include buffers, overlays, networks, map algebra, and raster analysis as well as interpolation, simulation, and modeling. The chapter concludes with a discussion of some common pitfalls to be aware of in your analysis and interpretation of results.

Chapter 10: Future Opportunities
for Social Research and GIS

This chapter explores the important role that GIS can play in the toolbox of the social scientist. As a research tool in the social sciences, GIS has not been explored and applied to nearly the same depth relative to applications in the natural resource sciences, where the technology has a longer history. Current and future opportunities for the application of GIS in the social sciences are tremendous; the surface has just been scratched. As a means to analyze societal structure and change, GIS provides an additional and often unconsidered geographic variable in the mix of applied social science research. GIS has an extremely valuable role to play in assisting social science researchers in their quest to study issues such as inequality, social capital, crime, social services, and historic change, as well as many other societal issues. GIS also has great potential to incorporate and visualize the concerns, goals, and ideas of various stakeholder groups. This chapter presents opportunities to incorporate GIS as a tool for governments, service organizations, and community groups to examine and plan for their communities' needs and to improve their effectiveness in managing information. Finally, we present a brief discussion of some of the future directions of GIS, including a move toward common, open standards for spatial data and availability of open source software tools.

Acknowledgments

We would first like to thank Lisa Cuevas-Shaw, our editor at Sage Publications, for providing an in-depth review of our book as well as guidance and suggestions. It was a pleasure to work with Lisa, and we sincerely appreciated her positive encouragement throughout the writing process. We also want to thank Margo Crouppen for locating reviewers for the early versions of the text and for her helpful summaries of those reviews and suggestions for improving the book. Additionally, we owe a very special thank you to C. Deborah Laughton for her initial vision of the value of this book and her belief in its potential to make a valuable contribution to the social sciences. We also want to acknowledge Michael O. Gough for his assistance with the cover artwork and Doug Renwick of HostGIS for providing Web support for this text. Finally, we want to thank the reviewers of this book for their thoughtful feedback: Theresa K. Burcsu, University of Florida; Todd Fritch, Northeastern University; and Xun Shi, Dartmouth University.

Introduction

The headline on this morning's paper reads, "Westside Mugger Caught!" Given that this is the part of town you work in, you feel a great a sense of relief as you begin to read the article. A rash of muggings had taken place during the past few weeks; every couple of days another victim was attacked, and it seemed as though the assailant was always a step ahead of the police. You've always wondered how the police catch up with criminals, and as you read the story you come across a sentence that piques your interest: "'We never would have caught the person behind these attacks without our new CompStat system,' stated the chief of police." The article goes on to explain that CompStat is a computer-based analysis system built around crime statistics mapped in a geographic information system.

Interesting. You begin to wonder exactly what they mean by mapping crime statistics. How would that help catch a criminal? You've always found maps to be interesting, and they certainly help you find your way when traveling. You've even heard about those maps to the movie stars' homes you can buy in Hollywood, but you don't recall ever seeing a map to criminals' homes!

It turns out that the geographic information system behind CompStat wasn't exactly used to find the home of the criminal, but almost. The police took advantage of a variety of basic information, or data, about the area the crimes were occurring in, along with information about the locations of each of the muggings as they were reported. As the locations of the crimes were mapped, some interesting patterns began to develop.

For example, all of the muggings occurred within 2 blocks of an ATM machine. That seems sensible to you; the mugger might well have been targeting people who were getting cash. The attacks were always late in the evening, after 10:00 p.m., and the victims were always confronted on streets that had little traffic. What streets don't have lots of traffic at that time of night? Maybe residential areas where folks are in bed? Maybe. But wouldn't someone hear the commotion? More likely, the area is around the financial district, where everything closes at 5:00 p.m., and there's not a lot going on at night.

You start to realize that by looking at some basic map information you might be able to narrow down areas that meet a particular profile that seems to be developing. But as you think about it, you wonder, "Aren't there lots of areas in Westside where there's little activity in business districts at that time of night? And ATMs? It seems there's one on almost every corner.

What else could have helped the police to get the bad guy?" It turns out that all of the crimes also seemed to be clustered in a 10-block area. Perhaps the mugger lives near that area, or, better still, he probably lives near the middle of that area, so he didn't have to walk too far to find his victims; after all, aren't criminals lazy? That's why they steal rather than work!

Of course, the police know some other things that might have helped. Who do they know of in that area with a record for mugging, robbery, burglary, or other similar crimes? Are there any recent parolees living near there? Are there any other clues that match known offenders? Odds are this wasn't someone who woke up one day and decided to become a mugger—someone like this probably has a history!

So, as you ponder all this, you begin to understand how a system like CompStat would be helpful. Of course, if you could somehow put all of the data together on a map, defining areas that meet criteria such as those discussed earlier, you might be able to narrow the search area down to a manageable level. Sure, you might not come up with the criminal's home address, but you would certainly know where to put extra police on the beat to catch the criminal. But one thing still bothers you: the complexity of getting all of this information onto a map and doing the analysis to get to this point. Wouldn't that be a major task? It was hard enough for you to draw a readable map for your friends to find their way to your new apartment for your last Super Bowl party!

It must be that computer thing the police chief mentioned in the article, that geographic information system, that performs such a complex task. It all sounds very complicated! But you're intrigued and want to find out more about these geographic information systems. Maybe they could be useful in other ways. After all, if you can use them to narrow down locations of criminals, what other kinds of analysis might they be useful for?

The use of geographic information systems in applied social science research is what this book is about—not only for crime analysis, although that is one very valuable application. Geographic information systems, or GIS, can be useful in all kinds of social science applications. Public health, social services, community and economic development, social change, public planning processes, historical studies, and many other disciplines can benefit from the inclusion of mapped information as part of analyses. As a technology, GIS has been around for more than 40 years; however, it has only been in the last decade or so that it has made significant inroads in the social sciences.

This book introduces GIS technology as a tool for the social scientist. Whether you are an academic researcher, a student, or a person out there on the ground working in a social science field, this book is for you. The value of spatial relationships, patterns, and connections represented with maps have a long history in all of the disciplines clustered within the social sciences, but it is only more recently that we can take this information and put it all into a computer-analysis environment that understands and can analyze space in meaningful ways.

Although GIS is a relatively new tool, the concept of conducting a geographically based spatial analysis of social issues is fairly old. Past social science researchers from a variety of disciplines, such as anthropology, public health, history, political science, urban planning, geography, economics, and sociology, have incorporated spatial analysis into their social science research projects. Keep in mind that much of this incorporation of the geographically based spatial approach occurred prior to the existence of fancy computer programs that we now have today. In the following sections, we highlight just a few of these historic studies as examples.

Social Inequality in Chicago Slums

Florence Kelly is a name that should be a household name because of the social advocacy work Kelly accomplished during her lifetime. Kelly was a women's rights activist, a child labor law advocate, and one of the original founders of the National Association for the Advancement of Colored People (NAACP). Kelly was an original, applied researcher who sincerely believed in the power of research to help improve conditions in society.

Kelly's goal was to identify some of the areas where people were suffering and combine that information with the idea of improved social conditions. She ultimately created a map that indicated patterns of social conditions. Her idea was that the clear identification of the pockets of social inequality would lead to policies to help rectify these situations of social inequality.

In 1893, she used geographic analysis to map the "Slums of the Great Cities Survey Maps." Kelly was a resident of Chicago's famous Hull House, run by Jane Addams, which was a magnet for providing aid and social organizational skills to Chicago's poor. Kelly was chosen to lead a federally funded study to identify poverty in urban areas (Brown, 2004). The study involved interviewing all of the residents who lived near Hull House in Chicago and finding out whether they lived in tenements, rented rooms, or their own homes (Addams, 1895).

A very important aspect of this study was Kelly's recording of the geographic location of the respondents whom she interviewed. Kelly was unique in that she transferred much of the sociodemographic, employment, and housing data collected by individual households onto maps of the city to illustrate geographic patterns of poverty. She was a pioneer in integrating geographic variables into the study of social inequality. This was a very early application of spatial analysis techniques, albeit without the benefit of a GIS to study social inequality. Kelly believed that the scientific documentation of social inequalities could help lead to improved working and housing conditions for the poor. Thus, geographic location can be a very important factor to consider when studying social problems.

Today, researchers can employ the same approach, but the work would be much easier given the advances in GIS technology that have been made.

Railroads as Indicators of Civilized Society _____

Mark Jefferson is another early pioneer of geographic variables and spatial analysis in the study of social issues. In 1928, Jefferson, a geographer, conducted research in which he used the geographic concept of buffers to help analyze the influence of the railroad on settlement patterns in different societies. His study was unique because he operationalized the modernization or "civilization" of different societies based on the networks of rails (Jefferson, 1928). He attempted to analyze societies' levels of civilization based on proximity to railroad lines (Corbett, 2004). His assumption was that the networks of railroads were indicative of "civilized" society.

Jefferson drew buffer zones (mapping a 10-mile distance) around the railroads in different countries throughout the world (Jefferson, 1928). The notion of buffers was used to extend the examination of the geographic lines caused by the railroads. His use of buffers in the study helped people to understand the dual concept of where railroads both existed and did not exist (Arlinghaus, Goodman, & Jacobs, 2004). Buffering around the railroad tracks spread the width of the line, which assisted in mapping and comprehending the significant impact that railroads had on communal development and the "civilization" of societies.

Jefferson found that places that had more extensive railway systems were more "civilized" than places with fewer railway systems. Today, such a study would be viewed as ethnocentric and biased because it favors traits of development that are partial to Western societies (the railroad). Nevertheless, Jefferson was an early applied social scientist who adopted a creative approach to integrating geographic spatial variables into a social science study.

Early Social Ecology: Spatial Studies of Chicago _____

In 1925, Robert Park and Ernest Burgess conducted a series of research projects around spatial settlement patterns in the City of Chicago. They were both affiliated with the University of Chicago. They were early applied researchers in the field of urban ecology and were not content to conduct their research from within the confines of the university. Rather, they felt it important to actually go out into the social field and map the social and physical contexts that they were studying.

Park and Burgess's work centered on mapping ethnic communal patterns of settlement throughout the city. Their work was central to the development of the field of social ecology, which is described as the relationship between people and their social environment. They conceptualized much of the social and physical organization of Chicago as based on the competition between groups, which drove the geographical division of land use and space within a city (Brown, 2004). They used geographic spatial data of settlement patterns to study urban social groupings. Park and Burgess (Park, Burgess, & McKenzie, 1925) found that people grouped together shared similar social characteristics. Their analysis took physical ecological concepts and applied them to human settlement patterns in the cities.

Their work produced something know as the concentric zone theory. This theory was used to describe why certain groups geographically cluster and is based on the competition for good land (Schaefer, 2004). Their model ties land use to wealth and power. Social groups who possessed power and wealth tended to cluster in the more geographically desirable places in the city, whereas the poor were left to live in the geographically less desirable areas (Schaefer, 2004).

Their studies also applied ecological concepts such as succession and invasion to the study of ethnic population settlement and demographic patterns. This is a model that has since been adopted by many of today's researchers of urban communities.

This book is about doing analysis of social science data in a spatial context. We begin by introducing the concepts behind GIS and mapping. We discuss the processes of developing your research question and operationalizing variables. This is followed by a discussion of data, be it collecting your own or locating existing data necessary to conduct your analysis. Finally, we discuss processes for analyzing the data to get an answer that will be useful in informing hypothesis testing, decision making, social change, and city- or county-level planning decisions.

We hope this book sparks your interest in GIS and that you add it to your toolbox for social science research. GIS is a powerful technology and has much to offer. Like any new tool you encounter, GIS must be handled with care so as not to misuse it. But with a little patience and practice, GIS can serve you well and provide a whole new set of analytical capabilities that would otherwise be missing from your analytical toolbox.

Relevant Web Sites

Archives of the [New York City] Mayor's Press Office, May 13, 1997: This press release from the New York City Mayor's Office discusses the use of CompStat in reducing crime to its lowest level in 30 years. http://www.ci.nyc.ny.us/html/om/html/97/sp268–97.html

"CompStat: From Humble Beginnings, Baseline, September 9, 2002": This article is about the history and development of CompStat as a spatial analysis tool for crime. http://www.baselinemag.com/article2/0,1397,538007,00.asp

New York City Police Department: CompStat Process: This site describes how CompStat is incorporated into the processes of community-level crime analysis, enforcement planning, and prevention. http://www.nyc.gov/html/nypd/html/chfdept/compstat-process.html

1 Introduction to Geographic Information Systems

Chapter Description

This chapter introduces, defines, and explains three primary components and associated concepts common to any geographic information system (GIS), including appropriate examples relevant to social science research methods. The chapter serves as a foundation for the following sections of the text. We illustrate the versatility and wide-ranging applicability of GIS.

Chapter Objectives

- Present a working definition of a geographic information system.
- Demonstrate the use of GIS as a social science research method.
- Present examples showing how GIS can be used in social science research situations.

After reading this chapter, you should be able to perform the following tasks:

- Identify spatial perspectives in your own area of social science research.
- Present your own definition of a GIS.
- Understand how a GIS is different from other analysis environments you are familiar with.

What Is a Geographic Information System?

In its simplest form, a geographic information system (GIS) is a system designed to store, manipulate, analyze, and output map-based, or spatial, information. In practice, the functions of a GIS can be carried out by hand, using only paper,

Data Sheet

Survey Number: 294

Street Address: 325 Burnaby Court

City, State: Fraser, TX

Age of respondent: 37

Gender of respondent: Male

Highest level of education: B.A.

Number of adults living in household: 2

Profession of respondent: Stock Broker

Profession of other adults in household: Teacher

Annual Household Income: $86,000

Number of children under 18 in household: 3

Figure 1.1   Linking real-world locations to data via a GIS-compatible spatial reference. On the left is an example of a United States Geological Survey aerial photograph of a suburban location. This photo shows the world in much the same manner as you might see from the window of an airplane. When collecting data in this area—for example, via a mailed survey—you would have the option of retaining spatial information by recording something about the specific place the data were collected (e.g., street address, census block, neighborhood). On the right are tabular data that are associated with one such surveyed household, as recorded on a survey form. Used together, this spatial and tabular information would be useful in doing a GIS-based analysis.

pencil, and a ruler (a surprising number of people still do it this way!). Of course, this is not practical or efficient for many research applications.

When we refer to spatial information or data, we simply mean that the information is linked to a specific location, for example, a street address. Figure 1.1 provides an example of a real-life view of the world, as represented in an aerial photograph tied to the associated data about the world similar to what you might choose to collect or analyze. These tabular data are related to the world via its location, or spatial information.

Although there is no single universally agreed-on definition of a GIS, GIS professionals do agree on several general principles. First, a GIS requires a combination of computer hardware and software tools. Second, a GIS requires data, and these data must posses a spatial or location component. Third, a GIS requires knowledgeable individuals to develop the database and carry out the data processing. Most of these tasks can be accomplished by anyone with a little basic computer knowledge, which we discuss in this book. Although GIS software has become much easier to use since the introduction of graphical user interfaces, GIS programs and much of the underlying geographic theory require people to have a basic understanding of maps and map analysis. Last, and perhaps most important, a GIS is a system for analysis. That is, a GIS is useful for the examination, display, and output of information gleaned from the data that are stored and maintained in the system. The focus of this book is to provide you with the necessary understanding of mapping concepts and spatial analysis as well as the analytical approach needed to perform GIS-based research.

Understanding GIS

GIS are best understood by breaking down the terminology and developing an appreciation for the application of GIS to various analysis situations. In particular, how can a researcher's area of interest and the associated data be placed into a GIS context and how can GIS technology enhance the analysis and understanding of data? In the following sections, we review GIS in detail to establish a basis for successful use of GIS in applied social science research.

The "G" in GIS

The geographic component of GIS is simultaneously obvious, confusing, and difficult to get a handle on. From an early age, we all develop an understanding that the location of people and places can be marked on a map and, furthermore, that connections can be made between these locations. What we may not have is a good understanding of the scientific basis for mapping—that is, the numerous issues of scale, coordinates, control datums, and so forth. Even to those readers familiar with some of these concepts, very few, other than mapping professionals, have a deep conceptual understanding of the mathematical algorithms behind these concepts and the potential errors that result from various combinations and interactions of such data.

Fortunately, most of these underlying issues are addressed for us through the GIS software, so it is not essential to have a deep understanding of these concepts. What is important for you to understand is that there are a few concepts that will be important to pay attention to, even if you don't understand the intimate details of how they work. You can think of this as analogous to knowing the difference between VCRs and DVD players. You know these are different tools with different strengths and weaknesses, but selecting the right one does not require you to understand the intricate details of their function. What is important is that you know which format to ask for when you go to rent a movie at the local video shop so that the media selected fits the player you own.

In social science research, the value of the geographic context may not always provide an obvious research benefit. Many social science studies focus on social, economic, cultural, and survey data that have limited if any spatial question associated with them. For example, do pregnant women who are better educated or wealthier receive higher quality prenatal care? Perhaps the more telling question would be, where are the prenatal clinics located relative to available public transportation, child care, and so on? One might use census data to conduct a statistical analysis of census block groups and levels of prenatal care, but this analysis may miss an important location component. Often, when explored in conjunction with other map-based location information (e.g., where the blocks are located relative to other important components), a more complete understanding of the causative relationships can be obtained. Furthermore, from an applied standpoint, the geographic component can help in determining where to best locate and spend limited resources to help improve the situation.

In reality, almost all information researchers collect about people, their communities, and their environments can be tied to a geographic location. For example, we may survey people at their home address or by a geographic unit such as a census block or city of residence. All of these locations can be easily mapped to a location. Furthermore, if privacy is a concern, data may be aggregated to a larger geographic unit to mask specific, personal information. In short, if you can answer the question, "Where was the data collected?" then GIS is an appropriate means for storing and analyzing the data.

Difficulties With the "G"

The geographic context may be difficult to collect because determining the exact location of a piece of data on the ground is not always easy to accomplish or, for reasons of privacy, may not be permissible. When mapping people, we face an additional challenge: People move around, may be without a home, or otherwise may be difficult to tie to a particular location. However, because geographic data are the heart of the GIS, knowing a location of some kind is an essential part of the GIS process (even if it must be spatially degraded or detached from the exact, true location).

For example, if you were doing a study of homeless individuals, you might be better able to define their location at the level of a particular neighborhood they call home than you could a particular street address. Furthermore, even in studies where mappable locations are available, there may be privacy issues that necessitate degrading that information. In other words, even if you have specific addresses of your respondents, you might choose to degrade the data to census blocks, neighborhood, or even the city level to maintain privacy dictated in ethical research. Choosing the level of spatial detail (which is actually a scale question, as discussed in further detail in Chapter 2) is an important part of the GIS process.

Perhaps more difficult to map, though equally important in social research, are conceptually mapped features. Such features might include data about perceptions, ideas, or interactions. For example, social networks or interactions between individuals may be mapped in such a way that people who are emotionally close are located conceptually close together, whereas individuals who are casual acquaintances are mapped at a greater distance. Lines connecting people on the map could represent a social distance rather than true geographic distance. On such maps, referred to as cartograms, the distance between mapped data is scaled to a variable or index value other than distance. In the case of social ties, this might be an index representing the strength of a particular relationship.

A second difficulty in GIS mapping relates to the variability that occurs in time and space. Most data at present are collected as a snapshot in time. We have a more difficult task obtaining data over a series of short time steps to reliably map changes or trends in the data. Furthermore, because many of the things that we may map—especially individual people—move over time, there is an extra dimension of analysis to consider. Do we locate survey respondents based on their home address or place of employment or on where the respondents are most likely to be at a particular time of the day or week? This decision would be most significantly influenced by the question under study; there are no set answers.

Using computer animation, map data can be transitioned from static to dynamic. However, this type of mapping is still limited by the difficulty and expense of collecting data at a high frequency (temporal scale) as well as by software limitations in incorporating data instantly as it is collected. Fortunately, there are few social science applications that necessitate true real-time analysis. The primary goal for researchers considering GIS as a tool in their analysis is to make such decisions before collecting the data.

Additional considerations relate to the spatial representation of data. Often, in social science research, privacy is of the utmost concern. Data are typically lumped to mask individual data points representing individual respondents. A serious trade-off resulting from the lumping, or degrading, of data in this fashion is that the true, raw data may be permanently lost and no longer available for future research. One result of this process is that an enormous amount of redundant data collection occurs in situations where the simple recategorization of existing data in different but equally valuable combinations could provide for the exploration of vastly different questions.

A simple example of data degradation is the grouping of income levels into categories, a common practice in survey research. Categorical information such as < $15,000 and $15,001–$35,000 provides no means for a later study to distinguish individuals with incomes between $20,001 and $30,000. In a mapping context, it could be useful to link people or ideas to specific locations, but, more commonly, data are collected by larger geographic regions, such as census blocks or other political boundaries. The same problem as demonstrated with income occurs with census blocks. A census block doesn't show the internal distribution of data in the census block. Are the households equally distributed across the area, or is clustering of the households hidden in the simplified data? Data that are degraded can no longer be recategorized to explore new or different questions. Of course, these are not simple issues to address because anonymity is an essential component of many social science questions; however, to the extent possible, when data are maintained in near-original, detailed form, the possibilities for analyses both within and outside the GIS become much greater.

Expanding the "G"

Mapping attitudes, ideas, social networks, and countless other human constructs should be viewed as equally valid as mapping the latitude and longitude of a data point on the ground. Numerous opportunities, limited only by the creativity of the researcher, allow GIS to extend into realms not envisioned by the traditional geographies originally programmed into the software. The question that remains to be addressed is how one can develop an appropriate mapping context to represent concepts such as social interaction, desirability of a community, or social ties. Developing an index value or relationship between data points that can be used in place of physical distance as traditionally mapped is one means for visualizing data in a mapping context.

The "I" in GIS

The information component of GIS relates to the database aspect of the software. Databases are specialized software programs designed for the storage, organization, and retrieval of information. GIS software packages can read or directly interact with data from almost any data management and analysis software. There may be some data translations necessary to facilitate the movement of an existing research database into a GIS software package. It is useful to note that many of the fundamental baseline data sets one might need in answering a question are already available in GIS-ready formats.

In particular, data from the United States Census, as well as data from many state- and local-level data sets, are available through online sources or via the appropriate government office. Numerous university sources also provide GIS-ready data, as do a variety of private firms. Much of the data are freely accessible, whereas a good number of commercial databases are available for purchase. Deciding to use free versus commercial data most often comes down to your needs and experience. Commercial data are often reviewed for quality control purposes and are presented in ready-to-use formats directly compatible with commercial GIS software packages. Many free sources are similarly prepared, although some free sources may require more effort and manipulation to make them compatible with a particular GIS package. Your choice of data source may depend only on your budget. If you do not have the resources to purchase data or to collect your own new data, you may need to explore free options. Of course, if you use free data, there could be a trade-off in the time it takes to prepare the data for use in your analysis, or the necessary data simply may not be available.

Of course, you can also use any of your own data collected via surveys, interviews, observations, or almost any other means, which become vastly useful input to the GIS. In fact, as long as a researcher intends the data to end up in a computer in digital form, regardless of the particular software involved, it will be accessible to a GIS. Chapter 6 discusses data preparation in detail, including the import and export of data between software packages. In fact, with a little foresight, perhaps through one or two additional questions or notations on the data sheet, data can be collected to facilitate its easy incorporation into GIS. These additional data are the collection of some form of either real or conceptual location information tied to a base map chosen by the researcher. Thus, the information aspect of GIS is the easy part because almost everyone working in social sciences is already familiar with the process of collecting and coding data. Most are also familiar with entering data into a computer for analysis of one kind or another.

Extending the "I"

Most of the issues related to making information more accessible to GIS relate to the upfront organization and structure of data storage, coding, and format. These issues are not unique to GIS but are essential considerations for all data collection and analysis. Additional benefits of the computer and GIS are the additional storage opportunities available. Multimedia capabilities of the computer allow the linkage of photographs, sound or movie files, and scanned information. This provides a significant opportunity for raw data preservation, thus maintaining complete, detailed information.

For example, a key-informant interview or oral history could be recorded on tape in its entirety or a traditional dance recorded on video. These records can be converted into sound and video computer data files and linked to the GIS map as discussed in Chapter 6. When the location associated with that video or sound file is clicked on the GIS map, the complete recording becomes available to the researcher. Data that are coded or summarized from open-ended surveys or interviews for purposes of analysis are simultaneously available in their entirety to a researcher who may opt for a different coding scheme or analysis at a later time.

Thus, beyond the many analytical and data presentation benefits we explore in this text, the GIS can serve as a place to store a wide variety of digital data sets collected in the course of a particular study. And so far as these data can be maintained in raw form, this information can be used in new and different analyses at a later time. As one builds a library of GIS data sets, opportunities for extending the life and use of any individual data set are greatly enhanced.

The "S" in GIS

The system necessary to carry out the development and analysis in GIS includes a variety of hardware and software components, in addition to people who can make them work. Most academic institutions and government agencies and many private consultants may have these capabilities. Building GIS from the ground up varies greatly in cost and required training. The important considerations for a researcher are the trade-offs between doing the GIS work on your own and turning some aspects over to a more highly trained GIS analyst. Regardless of the decision made, it is most important to ensure that there is an upfront understanding of the data structure and format necessary to achieve compatibility with a minimum of difficulty, this being a component that you, the researcher, needs to take charge of. We discuss the conceptualization of a GIS-based analysis in detail in Chapter 8.

Difficulties With the "S"

GIS were largely developed with traditional geography in mind, and these original systems have areas of improvement. Since the initial development of GIS, the use and thus the capabilities of GIS have expanded across a wide variety of disciplines and applications in both the public and private sectors. These systems are further limited by the map data model, consisting of points, lines, and polygons (discussed in Chapter 2). This model assumes that all data can be linked to a very specific, discreet location and that lines can be drawn to explicitly delineate the boundary between data categories. Of course, many data sets are not so clearly defined, especially when dealing with social science data, which tend to be less geographically specific, either because they must be degraded to protect privacy or because you are analyzing conceptual maps as opposed to geographic maps.

Although there have been efforts to develop fuzzy GIS systems that allow locations and boundaries to be less definite, these systems are not yet available in the mainstream. Therefore, the existing GIS data models do not necessarily fit the analysis being conducted, and a researcher is sometimes forced to come up with a creative solution to make nondiscreet data fit into a discreet data model (data models are discussed in detail in Chapter 2). Therefore, one caution is that it is all too easy to allow the capabilities of the software to dictate the analysis carried out, or conversely, the analysis never attempted. This is one reason why GIS technology has taken longer to make its way into social science research than it did the natural sciences (as much as 40 years). Nonetheless, GIS did begin to find their niche in social science applications soon after their early development, most notably their use as a tool for the collection, storage, and analysis of U.S. census data beginning with the 1970 U.S. Census.

Those early years of GIS focused on natural resources for two simple reasons. Natural resource managers in Canada, with vast amounts of information to map, originated GIS technology in the 1960s. It was relatively easy to map the location of a forest, which doesn't move and doesn't change quickly, and the computer provided an excellent platform to accomplish that task in a large government agency. Working out methods to map nondiscreet data, such as mobile human populations, concepts, and attitudes more typical of social science research, would come later, thus explaining why GIS have taken substantially longer to make their way into daily use by social science researchers.

Furthermore, early GIS were traditionally expensive and complicated to use. This made GIS a difficult technology to bring to small community groups or individuals and often required a researcher to act as an intermediary between the data provider and the GIS analysis system. To provide the additional capabilities of a spatial analysis requires the researcher to develop an understanding of spatial data characteristics, a multitude of data types, spatial and topological analyses, and spatial modeling. It is crucial that the social scientist be equipped to discuss the application of GIS technology to their data, even if a GIS expert eventually is employed to carry out the database development, analysis, or output of results from the GIS. Fortunately, powerful personal computers are now relatively inexpensive (especially compared to computers of the 1960s and 1970s, when GIS technology was in early development). In combination with easier-to-use GIS software, the technology is much more accessible to the end user. Many spatial analysis questions that may previously have required the expertise of a GIS specialist can now be performed directly by the researcher. Learning the ins and outs of any GIS program, as well as the essential underlying concepts, is still a relatively time-consuming process. However, with some time and effort put into learning the fundamental concepts and organization of GIS and spatial analysis, you can go a long way in answering interesting and important questions in the social sciences.

As GIS has grown in popularity, the number of trained GIS professionals has also expanded tremendously. Thus, when your questions or analyses go beyond your own experience, there are a number of people you can go to for additional assistance. In particular, check for experts in GIS at local universities, community or technical colleges, and government agencies. In many areas, there are even GIS user groups that meet regularly to share ideas, assist with questions, or show off new projects and capabilities of their favorite GIS software. Visiting the Web site of your GIS software can often provide information on these local groups as well as access to online communities of users who can be of assistance.

Summary

As a research tool, GIS provide a wide range of opportunities for examining relationships in space, often by incorporating additional information not traditionally considered in social science research. As GIS continues to become more accessible to nonexpert users, there are a wide range of new and creative opportunities in social science research. As with any new tool, GIS can be used incorrectly and can provide misleading results. Any researcher familiar with standard statistical analysis software can relate to this concept. Use of the tool is not simply a matter of collecting a data set and pushing buttons in the software. Good research requires collecting appropriate data in an appropriate fashion and then conducting an intelligently thought out analysis that makes sense in light of the hypothesis or question being addressed.

In the following chapters, we discuss several of the essential concepts all GIS users should keep in mind when developing a data set for analysis in a GIS. We also address the major GIS data formats along with their strengths, weaknesses, and applications. With these few, but important pieces of information, you will be better prepared to use GIS as a tool in your own research applications, while avoiding many of the common pitfalls encountered by new users of these tools.

Relevant Web Sites

The first two Web sites listed in this section are portals to all things GIS. In addition to basic information about GIS, they link to information about software, training, data, and a variety of other useful resources.

GIS.com: This is a general GIS portal managed by the Environmental Systems Research Institute (ESRI), one of the major GIS software providers. The site offers a variety of general information and resources relevant to getting started with GIS technology. http://www.gis.com/

The GIS Lounge: This is a general GIS portal offering a variety of general information and links related to GIS technology, software, data, and other related resources. http://gislounge.com/

Cartographic Communication: This link regarding cartographic communication is part of a larger geography education Web site developed by Kenneth E. Foote and Shannon Crum, The Geographer's Craft Project, Department of Geography, The University of Colorado at Boulder. http://www.colorado.edu/geography/gcraft/notes/cartocom/cartocom_f.html

Center for Spatially Integrated Social Sciences (CSISS): CSISS recognizes the growing significance of space, spatiality, location, and place in social science research. It seeks to develop unrestricted access to tools and perspectives that will advance the spatial analytic capabilities of researchers throughout the social sciences. CSISS is funded by the National Science Foundation under its program of support for infrastructure in the social and behavioral sciences. http://www.csiss.org/

2

GIS Basics

Chapter Description

This chapter on fundamental GIS theory and concepts covers the essential information regarding the use of GIS for analysis. The chapter begins with an example of spatial data analysis to give readers an understanding of how GIS applies to areas of research they may be engaged in. The chapter then provides guidance in developing questions one might examine using GIS. This is followed by a discussion of the common GIS data models. The chapter concludes with a discussion of geographic and mapping concepts essential to proper data analysis and the presentation of results in GIS.

Chapter Objectives

- Develop an understanding of the two primary GIS data models.
- Provide guidance regarding strengths of each data model for particular forms of analysis in GIS.
- Present some common file formats encountered while searching for GIS data.
- Review the essential mapping concepts that influence your work with mapped data.
- Introduce forms of data output that can be developed in GIS.

After reading this chapter, you should be able to perform the following tasks:

- Develop a spatial question related to your own interests in the social sciences.
- Explain the differences between the vector and raster data models and choose the appropriate model for a specific research question.
- Choose between topological and map algebra approaches to analysis.
- Recognize several of the major file formats common in spatial data and data compression.

- Explain how map scale influences detail and accuracy in a data set.
- Discuss why the coordinates, projections, and datums of your maps or source data must match and how to make suitable choices for an analysis.
- Describe several output formats, in addition to a printed map, that you might seek to obtain from a GIS analysis.

An Example of a Spatially Based Study

One of the best known and widely cited examples of spatial analysis occurred long before computers of GIS were available—the work of John Snow, M.D. (1813–1858), whose book *On the Mode of Communication of Cholera* (Snow, 1855) was one of the earliest scientific uses of mapping in an epidemiological study. Snow used map analysis techniques very similar to those used in GIS today to determine likely sources of cholera in London, England. Although the details of cholera's transmission and life cycle were not understood at the time, by exploring the commonalities of individuals suffering from the outbreak, Snow was able to pinpoint the likely source of the disease. He identified the Broad Street water pump as the likely source, this pump serving as a primary, shared water source for most members of the local community. By mapping the addresses of individuals who contracted the disease, Snow found a cluster clearly apparent around that particular pump. Exceptions were noted for individuals who had access to separate wells or who, although not living in the immediate vicinity, had been in the area and may have used the pump in question. By using maps and simple spatial analysis techniques, Snow was able to find a correlation between the pump location that was the source of the disease outbreak and the homes of those afflicted with the illness, based on geographic information. Of course, similar studies today would more likely be mapped in a GIS.

As GIS technology continues to develop, its application expands into a wide variety of social science research applications, often in situations that cross disciplines—a wide range of applications in social justice, public participation GIS (PPGIS), demographic and anthropological research, and many others. In fact, an Internet search combining any of these disciplinary descriptors along with GIS returns thousands of sites, including many research- and community-based organizations, academic programs of study, and data sources.

Students in GIS classes or workshops often ask, "What can I do with GIS?" Perhaps the most appropriate answer to that is "You can do almost anything." Although this may be a slight overstatement (GIS won't do the laundry or take out the trash), the technology is applicable to a vast array of questions, the only requirement being that the questions have a spatial component. To be fair, GIS is not a panacea; like any tool, it may not be the best choice in every situation. The most common reason GIS may not be appropriate has to do with the expectations you have for it. The most difficult part of doing a GIS-based study is getting all of the data together and in a consistent and appropriate format for the software that you plan to use. In fact, you should expect that the majority of your effort in completing a GIS analysis will be related to data preparation. Once this aspect is out of the way, the analysis and output phases come relatively easily.

For large implementations, the data preparation portion may, quite literally, take months or years. This is especially true if you require historic data that are not already available in a digital form and must be coded into the computer. One step in the research process that many individuals are surprised by is that, even when data are available in digital form, the data may still require extensive manipulation to make it useful in a GIS analysis. To make a long story short, regardless of the sales literature or demonstrations, you will probably not sit down and start doing applied research in a GIS in a matter of minutes. Unless you are fortunate to work in a place where someone has already completed the difficult task of building a GIS database with exactly the data you require to answer your particular questions, starting to use GIS will take a reasonable amount of upfront preparation. However, with the growing availability of GIS at government

> Despite all of the online digital data now available and the vastly increased power of GIS, it is still common to spend 80% or more of a project's resources on searching, discovering, assessing, retrieving, and reformatting data.
>
> —Michael F. Goodchild (2003)
> *University of California, Santa Barbara*

agencies, consulting firms, schools (including K–12 schools), and nonprofit organizations, it is highly likely you already have access to some or all of the tools and expertise to start using GIS, if not in your own location, then somewhere close by.

Ultimately, if you are contemplating GIS for your own applied research, you need to consider three fundamental questions: (1) Would my question require or benefit from the spatial analysis component in some way? (2) Do I have access to or can I afford the investment in the required GIS software and training? (3) Does the data I need to carry out this analysis already exist, or, if not, do I have the time to collect or prepare the necessary data?

Let's answer these questions in turn, for now just in a general sense.(We discuss specific scenarios in other chapters.) The first question is about the value of the spatial component; however, when we think of space, we must consider more than just the three dimensions we are most familiar with: length, width, and height *(X, Y,* and *Z)*. Also consider that time is a valuable dimension. In Chapter 8, we discuss the concept of nontraditional geographies, that is, the use of space to represent concepts that are nonspatial. Nonetheless, almost everything we study can be located on a map, and for almost every study a spatial question can be developed. Some examples of spatial questions include the following:

- What elementary school is the nearest to my home?
- How many major streets will my child need to cross to get to school?
- Are schools close to neighborhoods of lower socioeconomic class correlated with higher dropout rates?
- Are individuals of higher socioeconomic class less likely to live downwind or downstream from industries that have higher levels of pollution than individuals of lower socioeconomic class?
- How many restaurants serving ethnic foods are within a mile of my workplace?

Putting these into more generic terms, spatial questions ask about issues such as the following:

- Nearness: questions relating to the item that is closest and how close it is
- Adjacency: questions relating to what is next to or touching
- Within a distance of: questions relating to everything near a particular location
- Correspondence: questions relating to where items coincide in space (e.g., occur together and possibly indicate cause and effect relationships)
- Directionality: questions relating to which features are in a particular direction from a place of interest (e.g., downstream)
- Categorization and query: questions relating to the organization, grouping, and sorting of data in space (e.g., the number of items at elevations above 1,000 ft)

GIS Data Formats

One of the most fundamental decisions in a GIS is the choice of data model to be used. In most cases, this decision will be driven by the software you are going to use. Thus, if you are going to be working in an existing GIS environment, it is important to know which software package and which type or types of data it is capable of working with. Beyond the particulars of the GIS software and data, there is the added complexity of data packaging and compression for the purpose of distributing GIS data sets on the Internet.

Unfortunately, this means that if you don't have the knowledge or capability to access, or open, certain data formats, some commonly available and potentially very useful data sets will be of little or no use. When the data sets can be opened, it is often after a variety of manipulations, conversions, and overly complicated contortions. This may sound a bit overly dramatic, but the fact is you will often encounter data sets on the Internet that require as many as three or four separate operations, using three or four separate software programs, just to get them to open up in your favorite GIS package.

Fortunately, the most popular commercial software packages offer support for most or all of the common data formats. Unfortunately, this support does not necessarily come with the basic software license and may require you to purchase additional components. In short, there are a whole host of issues (and potentially costs) related to the seemingly simple act of accessing a data set with your particular software. The following sections address the most common of these issues.

Spatial Data Formats

When you first obtain spatial data it is typically stored in a format defined for one of the leading GIS software packages or one of the formats defined by the federal government. The file extension, referring to the three or more letters at the end of the file name following the period, is your key to determining the file type. It is important to recognize the file extensions used, so you can determine which software capabilities, tools, and conversions are required for you to use the data in your own software. Most GIS packages are capable of reading or translating a variety of the most common formats; however, in some cases you may need to obtain a separate data conversion tool to accomplish this task.

This list, shown in Table 2.1, is by no means complete; there are literally dozens of software packages and file formats in use today. Fortunately, most of them include tools to import or export one or more of the listed formats, thereby facilitating exchange and translation of the more common formats. There are also a variety of stand-alone tools available on the Internet to assist in the conversion of a variety of spatial data formats, such as those in Table 2.1.

GIS Data Models

Two data models are commonly used in GIS. Although these go by a variety of jargon terms, they are most frequently referred to as the vector and raster models. The data model used has a significant influence on the structure of

Table 2.1   Common spatial data formats and file extensions

Name	Native Software Packages	File Extension(s)
Shapefile	ArcView®, ArcGIS®	*.shp, *.shx, *.dbf
Export File	ArcInfo®, ArcGIS®	*.e00, *.e01, and so on
MapInfo File	MapInfo®	*.mif, *.mid
Drawing Exchange File	AutoCAD®	*.dxf, *.dwg
SDTS Files (Spatial Data Transfer Standard)	National Institute of Standards and Technology Federal agencies and others	*.sdts, *.ddf
TIGER/Line® Files	U.S. Census Bureau	trg#####.zip

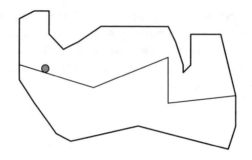

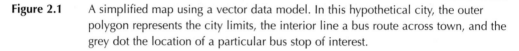

Figure 2.1   A simplified map using a vector data model. In this hypothetical city, the outer polygon represents the city limits, the interior line a bus route across town, and the grey dot the location of a particular bus stop of interest.

data in the GIS software and in the kinds of data analysis that can be carried out. For this reason, it is important to have an understanding of these two data models. As mentioned previously, not every GIS software program has the ability to use both vector and raster data. Therefore, the choice of software, whether it is your choice or your organization's, may force you into one of these two approaches. In this situation, changing models may require the acquisition of additional software components or even an entirely different GIS package.

Vector GIS

The vector data model is the model most like a traditional paper map. Items marked on the map are represented by one of three fundamental feature types: point, line, or polygon. Thus, when placing your data on the map, you can represent each item using the most geographically appropriate feature. For example, the location of a bus stop might be marked by a point, the streets on the bus route may be represented by lines, and the area comprising the city limits may be noted with a polygon. Figure 2.1 shows a simplified map in vector format. Each of the items shown on the map is commonly referred to as an entity in the data set.

A variety of information can be collected and stored about each entity in the GIS; these other pieces of data are referred to as attributes. Attributes can be described as characteristics of a particular variable. For example, a line representing a street might have attributes such as street name, speed limit, road surface, traffic levels, parking status, and the number of currently unfilled potholes. The variety of attributes collected is determined by the parameters of the research and is stored as part of the GIS database in an attribute table. Often these tables of data already exist in a digital format outside of the GIS and can be imported or even attached to the map data with minimal difficulty.

Raster GIS

The second data model is the raster format. In this data model, information is stored using a single feature type called a cell or pixel. Cells are most often represented as squares of a fixed dimension, and the resulting data and maps can sometimes appear blocky. Furthermore, features on the map that we might conceptualize as linear or polygonal are represented as a group of cells in the raster model. Figure 2.2 shows a simple example of a raster version of the bus map in Figure 2.1. On first glance, the raster map loses something visually; it also results in a different means of working with the data. Attributes are no longer stored in a data table (in most cases) but rather are coded directly into the cells. As represented in Figure 2.2, the shading tells us what occupies a particular cell, but coding individual cells in this manner limits us to a single attribute in each of the cells on the map. If more attributes are required, additional data sets will be necessary.

What raster data gives up in detail it gains in speed. Therefore, if the needs of a particular study don't require highly detailed maps (or, indeed, confidentiality demands less detailed mapping), the raster format may be preferred. Conversely, if the spatial detail and the appearance of the map output are more crucial, the vector format is desirable.

Of course, in some cases, you will find that the existing data sets you would like to use are in the wrong format. It is possible to convert vector and raster data models; however, as you might expect from looking at Figures 2.1 and 2.2, this may result in less accurate data, thus affecting the quality of your results. The size of the raster cells has a lot to do with the detail retained, but at a trade-off to file size (thus requirements for larger hard drives and faster computers).

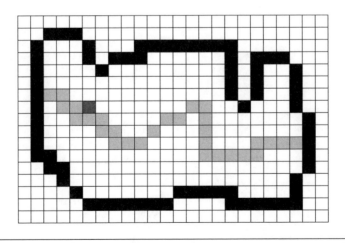

Figure 2.2   A simplified map using a raster data model. In this hypothetical city, the black cells represent the city limits, the light grey cells a bus route across town, and the charcoal grey dot the location of a particular bus stop of interest. The cells in a raster may represent any size; thus, on this map a cell might represent a square kilometer.

Topological and Raster Data Models and Analysis Approaches

Is one of these data models preferable? There is no single answer to this question; your choice should be determined by your analysis goals. In very simple terms, vector data are well suited to analyses that require topological characteristics. Topology is an area of mathematics used to analyze connectivity in the geometry independent of changes caused by warping of the data. Conceptually, if there is a connected set of lines on a map and one line is pulled, the other connected lines will also be pulled and potentially warped to maintain the connections that exist in the data (see Figure 2.3). All locations, or nodes, that are initially connected will remain connected, and any starting node (beginning of the line) will remain fixed at the appropriate locations.

By contrast, in the raster model, maintenance of the gridded structure of the data, not connections, is the primary interest. The advantage is that multiple layers can be manipulated mathematically by the computer on a cell-to-cell basis, a process known as map algebra (see Figure 2.4). In raster modeling, it is up to the researcher to develop a coding scheme that provides useful results. For many studies, numeric coding is preferred, especially in situations where complete knowledge of the contributing factors is not as important as the end result. For example, some of the mathematical results shown in Figure 2.4 can result from combinations that may not actually represent the same things. For example, a result of 3 may come from 1 + 2 or from 2 + 1, or a result of 2 could come from 1 + 1, 2 + 0, or 0 + 2. Careful examination of Figure 2.4 shows all of these results in Layer 3.

The trick when doing a raster-based analysis is to develop a coding scheme that gives you results that are sensible for your application and need.

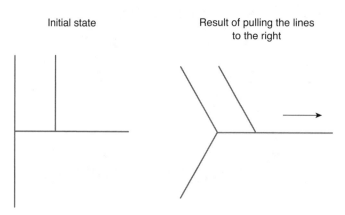

Initial state   Result of pulling the lines to the right

Figure 2.3   A topologically connected vector GIS data model. When one line is moved to the right, all connected lines are pulled along, thus maintaining established connections in the data.

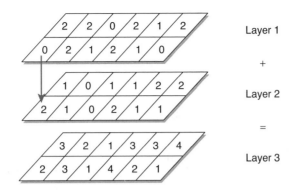

Figure 2.4 The mathematical combination of raster data layers using map algebra. In a raster GIS, layers of information are coded into grids of equal-size cells. A mathematical combination of these grids provides a fast and powerful map-based modeling environment. This example shows an additive combination of two sets of data, resulting in a new, third data set. The coded values may represent any data value the researcher chooses to assign.

The simple example in Figure 2.4 may be just fine if you are interested in the total population of a region under study where Layer 1 represents adults over 18 and Layer 2 represents children. However, this same coding scheme may not be relevant if the layers represent the average number of bathrooms per household and the average number of years of residence, presumably noncorrelated attributes.

To make things slightly more complex, the operations carried out between raster layers can include other mathematical computations, from the simple (+, −, ×, ÷) to the complex (log-, power-, and root-based operations). The advantage to using mathematical operations in the combination of the raster data layers is that it provides the capability to implement complex, statistical models (perhaps developed via previous research) in the GIS environment and makes raster analysis very useful, even though the visual and spatial quality of the resulting maps may not be as attractive and accurate as in a vector-based approach.

Data Compression and Packaging

When downloading data from the Internet, the first hurdle is most often data compression (see Table 2.2). Many data sets are compressed to make them smaller and faster to download. Although this is helpful in saving downloading time, it adds to the steps you will need to carry out.

And to further complicate matters, you may see the file extensions combined; for example, a TAR file may subsequently be nested inside a Zip file. There are a host of freely available and commercial software programs that can decompress these files. WinZip® is one relatively inexpensive package with an easy-to-use interface that decompresses all of the formats listed in Table 2.2.

Table 2.2	Common compression formats and file extensions
Name	*Common File Extension(s)*
Zip	*.ZIP, *.Z, *.GZ
Tar	*.TAR

Essential Mapping Concepts

Most everyone is familiar with maps in some form, be it a road map used to plan your family vacation, a subway map posted in the station, or a globe used in an elementary school classroom. However, there are a variety of fundamental mapping concepts that are essential to your success in a GIS context: scale, projections, and coordinates.

Scale

Scale relates to the miniaturization of the world to a size that is small enough to fit onto a sheet of paper or a manageable globe. When working in a GIS environment, many people incorrectly assume that scale is not important because it is so simple to zoom in or out on the computer screen. Although it is true that you can zoom in and out, it does not mean that the data are scaleless. All data collected in space have an associated source scale. That is, the original map or groundwork that the digital data were originally derived from has an associated scale, or level of detail, and this is maintained when the data are placed into the computer.

Why is this important to you? Scale of the source map influences spatial accuracy and map completeness. Maps that are at small scale (covering a large geographic area) tend to be less detailed, whereas maps at large scale (covering a small geographic area) tend to be more detailed. Consider the difference between a national map of the United States and a map of your community. On the U.S. map, it is possible your town will not be shown at all, but if it is marked on the map, odds are it will be represented by a point symbol. At the national scale, there isn't enough space on the page to include every city and town without making the map overly cluttered, and certainly there is not space to include every local street, park, and school on the map. However, on a map that shows a single city, this additional detail can be more readily drawn.

Cartographic concepts influenced by scale are generalization, abstraction, displacement, and simplification. Cartographers designing maps at smaller scales may need to give up a substantial amount of detail and accuracy to make everything fit the page. For example, city boundaries that are, in reality, multisided polygons may be abstracted, or represented, as a dot on the map. The river that runs near or even through the city may be displaced, or offset, and straightened when drawn as a line on the map. Small features may be grouped together into larger symbols, or they may be completely left off the map. Although all of these alterations make sense from a cartographic design standpoint, they can represent lost or spatially inaccurate information when viewed in the GIS.

The bottom line with scale is this: At any given scale, a map is accurate to a specified level (give or take some measured distance). If you try to make more detailed measurements from that map, you are doing so at your own peril. Furthermore, mixing together mapped data from vastly different source scales will lead to results only as good, and potentially a bit worse, as the least accurate map incorporated into the study. Therefore, it is worthwhile to seek out data that are mapped at a scale appropriate to your research question. For example, if you are making decisions or carrying out an analysis where it is important to know the location down to the specific household or individual, data available from the U.S. Census will not be sufficient. However, if your analysis is being carried out at the county level, you may be able to use that same U.S. Census data quite effectively because it is more detailed than you need. The excess detail in the data can be retained for future analysis or simplified (in this case by aggregating all of the census blocks in each county into a single unit).

From the data collection perspective, this means locating your sample units to an appropriate level of accuracy. It may be easier, and just as useful, to map survey respondents to the neighborhood or census block rather than mapping the location of each respondent's front door to the nearest centimeter. Yes, the tools and technology exist (at great expense) to map locations to centimeter accuracy, but you need to determine if that detail is really useful before seeking out the "best" data available. Data development is discussed further in Chapters 6 and 7.

Realistically, most social science applications will never require accuracy anywhere close to centimeter accuracy; more often, neighborhoods, streets, or census blocks will be the greatest level of detail needed, and quite often even this will be more detailed than necessary. The bottom line in data detail is that data can always be simplified to be less detailed, but data that are generalized cannot easily be made more detailed. Once you have decided on the level of detail you require in your own analysis, then that level of detail should be set as a minimum target for all data to be assembled, located, or collected. Data of greater detail are fine, but data of lesser detail will simply decrease the final quality of your analysis results.

Projections and Coordinates

As is the case for scale, maps also come in a variety of projections. Projection is a process by which the relatively spherical earth is flattened to a flat page or computer screen. Numerous projections exist, and conversions between them are relatively easy to accomplish in most GIS software programs. Some GIS packages even do the conversions automatically (called on-the-fly projection) when the data format can be determined by the software. When data sets are not in the same projection, problems occur. Features may not line up as they should and thus may contribute error to your analysis results.

You need not be an expert in map projections to avoid these problems, but you should be aware that it is important to know the projection information for your data sets and when possible to obtain data sets that were originally developed in one consistent projection. If you do convert projections, the error will typically be minimal, especially when analyzing small areas (e.g., city level). However, as the geographic size of your study increases, projection errors can accumulate.

Although there are dozens of commonly used projections (and with the advent of computerized mapping, literally infinite possibilities to develop new ones), projections can be classified into three primary families: azimuthal (planar), cylindrical, and conical, as shown in Figure 2.5. Each of these three

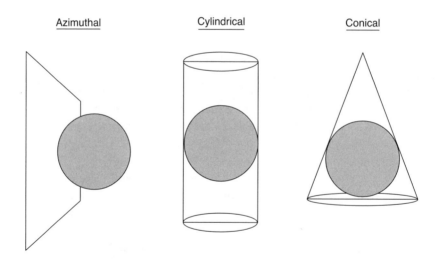

Figure 2.5   Examples of the three primary projection families. An azimuthal projection can be thought of as a flat piece of paper held against the side of the globe that is being mapped. Only the portion of the globe facing the paper would be mapped using this projection, with the greatest accuracy at the point where the paper touches the globe. The cylindrical projection can be thought of as a piece of paper wrapped around the globe in the shape of a cylinder. This permits one to map the entire globe. As with the azimuthal, the area along the point of contact (often the equator) is mapped most accurately with distortions occurring as one moves toward either of the poles. The conical projection can be thought of as a cone of paper placed over the globe. This approach is again most accurate at the point of contact between the cone and the globe and does a relatively good job in mapping the hemisphere encircled by the narrower portion of the cone (in this case the northern hemisphere). Areas toward the open end of the cone are more drastically distorted.

basic projections can be oriented in a variety of ways relative to the globe. For example, many maps use a projection oriented to the poles (the north/south axes of the globe). However, in some mapping applications, it may be desirable to orient the projection along the equator or at another angle between the poles and the equator (oblique). For a further discussion of map projections, visit one or more of the Web sites referenced at the end of this chapter.

Depending on where your data come from, information about the projection and any conversions may be documented as part of the digital data itself (most common for GIS-ready data), or it may be documented in a separate document or location on a Web site. For many government organizations, standards for data are consistent across the agency and may not be included with each individual data set. In general, you will find the relevant information in a metadata file. If no metadata exist, you may need to contact the provider of the data directly or do some comparisons to other known data sources to assess the use of the data for your particular application.

Coordinates are the means to locate data on a map. Most of us are familiar with concepts of latitude and longitude as a common example. All coordinate systems have an origin that is the zero point from which coordinates are measured. For latitude/longitude measurements, this point is located at the intersection of the prime meridian (running north to south through Greenwich, England) and the equator. One might ask, "Why Greenwich?" At some level, one could argue that this decision was arbitrary, although it was decided in October of 1884 at an international conference called to develop standards for location and time. Could the meridian have been just as functional if placed elsewhere? Yes, and indeed when we use one of the other numerous coordinate systems, that is exactly what we see.

Many GIS users work in a coordinate system more relevant to their local area and needs. In the United States, two commonly used systems are State Plane Coordinates (SPC) and Universal Transverse Mercator (UTM). State Plane Coordinates, as the name implies, are tied to the individual states and in each case are optimized for the state, depending on its dominant orientation (north/south vs. east/west). States are divided into zones, each with its own origin. The reason for establishing multiple zones comes from the desire to minimize error in survey measurements; in simple terms, if you can measure from a (relatively) nearby origin, you are less likely to accumulate error over shorter distances. The UTM system uses a similar approach but on a global scale. The globe is divided into 60 zones, and to avoid the use of negative values all coordinates are based on standards that ensure that the zero point actually falls to the south and west of the zone border. The contiguous United States falls in UTM zones 10 through 19 as one goes from the West Coast to the East; each of these 10 zones has its own origin and the same coordinate *(X, Y)* locations appear in each zone.

It is not our goal to describe the complete details and structure of coordinate systems but rather to make it clear that these important issues exist. A good book on mapping or a visit to the United States Geological Survey

Web site will provide you with details, if you are interested in how these coordinate grids are established and defined. Regardless, if you are conducting a study using data from multiple sources and the data are not provided in the same coordinate system or the same zone of a particular system, the data will be misaligned. The GIS software can typically make conversions between coordinates and zones as long as you are aware to be watching for these issues and are able to provide the necessary parameters for the desired conversions.

If you are working with data outside of the United States, there are national coordinate systems defined by most nations of the world. Regardless of the system used, the issues are the same. You need to know which system the data are provided in and, if necessary, convert it to match your other data.

A Bit About Datums

An issue related to coordinate systems, particularly in the United States, concerns datums. Datums are sets of control points used by surveyors to tie their mapping to the particulars of the earth's surface. Although there are numerous datums in use, two of the most common are the North American Datum 1927 (NAD27) and the North American Datum 1983 (NAD83). Because global positioning system (GPS)–based data collection is affordable and common, more people are using the World Geodetic System 1984 (WGS84). The WGS84 system, as the name implies, is globally consistent. Many countries have their own international datums as well. The positional differences observed due to use of different datums are often small enough that you may suspect it is actually a problem caused by one of the other issues discussed previously. However, the shifts may be as much as hundreds of meters or more and will be generally consistent in direction. As with the other aspects of data, having a sense of the datum being used with a particular data set, and using the same datum for all data in an analysis, will remove these errors.

So What Do I Do?

Ultimately, all issues involving matched data relate to understanding the data sets you are working with. Data that meet national standards and include compliant metadata will be easiest to work with. Again, depending on the source of a particular data set, the details and format of metadata can vary. In the United States, the Federal Geographic Data Committee (FGDC), as well as other federal agencies, has defined metadata standards to use when creating new data for GIS. Older data may or may not be compliant.

Many state- and local-level agencies and organizations also follow FGDC standards. Internationally, several countries have their own standards. The International Standards Organization (ISO) has also defined norms for the documentation of spatial data (ISO 19115), and at present many countries, including the United States, are working to harmonize their standards with those defined by ISO 19115.

Whatever standards are being followed, it is important that the metadata file contains all of the essential information regarding scale, projection, coordinate systems, and datums as well as a wide variety of other useful details about the data set, its sources, and its methods of creation. In short, metadata are documentation about a data set that specify the answers to all of the previous questions and provide information about the source and method of the data collection and input, the coding used in the database, and a host of other relevant information. If the data you have lack a metadata file, you should be wary of using them. Unfortunately, there are vast quantities of GIS data available, especially on the Internet, that do not include formal metadata. You may find that a little digging on the Internet or direct communication with the agency or organization that created the data will provide answers to many of these questions. Chapter 5 goes into detail about locating existing data as well as how you can create your own GIS data.

GIS Output

The final phase of GIS is output, and for most people that means a map. Maps produced in a GIS can be quite attractive and do an excellent job of communicating key results. As the saying goes, a picture is worth 1,000 words. Good map design is based on a whole host of principles that, unfortunately, are not programmed effectively in most GIS packages. In particular, many GIS packages assign random color palettes to features on your map. Often the colors are too similar to tell apart when viewing the map, or they just don't make sense. You may see blue land areas and purple water bodies pop onto your screen, which is not only counterintuitive (most people would expect water to be represented in blue) but also downright ugly.

Pay attention to the colors and symbols and take the time to assign them in a way that makes sense. One common error is the selection of colors that are too similar to be differentiated on the map. Another mistake novice map designers make is to put too much information on a single map. When using categorical data, five groupings is reasonable, and you can assign sufficiently different colors or patterns to make the map readable. Just because you have a vast amount of data in your final GIS database, you don't need to put it all on one map. Last, consider the space on the page. Try to use the white space outside the map for details such as titles, legends, and so on. Also, consider the orientation of the page so that you can effectively fill the space

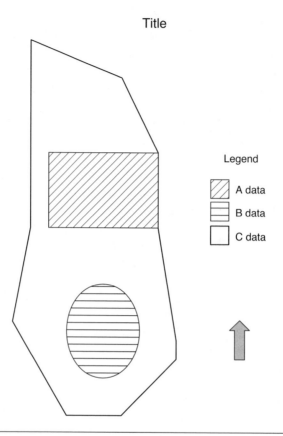

Figure 2.6   A simple map layout where the map, which is oriented in a north-south direction, is placed toward one side of the page. The remaining white space on the page is used to position other map information without cluttering the page.

(Figure 2.6). If your map fills the entire page, you may need to place text into white boxes overlain on the map to make the text readable.

There is extensive literature on the topic of cartographic design. You may want to delve more into this topic or even hire a cartographer to assist in designing your maps. However, for many GIS users, the map design tools included in the software serve well as long as a little thought and common sense go into the final output.

Through the use of computer animation, maps can also show change over time. Although animated maps are a valuable tool, they are not practical in all situations. Of course, if the tools to display an animated map are available (e.g., in a classroom, at a public meeting, or on a Web site), a map showing changes can be quite nice. Very often you will still find that the printed map or a set of printed maps can be just as effective in getting your message across, not to mention much easier to print in a final report.

Summary

In preparing to carry out a GIS analysis, it is essential that you consider a variety of basic mapping and data format concepts. Although these may appear intimidating at first read, you need not be overwhelmed by these issues. GIS software packages typically include tools for the conversion of data formats, projections, and datums, and when there are mismatches, most packages warn you of the discrepancies. The important point is to take note of such messages and understand what it means to allow these differences to remain or to convert data.

Although some GIS software programs make the conversions on-the-fly so that you don't need to do anything, this can be problematic when data are not properly documented in the metadata. The bottom line of any computer-based analysis is GIGO (garbage in, garbage out), and this is no less true for GIS. If you lack information about data you are using, or fail to be sure data from multiple sources are matched properly, you may get an answer out of the computer, but that answer may not be useful or correct. In a world of unlimited time and resources, you might personally collect and create all of your data yourself so that you fully understand its construction. The next best thing is to obtain data that are well documented with metadata. Think of metadata as a pedigree for the data set. If you were going to get a new puppy, you'd want to see its pedigree before paying top dollar for its supposed good breeding. By the same logic, you shouldn't trust a data set that lacks its papers either; otherwise, you might end up with a mutt!

Therefore, it is important to pay attention to issues of data format and quality and, when necessary, correct for them so that you can carry out your GIS data analysis. Of course, if one has the time and interest, there is much literature detailing these topics. Our goal here is to elucidate the key issues that you need to pay attention to so that you can move forward with GIS without getting bogged down in too many details.

Relevant Web Sites

Federal Geographic Data Committee: This is the official site of the FGDC, offering the latest information on metadata standards. http://fgdc.gov/

The Geographer's Craft: This site provides information about most key geographic mapping concepts included in this chapter as well as references and additional links. http://www.colorado.edu/geography/gcraft/contents.html

USGS Map Projection Decision Support System: This site offers an interactive Web interface to assist in determining an appropriate map

projection for any portion of the globe. http://helios.er.usgs.gov/research/
DSSMain/DSSApplet.html

Bibliography of Map Projections: This document is a bibliography of
nearly 3,000 articles related to map projections from the scientific and
professional literature. Although this goes far beyond the requirements of
most GIS users, the site does provide a sense of the vast array of projections and projection issues that one might consider. http://www.ilstu.edu/
microcam/map_projections/Reference/Bu111856.pdf

Notes Regarding the Principles of Cartographic Design: This site contains
an online discussion list of the Cartographic Society. http://www.shef. ac.uk/
uni/projects/sc/cartosoc/1999/Nov/msg00044.html

The following two sites provide an overview of the map projection concepts covered in this chapter:

The Geographer's Craft (Map Projections Overview): A direct link to the
section on map projections. http://www.colorado.edu/geography/gcraft/
notes/mapproj/mapproj_f.html

Map Projections: This site provides a good overview of projections as well
as references and software tools related to map projections and conversions. http://www.geography.hunter.cuny.edu/mp/

Suggested Reading

Goodchild, M. (2003). Foreword. In Z. R. Peng & M. H. Tsou (Eds.), *Internet GIS:
    Distributed geographic information services for the Internet and wireless net-
    works* (p. iv). Hoboken, NJ: Wiley.
MacEachren, A. M. (2004). *How maps work: Representation, visualization, and
    design.* New York: Guilford Press.
Slocum, T. A., McMaster, R. B., Kesssler, F. C., & Howard, H. H. (2004). *Thematic
    cartography and visualization* (2nd ed.). Upper Saddle River, NJ: Prentice Hall.

3

Topics for Sociospatial Research

Chapter Description

In this chapter, we explore how incorporating a spatial context into your investigation can enhance your analysis by providing additional insights and information not previously considered. We first explore approaches for defining project goals, and, based on the defined goals, we explore whether GIS analysis techniques enhance the outcome. The chapter includes sections on developing your project goals and approach, including relevant examples that explore the potential of spatial analysis as part of social science research. We also include suggestions for the application of these approaches when locating or collecting data for your own research. These examples illustrate how common data types can be tied to the spatial realm of the GIS.

Chapter Objectives

- Introduce GIS as a tool for the integration and analysis of social science data.
- Offer a series of considerations to use in defining the role GIS will play in your research.
- Provide examples of research that would benefit from a spatial perspective.

After reading this chapter you should be able to perform the following tasks:

- Select, organize, and begin to seek out relationships in a variety of data.
- Consider a variety of potential factors related to social data that might help to explain observed differences between locations.
- Define and begin to conceptualize goals for a GIS project, including the spatial extent of your study area, the data needed, and the approaches to analysis.
- Begin to plan approaches to data collection, including the value of taking a computer with you into the field.

Introduction

Although GIS does not have a long history in the social sciences, its value in social science research is beginning to be recognized. GIS is such a powerful tool for the social scientist because it allows for the integration and comparison of contextual data from a social as well as environmental or physical standpoint. Almost all data that the social scientist examines have an associated geographic point of location. The ability to identify where differences or similarities, correlations, and interactions exist is of major import to the social science researcher. Additionally, GIS can facilitate the incorporation of both qualitative and quantitative variables into one's study. This is discussed in more detail in Chapters 4 and 5.

What Value Does GIS Present in Social Science Research?

Analysis may, on the surface, seem an obvious reason for getting involved with a technology such as GIS. Indeed, the purpose of this book is to present a variety of ways that GIS can be effectively incorporated into your own research. Surprisingly, many people who use GIS use very few, if any, of the analysis tools offered in any of the commonly available software packages. Instead, the GIS is viewed simply as a tool for designing simple maps. Certainly, a well-designed map of your data can communicate a tremendous amount of information, and this is one component of the GIS. A good book on cartographic design will prove a valuable resource for map design. We address map design briefly in Chapter 2.

The real value of GIS to the researcher comes in the analytical capabilities added when incorporating the spatial component GIS provides. This is a major focus of this book, particularly in Chapter 9. Before discussing analysis, it is important to provide a basic overview of GIS organization and structure as well as data formats that can be most easily incorporated. One especially appealing benefit is that most, if not all, of the data already being collected by social science researchers can be easily integrated into a GIS, and, with a little extra up-front planning, all data can be prepared in a GIS-friendly format. Data are the focus of Chapter 2; data conceptualization in a spatial context is further discussed in Chapter 4. Chapter 6 focuses on the collection of spatial data in your research process and the location or entry of data that will be GIS friendly when it comes time to incorporate the data into your GIS analysis.

Exploring and Integrating Information

Studies taking into account a variety of contextual- and individual-level variables would benefit from using GIS. Why? GIS allow researchers to establish a context for their individual-level data. For example, if you were to survey a group of people living in a particular state, a GIS would allow for the specific connection of each individual's responses to a geographic location, such as a particular community within that state. These individuals do not exist in a vacuum; they live in particular places. Although it may be perfectly desirable to understand attitudes of respondents statewide, there is potentially much to be gained by understanding differences in different regions of the state (e.g., urban vs. rural counties). Similarly, any study can be examined at a variety of spatial scales, and the unit of analysis appropriate for one study may be entirely different from that of another study.

Capturing the additional location information is useful when conducting more targeted analyses, for understanding the social context pertaining to a particular geographic area, or for understanding characteristics of an area that might influence the social situation. A GIS facilitates the integration of spatial and nonspatial data because the researcher identifies which variables (environmental, physical, individual) to incorporate into the analysis. As long as the variables in your study can be tied to a geographic location, they can be incorporated into a GIS. Later in the book we also discuss how GIS can be used to analyze data that are not linked to a geographic location.

A GIS is perfect for integrating physical, environmental, and social data in one unified analysis environment. One benefit comes via the visualization of the data as your analysis proceeds; that is, you can see how things appear to relate in space by viewing them on a map before moving forward with a formal analysis to explore the statistical significance of the relationship. A GIS may also allow the researcher to examine how previously unconsidered geographic variables integrate into the system, making the GIS an excellent data exploration tool. Because a GIS can integrate data from a variety of sources, it allows the researcher to develop a holistic view of the many different contextual variables that may be important to addressing a particular social issue or research question.

For instance, let's say that you are studying a community where homelessness is considered a major problem. Residents of the local community complain to city officials about the constant panhandling that occurs around the community as the homeless try to make ends meet. City officials could commission a study of the migration pattern of the homeless by conducting interviews to determine where geographically these individuals are spending their time, where they are sleeping, and what sorts of needs they have (e.g., public bathrooms and food distribution). Using a GIS to map the location and needs of the homeless community and the areas that currently serve some of their needs, gaps, or shortfalls in services might be identified. In concert with a variety of social, environmental, and physical data, in combination with public input, the GIS could be used to identify optimal and willing locations to provide additional services to the homeless community and to more effectively help them to get back on their feet.

Seeking Relationships

A GIS facilitates the examination of relationships between different types of data. A GIS allows for the connection of both qualitative and quantitative data in a geographic context. An example of the incorporation of qualitative data might be the oral histories or stories told by the elders of a particular tribe or community about the importance of nature to their local community. This data could be linked to specific geographic locations within the community, for example, locations of traditional hunting and fishing grounds, ceremonial sites, or significant landmarks of cultural or personal significance. The GIS would facilitate the exploration of relationships between individuals' geographic locations within the community and the importance the individuals place on nature. For instance, elders who live closer to the edges of the community and in closer proximity to the surrounding natural forest may emphasize the importance of nature more than those who live in the more urban or central part of the community.

Another interesting function of the GIS might be to identify areas consistently mentioned by multiple respondents interviewed during the study to identify the common, shared history and understanding of the community. Using a GIS facilitates the visualization of such relationships. Correlations that may not be readily apparent in a traditional analysis may jump out when viewed spatially on a map. Furthermore, if the GIS is available in the field during the interview process, respondents could point out locations on the map, further enhancing the process of data collection and analysis. Using maps, photos, or other visual information can be especially useful in situations where language is a barrier to data collection.

Thinking Critically

The ability to think critically is a skill needed not only in academia but also in the corporate world. But what does it mean to think critically? Thinking critically means not relying solely on other people's explanations or rationalizations for phenomena. Critical thinking is a major skill that is stressed in many universities throughout the country. Using a GIS facilitates critical thinking because it allows for the integration of previously unconsidered geographically based variables into one's study. This integration contributes to critical thinking because it helps the researcher to move beyond the consideration of traditional variables or explanations for observed changes and explanations in one's study. It facilitates the inclusion of both qualitative and quantitative analyses into a study.

Qualitative analysis is defined as "the nonnumerical examination and interpretation of observations for the purpose of discovering underlying meanings and patterns of relationships" (Babbie, 2003, p. G6), whereas quantitative analysis is defined as "the numerical representation and manipulation of observations for the purpose of describing and explaining the phenomena that those observations reflect" (Babbie, 2003, p. G6).

Acknowledging Differences

A GIS can be very useful for examining differences that exist between variables in your study. A GIS could help a researcher to identify differences between groups, places, organizations, and resources. The list is almost endless. As long as the data can be linked to a geographic point, they can be examined using GIS. In Figure 3.1 we considered the possibility that differences across the state of Illinois might have something to do with urban versus rural settings as defined by population. Further analysis might explore relationships to other variables that are socioeconomic (age, income, education), environmental (proximity to Lake Michigan, inland lakes or rivers, forest, parks), or physical (roads, telecommunications, housing). We might find that a variety of variables interrelate in space in a meaningful way and are worthy of further exploration.

For example, a GIS can be used to compare variable attributes at different points in time (assuming that you have data for these different time

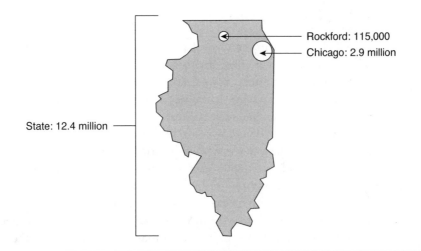

Figure 3.1   An analysis of Illinois could be easily biased by the large urban population in the greater Chicago area if the spatial component of sample data is not recorded for inclusion in a spatial analysis. In a state such as Illinois, Chicago is the single largest city by far. Chicago has nearly 2.9 million people and represents about 23% of the population of the entire state. The next largest city, Rockford, has a population just over 150,000, about 5% of Chicago's population (U.S. Census, 2000). An analysis of Illinois that did not incorporate spatial information could be biased by the large urban population in the greater Chicago area, representing much of the northeastern part of the state. The geographic location of respondents in a survey in Illinois might significantly influence the kind of responses obtained and could be overlooked if the spatial component is not recorded for inclusion in a spatial analysis.

periods). An overlay of variables for two or more points in time can be used to analyze actual social and environmental changes that have occurred for a particular study site over a period of time. This type of longitudinal study is sometimes termed a temporal analysis. If we were to consider just the example of Chicago with its 2.9 million people in 2000, one might ask how Chicago changed in the 10 years from 1990 to 2000. The census shows an increase of 3%, or about 112,000 people, enough people to match the size of the fifth largest city in the state! Granted Chicago is a large city, so one might reasonably ask, "Where in the city, into which neighborhoods did all these new people move?" With the data as stated here, you would have no idea, but with a little additional information (census block data), you could identify those areas of the city that experienced the most growth, those that stayed the same, and those with a decreased population over those years.

Census-based analyses of this sort are convenient because the data are already collected in a manner appropriate to these questions and are therefore an excellent source for many GIS-based analyses of social science data. It can be slightly more difficult to assemble data necessary to investigate other questions where the data are not quite so easily acquired from one source, but the process would be similar.

Finding Common Ground

A GIS can assist in the identification of common ground between social and environmental variables. In other words, it allows for discovering where different groups, clusters, towns, and corporations share common issues. GIS technology allows for examining the geographic intersection between different environmental and social features.

Additionally, a GIS allows for the visual portrayal of data. Having this ability is essential for communications between people of different backgrounds and can help groups to realize that they share things in common. Identifying common ground is often the first step toward building a consensus out of conflicts that often occur in planning. For instance, let's say that you have a consortium of service organizations that meets with the goal of streamlining the organizations' contributions to the community. Using a GIS enables the entire collection of service organizations to break up services to the community by the area of town that is closest to their club (Figure 3.2). So, for instance, the Southside Rotary Club would put its resources into improving playgrounds on the south side of town, whereas the Northeast Lions Club would focus on improving services for senior citizens on the northeastern side of town. This would be an approach based on separating the city into areas in nearest proximity to each organization, also known as proximity polygons (discussed further in Chapter 9).

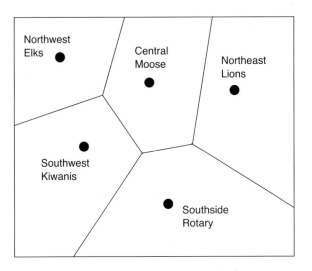

Figure 3.2   Proximity polygons delineate the areas nearest to each of the service organizations in the community. Everything within the polygon surrounding a particular point is closer to that point than to any other point on the map.

Determining Project Goals

Any person interested in conducting research ultimately begins determining the main idea, or purpose, of one's research. For the social sciences, the possibilities are endless, especially when it comes to incorporating GIS into the research plan. There are many different factors that can affect the purpose of your research. Some of these include your own personal interests and the interests of the sponsoring organization or agency. Applied research projects may have more than one single purpose, setting out to answer a series of questions or to work toward a solution to specific social problems.

Anytime you engage in a research project, you need a clear conceptualization of what the research goals are. A surprising number of people carrying out an analysis cannot easily answer the simple question, what is the purpose of this study? Having a clear project goal is very important because, beyond being the reason for why you are engaging in research in the first place, the goal directly informs the data you need to locate, collect, and prepare for the eventual analysis. A project may have more than one goal and different participants in and funders of the project may have different goals. If this is the case, it is useful to develop a set of overarching project objectives and a list of needed data prior to beginning the data collection process. One of the most troublesome things that can occur in carrying out an analysis is realizing after the fact that an essential and easy-to-acquire piece of data was not collected as part of the original design. Going back to fill in missing data after the fact, assuming it is possible at all, can be time consuming, expensive, and of course embarrassing. In the GIS realm, you will also need to determine how you will encode the data in a GIS-compatible format that simultaneously works within the GIS and effectively meets the requirements of your study. Chapter 2 addresses these issues in more detail.

Some questions you might ask yourself in developing goals for your study include the following:

- Why are you engaging in this study?
- What sorts of relationships do you want to examine as a part of your study?
- What causes or organizations might your study benefit?
- Who is funding your study?
- Are you studying patterns of human behavior?

If you are able to answer these questions clearly and up front, you will have a much easier time defining the specific goals of the project and thus the data and variables you will require in achieving your objectives.

Guiding Questions

To begin to discover whether your proposed study could be enhanced by integrating geographic information, you can answer a few questions.

The following sections describe four different sets of questions for researchers to consider in determining how a GIS can be integrated into their study. The sections include questions about concept, questions about data, questions about location, and questions for analysis.

Questions About Concept

The questions in this section focus on the ideological structure of your study. These questions are designed to be asked early in the research process, usually before you begin implementing your research methodology. When answering these questions, some background research may be necessary; this research should be done before beginning the actual project and going out into the field. You may be able to conduct much of your background research through a literature review and an Internet search or through talks with local experts and other individuals familiar with the study site to gain a good understanding of the existing relationships. However, your contact with people in your study site will depend on whether or not you have established social ties there, how accessible or remote your study site is, and the availability and access to technology (phones, the Internet, etc.) at the site. Sometimes a small pilot study is useful to ensure your approach is acquiring the necessary data and is not confusing to those doing the collection or to those responding to questions. Pilot testing of the analysis can also be helpful to ensure that the data can be analyzed as expected. Planning and carrying out the GIS analysis is discussed in detail in Chapters 4 and 9.

Of course, it is important to collect the proper information from each location, respondent, or unit of analysis in your study. This information is commonly referred to as variables. What is a variable? A variable can be defined as a domain of attributes that relate to a particular concept. For example, the variable Gender might be defined as the three attributes: male, female, or other. So what is an attribute? An attribute is a characteristic that is associated with a particular object or person. The following questions might help you in defining the concepts to be used in your study:

- What is your research question?
- What is your main dependent variable?
- What are your independent variables?
- What are the main hypotheses of your study?
- Are there any geographic features that you have already identified as variables in your study? If so, what are they? Are they man-made or natural features?
- Could any of the geographic features contained in your study site potentially affect the issue that you are studying?

Questions About Data

The questions in this section relate to the data collection portion of your project. Once again, it would benefit the researcher to find out answers to these questions prior to going into the field. This information should be available from local government agencies (local, state, county, federal) that have responsibility for the area, including your study site. In addition, contacting private businesses or local interest groups may turn up even more of the information you require. As was mentioned earlier, one of the keys to the successful use of GIS is being able to be a creative thinker and seeking creative avenues to find the data that you might need for your study. Although you may want to simply search the Internet for agency and organizational Web sites to get all the data you need, this process will rarely provide anything close to a complete list of the data that are actually available. More likely, you will need to make direct contact with the appropriate people at each agency or organization to find out answers to these questions. Because the collection and development of quality data sets are time-consuming and expensive processes, some people will be reluctant to provide their data to you. Therefore, it is often worthwhile to have something to offer in exchange for the data. Data trades, access to related data to be developed during the study, or access to the final report results are all valuable offers you can make to those who assist you. When considering the use of GIS for any particular study, some items to consider include the following:

- Do GIS data exist in any form for your study site?
- If not, what sort of data exists that might be GIS compatible?
- Do you have access to this data and, if so, under what conditions?
- What was the original purpose for which the data were collected?
- What variable attributes are included in the data set that you are interested in examining?
- How old are the data? Were the data collected at only one time, or are the data longitudinal?
- What sort of metadata exists for these data?
- Has any type of accuracy assessment been completed, or have the data been ground truthed?

Assuming that you can find and access data appropriate to your study, the time spent locating useful data, especially if it is already in a GIS format, will be well worth the effort. Even finding out that none of the required data exists or is available is still important information in planning your study. Knowing what you will need to collect and input data yourself is important in adequate budgeting of both time and money for your study. Considerations of data quality are addressed in Chapters 2 and 8.

Questions About Location

This section contains a series of questions that should be asked about your geographic location. These questions may appear basic, but they help you in gathering information that is useful for integrating a GIS into your project. These questions will help you in the process of identifying important characteristics of your study location. Answering these questions beforehand assists you in your data collection process because it helps you establish those aspects of your location that are important and determine which type of data variables you require. It is important you answer these questions before data collection so that you can arrange the categories and measurement devices for your project. These issues are discussed in detail in later chapters. When evaluating the geographic aspects of your study, valuable considerations might include the following:

- Where does your research occur geographically?
- How would you offer a physical description of your study site(s)/research area (i.e., what is the geographic boundary of the study)?
- Which urban areas or cities are in close proximity to your study site? Are these relevant variables?
- Are there emotionally, spiritually, environmentally, physically, or culturally important units of analysis (neighborhoods, counties, valleys, mountains)?

- What are the different geographic locations associated with your independent variable(s)?
- Are there any unique natural geographic features that exist in your study site(s)?
- Are there any unique man-made geographic features or facilities that exist within your study site(s)?
- Are there any geographic features of the area that hold some special meaning for the people who live there?
- Are there boundaries associated with your data? How are these defined?
- Are the data stationary through the time frame of your analysis or do they move? How will you account for these changes?

Questions for Analysis

The following list of questions will aid in conducting your analysis. They focus on the issue of boundaries, time, and place. All of these issues are discussed in greater detail in later chapters, especially in Chapter 6, but are important to have in mind early on. A GIS is useful for conducting a comparative study of groups of people. It's up the researcher to determine boundaries for the study. Boundary choice is essential because changing the boundaries of an analysis can drastically alter the results obtained. Therefore, the boundaries of your study are best dictated by the research question you are investigating and should be set in advance as opposed to during the analysis phase.

Trying to determine whether or not geographic variables will be useful to your study can be tricky, but keep this in mind: Almost all units of analysis have an associated geographic location. Social scientists are often interested in measuring basic sociodemographic variables, such as age, income, gender, ethnicity, and so forth. These core variables can then be associated with geographic locations, such as neighborhoods, cities, and states. The possibilities are limitless. Anything that involves geographic boundaries can be studied using GIS. Sometimes boundaries are artificially created by the researcher, depending on the researcher's goals. At other times, the boundaries already exist and are based on man-made (e.g., streets) or existing (e.g., rivers, lakes, and mountains) geographic features.

The issue of boundaries is a very important one for GIS. One thing to keep in mind is that you are the boss when it comes to your data collection and the type of information that you want to include in your study. Therefore, the notion of appropriate boundaries in your study may require you to look back at your research questions or hypotheses. It is also important to consider whether or not you are dealing with socially constructed boundaries, such as political boundaries (e.g., city limits or state lines) or physical boundaries (e.g., mountain ranges, oceans, or rivers). Sometimes the two coincide, but often they do not. Sometimes we use boundaries defined more fluidly and conceptually (e.g., a traditional hunting ground, the heart of the community, or a gang's territory).

Questions for analysis include the following:

1. What is the primary unit of analysis in your study?

2. What are the physical boundaries for your unit of analysis?

3. What are the social (conceptual) boundaries for your unit of analysis?

4. Are your conceptual boundaries social, philosophical, or economic? Conceptual boundaries can be anything that reasonably organizes people into groups relevant to issues you are examining. Although conceptual boundaries are often physically defined, geographic boundaries (e.g., cities or neighborhoods), such boundaries may be self-defined, such as people who identify themselves as part of a particular group because of some perceived shared characteristic (e.g., a particular ethnic or religious group or a group of people with a similar hobby or interest, such as gardening or bird watching). You can identify the boundaries of the group you are studying based on these conceptually defined parameters.

5. What is the hypothesis or driving research question? What is the problem or issue your research addresses?

6. What is the main geographic feature or variable you will examine in your study?

7. How is this feature or issue related to your independent or dependent variable? (Also see Question 8 for assistance with answering this question.)

8. Can you identify any geographic pattern by unit of analysis (e.g., group, neighborhood, county) relative to the topic or issue under study? For instance, if you are studying poverty, are there certain neighborhoods in the study that are more poverty-stricken than others?

9. If your study involves a comparison of groups, are there differences or stratifications based on geographic location?

10. If your study does not indicate any geographically based patterns, are there geographic variables worthy of exploration that you failed to consider?

11. What themes emerge from your data? Do they emerge by unit of analysis?

12. Are there themes that emerge specific to certain geographic locations?

13. Are there clusters of specific social, economic, and political data that appear to be grouped together geographically?

14. If this information is not easily available in a spatial database format, could it be easily created?

How To: Steps in the Process

If you decide that you want to employ a GIS in your project, you need to do two things right away: identify the geographic region and develop a data dictionary.

Identifying the geographic region (or spatial extent) and features important to your study is the first thing you should do. This task includes identifying the categories, geographic features, and physical environmental features that you want to consider as a part of your study. Basically, it means drawing a study site boundary, having a good understanding of your topic, and determining which geographic features you want to measure.

Developing a data dictionary means developing a set of definitions and criteria for your particular categories. In other words, you need to develop descriptions that clearly define each of the attributes you will be recording in association with your variables. We explore research design and considerations for the incorporation of GIS further in Chapter 4.

For example, you might be doing a study of urban communities, but how exactly will you define these? You might use a definition based on population density, the percentage of the landscape covered by concrete, or the number of roads per square mile. Developing and documenting clear definitions for each variable and attribute to be included in your study are essential steps before going forward with data collection and analysis. Doing this in advance helps to ensure that everyone involved in the study understands the data to be collected and that each item will be mutually exclusive, thus avoiding confusion later in the process.

Public Health Example

The best way to determine the purpose of your research is to think about the central question that you want to have answered. For instance, maybe you are interested in examining whether people who live in a certain section of town (e.g., the poorer section) suffer from respiratory problems. The different parts of the town may be described as being "rich," "middle class," or "poor" based on the income level of residents who live there. The question of health connected to income is a question that could be addressed using a GIS. Following the previously mentioned guidelines for integrating GIS into a study, you would determine the study boundaries and relevant geographic features that are going to be a part of the study. In this case, you are interested in drawing your study boundaries based on income. In other words, you want to draw a boundary around the low-income section of town, the mideconomic section of town, and the upscale part. Where would you begin? You could begin by looking at the U.S. Census data for that town to determine the different clusters in town based on household income. You could then draw your boundaries based on the clustering observed in the

U.S. Census data. Step 1 in the process also calls for identifying other geographic features that might be important to your study. In this example, these geographic features would include the locations of different factories, incinerators, and other production facilities.

Step 2 in integrating GIS into your study calls for developing a data dictionary. You would determine what level of household income fits your categories: for example, rich might be over $45,000 per year, middle class might be $20,000–44,999 per year, and poor might be less than $19,999 per year. In a GIS you could also gather information on the level of emissions from the different facilities by looking at the U.S. Environmental Protection Agency's Web site. On that Web site, the agency indicates industrial sites that emit beyond a certain specified level. This valuable information regarding air quality could become a part of your GIS database.

You could interview people who live throughout the town and conduct a survey that inquires about their general health and income and specifically questions whether or not they suffer from any respiratory problems. As long as you know the geographic location of respondents, you can enter this information, along with the survey answers, into a database. That way, when you conduct your analysis, you'll be able to have geographic information for each unit of analysis (i.e., household). If you want to aggregate the data slightly to protect the privacy of the individuals, you can categorize respondents as living in a neighborhood rather than use actual street addresses as a categories. Upon further investigation, you may want to geographically locate various factories, incinerators, or other production-oriented facilities that could be emitting substances that affect people's respiratory health.

Another important thing to consider in determining your research purpose is the general theme that is a part of your research question. In the respiratory health example, some of the potential themes might be environmental health, social inequality, or environmental justice.

After determining the general purpose of your research, you can then ask the question, how would GIS be helpful to the project? In other words, how would using a GIS enhance the study? A GIS is useful because it facilitates a more holistic and contextual view of the research problem or issue. It accomplishes this by bringing together a variety of different data types. Any study that you choose to develop will most likely include a variety of important variables. The trick in using the GIS is to identify which variables will best be studied using a GIS. This topic is discussed in greater detail in the following chapter.

Relevant Web Sites

"Demystifying the Persistent Ambiguity of GIS as 'Tool' Versus 'Science'": An article by Dawn Wright, Michael F. Goodchild, and James D. Proctor. http://dusk.geo.orst.edu/annals.html

"Social Sciences: Interest in GIS Grows": An article by Michael F. Goodchild of the Center for Spatially Integrated Social Science. http://www.esri.com/news/arcnews/spring04articles/social-sciences.html

U.S. Department of Labor: Bureau of Labor Statistics, *Occupational Outlook Handbook,* Social Scientist section. http://stats.bls.gov/oco/ocos054.htm

4 Research Design

Chapter Description

This chapter explores the primary steps in narrowing the purpose of your sociospatial analysis and the approach to be taken. We begin with a discussion of important factors related to developing your research or analysis design, including key stages of the research process and examples using the spatial perspective provided by GIS. This chapter also examines different approaches to research and its operationalization. We also consider several common pitfalls of research design. The chapter concludes with a section on research ethics and confidentiality and accuracy when using spatially linked data in GIS.

Chapter Objectives

- Present key topics relating to research design in a GIS context.
- Offer suggestions for carrying out a research project.
- Provide points of caution to consider in the design and implementation of GIS-based social science research.

After reading this chapter, you should be able to perform the following tasks:

- Explain the difference between inductive and deductive research.
- Lay out the major steps and considerations in the design of a research process.
- Determine the relevance of time in your research question and methods to incorporate time if necessary.
- Identify and avoid common errors throughout the data collection and analysis processes.
- Recognize and find an appropriate ethical balance between research goals and the protection of individuals' privacy.

Inductive Versus Deductive Approach to Research

A GIS can be useful for both inductive and deductive approaches to social science research. In an inductive approach, the researcher's understanding of the research topic and potential hypotheses emerge from the data. In other words, the researcher does not go into the study with any preconceived notions or hypotheses. Instead, the researcher begins the research process by collecting data, and then the researcher seeks to develop an understanding of patterns observed. This ultimately leads the researcher to develop a theory to help explain the observed patterns.

In contrast, in a deductive approach, the researcher begins the research process by following a series of traditional steps. (See the 10 steps of the GIS research process listed later in this chapter.) In this kind of research, the researcher begins by reviewing the literature, generating a conceptual framework, developing a hypothesis, and then testing the hypothesis by gathering data.

What Is the Purpose of Your Research?

Research can have a variety of purposes. When doing applied social science research, we often are interested in descriptive research that shows the current state of things. Two additional purposes of research are to explore data and to attempt to explain why things are the way they are. Of course, the practical goal of many research projects in the social sciences is to solve a specific problem or suggest alternatives. A GIS is an excellent tool for all of these research goals, especially in situations where data from a variety of sources must be brought together. With the speed and analytical power of a GIS, it becomes feasible to explore many more alternatives and characteristics of the data than might be practical using other approaches.

Descriptive Research

In a descriptive study, the main goal of the research is to catalog and observe data. A descriptive study is useful for increasing one's understanding about something. An example of a descriptive study using a GIS would be to look at the number and geographic distribution of ethnic populations in an urban area, such as New York City. The goal of such a study might be to determine spatially where these different ethnic groups are located and why (e.g., Italians are located in Little Italy, the majority of Haitians are in Brooklyn). The value of a descriptive study is that it provides detailed information that could be used as baseline data. It is informational and can be used to make policy decisions, provide services, analyze crime, and track diseases as well as perform many other social science–related tasks. By tracking the occurrence and location of cases of West Nile virus in each county in the country using a GIS, you could determine where the virus is becoming a problem, how it is moving, and when it is likely to hit next. Using this information, one could alert local public heath agencies, take action to reduce mosquitoes in at-risk locations, and develop appropriate policies for treating and preventing further spread of the disease.

Exploration

When a study is exploratory, there may be little known about the topic. The goal of exploratory research is to begin to develop an understanding of the topic so that additional questions or hypotheses can be developed. Exploratory research is research at the tip of the iceberg. In other words, the researcher is trying out something for the first time. An example of this would be if you lived in a community where there is a shortage of affordable housing. The word on the street might be that only "old people" can afford to live in the nice section of the city anymore. As a researcher who is conducting exploratory research, you can create a GIS map that portrays the age distribution of people in particular areas of the city. You might accomplish this by using a GIS and integrating U.S. Census population data into the mix. Then you would be able to visualize where older people reside compared to younger people.

This type of exploratory research would be the starting point for a much more in-depth study on housing issues that could be conducted in the future. Exploratory research is a great place to start for researchers who are beginning to learn about a particular topic. It is also a good place to start for someone who is interested in making an empirical investigation of general knowledge held by members of the community. This provides a way for a researcher to further examine whether the word on the street has any validity and, if so, to what degree.

Explanation

When explanation is the goal of your research, you are seeking to examine relationships between variables. A researcher conducting an explanatory study is interested in developing a scientifically based understanding of why things happen. Explanatory studies still involve description, but with a different goal in mind. One goal might be to develop an understanding of connections that explain why something occurs in some locations but not in others. How does a GIS fit into this? It enables the researcher to consider spatial relationships as one potential component in the explanation of why observed relationships occur.

For example, let's say that you are interested in understanding why crime rates are higher in some neighborhoods than others. Is it due to socioeconomic issues, such as income and education? Are there spatial relationships, such as proximity to ATMs or convenience stores? Or negative correlations to locations of police stations, well-lit streets, or other physical factors? As a part of your study, you can create a geographic picture of these variables within the areas that experience varied crime rates. The GIS will show you where the different variables intersect with higher or lower crime rates and quite possibly show that certain variable combinations have a stronger correlation with crime than others. To avoid committing the ecological fallacy (see discussion later in this chapter), one might wish to follow up the analysis by conducting interviews or surveys of residents and viewing trends in crime in the context of the national economy and crime in other areas to develop a complete understanding of why these higher crime rates occur in specific types of neighborhoods.

Of course, one must be cautious when using a GIS to avoid the temptation to draw conclusions based solely on appearance. Although visualization of the data is a powerful method for showing relationships, one must be careful to follow this up with sound analysis—be it spatial analysis in the GIS, spatial and nonspatial statistical analyses, or other means appropriate to the data. To help in this process we suggest the 10 steps presented in the next section as a guide to conducting sociospatial research that is deductive in its approach.

Stages of Sociospatial Research for Deductive Research

In using a deductive research model, researchers have a clear idea or hypothesis that they want to investigate through the research process. We've developed a set of 10 steps in the research process, which is a variation of the 8 steps associated with the scientific method as mentioned by Henslin (2003).

1. Choose a topic.

2. Define the problem.

3. Conduct a literature review.

4. Develop a hypothesis.

5. Develop a conceptual framework.

6. Choose research methods.

7. Collect and prepare data.

8. Ground truth the data.

9. Analyze the data.

10. Share results.

Choose a Topic

The first step in conducting your research is to choose a topic. As a researcher, you may already have your topic chosen for you by an employer, an organization, a funding agency, or a foundation that hires you to conduct research. If you are independently choosing your topic, it is a good idea to select a subject or issue that you find personally interesting.

If you are a student, you may face some unique challenges. Many students report that they find almost every topic interesting. If you are one of those people, then it would be a good idea to keep a journal of research ideas. In this journal, you could jot down research ideas or thoughts as they come to you. Keep a journal like this for a month and then go back to it and look for themes that emerge. By reviewing your thoughts and ideas over an extended time period, you might find that one or two ideas surface along with developed options for further study. Of course, you may also need to consider time limitations. If you are a student, will your study be completed in the course of a semester or will it be more like a graduate thesis, extending over a longer period of time?

If your project is related to your professional role in the social sciences, what is your time frame? Are you working within the confines of a budget or policy cycle? Is there a pressing need that you are trying to address, or is this research going to be used for long-term planning?

It is also good to pick a topic that is feasible to study. For example, you may find a comparison of nontraditional sexual practices around the world to be interesting, but you may encounter some difficulty collecting primary data on this topic. When evaluating the feasibility of a particular topic, consider what, if any, prior work has been done on the subject and how you will go about locating or collecting the data necessary to complete the analysis. Once you have determined a topic, you can begin to think about choosing a study site, perhaps something close to home, so you can visit personally. To determine how a GIS would fit into your topic, think about which relevant variables can be collected in space and which boundaries of analysis are appropriate to exploring the data.

Define the Problem

In defining the problem, you want to think more specifically about how you can narrow your topic. Having a good, solid definition of the problem is something that will guide the rest of your research because it is something that you can refer back to as a guide as you proceed with the project. We advise writing out a problem statement that includes the following four components:

1. An introduction to the topic.

2. Established relevance or importance through cited literature.

3. Background on your topic.

4. A specific problem related to a particular issue or research hypothesis.

To include a GIS in your definition of the problem, you need to conceptualize what units of analysis you are interested in comparing. (See Chapter 6 for additional discussion of unit of analysis.) Are you interested in investigating an issue by looking at different groups who live in different places? Or would it be more fitting to examine the same group over time? How you want to investigate your research question—meaning what groups, geographic locations, and issues your study involves—is key to know up front. Once you've determined these issues, you can begin the process of pursing the collection of already existing GIS data that relate to your topic or creating data that pertain to your topic—or both.

Conduct a Literature Review

Conducting a literature review is an essential next step in the academic research process. Even if you are not conducting an academic research project, a review of some of the pertinent literature will help to inform and support the approaches used, which is important when you need to convince colleagues. The literature review should present relevant information from a variety of literatures. A broad review is especially important if you are dealing with an interdisciplinary topic where one source does not adequately address all of the issues you are interested in studying in your analysis. Because GIS-based projects by nature draw on information from a variety of disciplines, a review of several areas of the literature may be necessary.

For example, if you are using a GIS to analyze gaps in the public transportation system in a particular community, you will want to examine literature in fields as diverse as sociology, psychology, transportation, and GIS. Such sources might help in your understanding of which people use public transportation and in what ways, how public transportation systems are designed and routed, how GIS is used in modeling systems and behaviors, and perhaps other areas in addition to these. Ultimately, by reviewing how others have thought about modeling or analyzing social science data in a spatial context—even if they never used a GIS—you will be better able to develop an appropriate model to implement in a GIS. (An important side note: Social scientists have, for many years, thought about questions spatially. The presentation of Dr. John Snow's research in London in the mid-1800s is one of the earliest published examples. Although the advent of GIS was more than a century off, the design of Snow's analysis can be easily carried out in a GIS today. For additional, classic examples of spatial concepts in social sciences, visit the Center for Spatially Integrated Social Science Web site on classic research at http://www.csiss.org/classics/.)

In writing a literature review, be sure to include a thorough review of the relevant information that pertains to your topic. This involves searching for a variety of sources of relevant information. It is always good to involve a variety of different types of information in your literature review, ranging from refereed journals to books, news stories, and Web sites. One should be especially careful to check the source and credentials when relying on information from Web sites because anyone can put anything on the Web, regardless of its quality and credibility. It is up to you, the researcher, to make a critical assessment of the sources of information found on the Web, or anyplace else for that matter, before deciding which ones you will use.

When conducting your review of the literature, also try to search for studies that may have been conducted on your topic using a GIS. This kind of information will give you some additional ideas about how you might be able to incorporate a GIS into your own study. Very often you will find more success by searching in the sources related to your discipline and using "GIS" or "geographic information systems" as key words in the search. This approach is generally more successful than the reverse—going to journals specifically focused on GIS and looking for information particular to the discipline you are analyzing—although sometimes this method also provides some good resources.

Your literature review should contain common themes and specific, relevant ideas and concepts and should also present relevant debates that pertain to your problem statement. By conducting a thorough literature review, you will gain insight into possible research methodologies, study designs, and variables that may be directly relevant to your own study. You will also find that the literature can help you justify or legitimize the methods you will use in your own study.

Develop a Hypothesis

Research is guided by a question or issue that a researcher or group of researchers thinks is worth investigating or that needs to be addressed in some way. Regardless of your motivation, your research question is best guided by a hypothesis. A hypothesis is simply an idea about the research that seems reasonable and that you think explains the situation at hand, or it might be the underlying basis of debate about the topic. In other words, the hypothesis of your research is an educated guess about what you might find, but the validity of your hypothesis has yet to be proven.

When developing your hypothesis, think about the most important aspects of your proposed topic. A hypothesis is an educated guess about relationships you might find between variables. Once you can state your ideas about the research or analysis in one sentence, you know that you have narrowed your topic enough to create a hypothesis. Your hypothesis should clearly state the main idea or the crux of your research project. In other words, a hypothesis is simply a statement that conveys what you might find or the state of some set of events. A hypothesis presents something that can be tested, explored, and further investigated.

The following hypotheses incorporate a spatial question and can be effectively analyzed in a GIS:

1. A greater percentage of poor people live in polluted environments than do wealthier people.

2. Newcomers who move to rural areas tend to cluster in areas with people of similar socioeconomic backgrounds.

3. Rates of AIDS are lower in individuals with a college education.

4. Individuals with strong social ties in their local community are more likely to participate in local governance.

A final comment on the hypothesis is that it establishes what you believe to be important about your research project. As a researcher, you can think about how GIS might add to the understanding of your hypothesis by identifying key variables.

Every hypothesis should have a single dependent and one or more independent variables. In the first hypothesis listed previously, a GIS could be used to take census data overlaid with pollution data from the U.S. Environmental Protection Agency's Toxic Release Inventory database. Socioeconomic information would come from the census data, and you could define (according to whatever criteria are deemed appropriate) what areas are polluted (see Figure 4.1).

If you consider the spatial distribution of the pollution sources in Figure 4.1, several things might be apparent: First, the majority of the mid- and high-pollution facilities are somewhat clustered to the left of center on the map in Polygons 1, 2, and 7. It would be logical to assume that if the center of the map (Polygon 4) was the historic city center, industrial facilities, particularly the older, higher-polluting facilities, would have grown up around the city center. Over time, newer, cleaner facilities might be expected to grow on the edges of the city. Second, you will notice that facilities are generally located to the left side of the map, with no facilities sited on the right side of the map (Polygons 3, 5, and 8). Last, we might note that although the central polygon (Polygon 4) has no points inside it and Polygon 7 has only one light polluter, several other sources of pollution are just across the line in the adjacent polygons (Polygons 1, 2, and 6).

We further discuss this example as we go through the remaining stages of research. As a problem exercise, you might also consider the other three hypotheses presented earlier or others you are interested in exploring. What considerations might be important as you operationalize this for your spatial analysis of the data in each of these situations?

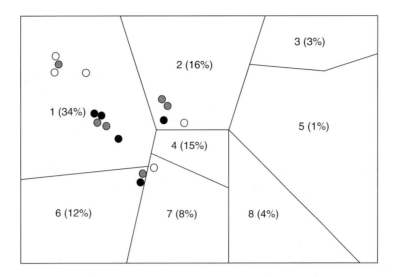

Figure 4.1 Facilities that are registered on the U.S. Environmental Protection Agency's Toxic Release Inventory are recorded as point locations in the database. Information regarding the specific pollutants released is also recorded. (Here these are coded on an ordinal scale from low toxicity—white circles—to high toxicity—black circles.) Assume the polygons on the map represent the census tracts with a specified percentage of the population classified as poor (as defined from census data). We could use the GIS to determine if there is a statistical difference based on solely the point locations of facilities releasing toxics (do they fall in the census tract or not) or based on other spatial concepts, such as nearness or adjacency.

Develop a Conceptual Framework

What is a conceptual framework? A conceptual framework is a working theoretical model that explains your view of the world. In essence, it provides your chance as a researcher to identify key variables in your study, to explain the links between these variables, and to explain the sequence and flow of relationships by using arrows. (The structure and creation of a flowchart for GIS analysis are discussed in detail in Chapter 9.)

Once you complete your literature review, you should have an easy time developing this framework. A conceptual framework is different from a literature review because it guides the research process of your specific project. The conceptual model establishes factors important to your study and indicates to all who read your study the predicted relationships between key variables.

Brainstorming is a good approach to begin developing a conceptual framework. You might start by writing down the important aspects of your study on a sheet of paper. Next, draw circles around these objects and use arrows to indicate relationships between these variables. As you identify your key variables, you can decide which type of contextual, geographic, or other information can facilitate a study of the relationships among these variables. When you identify relationships among the variables in your study, consider how geographic information might enhance your understanding of these relationships.

Consider our earlier example relating poverty and pollution. Given the spatial distribution of polluting facilities on the map, we would want to conceptualize what the actual locations really mean to our hypothesis: Is presence of a facility inside a polygon all that matters, or do sites affect people for some distance (perhaps in a neighboring polygon)? If there is an effect over a distance, how does the mode of transport (through air, water, or solid waste) influence the distance and direction of the effect? What about the poverty data? Are all of the people in the census block distributed equally, or does the housing cluster in certain portions of the polygon? (This relates to issues of boundaries and the modifiable area unit problem discussed more fully in Chapter 7.) The list could go on, but the important point is to think beyond what is directly visible, such as points falling inside particular polygons, to consider other factors or mechanisms that might be important in assessing the validity of your hypothesis.

A GIS is very useful for establishing the context of how different variables relate to one another conceptually. Some GIS software programs provide a flowchart tool as a means to develop your analysis approach and, once populated with data and analysis functions, to run your model. Even when the flowchart is simply drawn on paper, it guides you in developing a systematic or holistic approach to a particular issue under study.

For instance, suppose you are conducting a study about an individual's attitudes about environmental issues. You may hypothesize that the nature of the community and its geographic location (e.g., their proximity to unspoiled natural features, such as state or national parks or wilderness areas) influence community concern about environmental issues. Your conceptual framework would then incorporate the geographic variable of park and wilderness proximity into your model (see Figure 4.2). Using a GIS, one could map the locations of these natural features and overlay sociodemographic characteristics and residents' levels of environmental concern to see if indeed there are differences.

Choose Research Methods

What are the factors to consider in choosing a research method? One should first consider the project goal and the sort of data most appropriate in meeting it. Can you use existing data, or will you require new data (or both)? Should the data used in your study be quantitative or qualitative (or both)? What will the boundaries of your study be? Research can be conducted at the local, regional, national, or global level, or at any combination of the four levels. Will you be doing a descriptive study of one area or

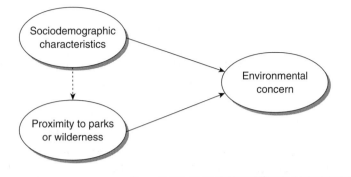

Figure 4.2   An example of a conceptual framework for environmental concern. Sociodemographic factors such as age, race, gender, and income might have a relationship with where individuals choose to live (dashed arrow) in addition to their environmental concern (solid arrow). Proximity to parks or wilderness is also expected to have an influence on environmental concern (solid arrow).

comparing multiple research locations? Is there one or are there several methods that might be used in the collection and analysis of the data?

If time and money allow, it is sometimes beneficial to incorporate multiple research methods in studying your topic because a variety of methods adds a greater empirical angle to your study. One popular approach is triangulation, or cross-examination, which is simply studying the same phenomena using three different research methods. Triangulation gives the researcher greater choice in gathering information on the topic. When data collected using multiple methods point to a similar result, your confidence in your results is strengthened.

Box 4.1   An Aside on Triangulation

Interestingly, the term triangulation is historically associated with geometry, not the social sciences. If you work primarily in the social sciences, you may be familiar with the term as it applies to using multiple sources or methods to arrive at a result or conclusion. However, if you do an Internet search on the term, you'll find the first several pages of resulting hits relate to mapping and geometry. The properties of triangles were well understood by the ancient Greeks and are the basis for many modern mapping and land surveying techniques. As we were writing this chapter, we realized an unintentional relationship between the mapping and social sciences may have originated in the translation of this geometric mapping term into the social science lexicon. In mapping, triangulation refers to the process of calculating a distance to a location by knowing the length of one side of a triangle and the related angles. This is accomplished with an instrument known as a theodolite, or its modern equivalents, including global positioning systems (GPS) or a surveyors' total station.

So you could approach your problem or issue using a variety of methods, such as surveys, key-informant interviews, external or participant observation, and a review of historic or archival data. A geographic component could be incorporated into some or all of these different methods. (Chapter 5 further discusses the incorporation of GIS in your research methods.)

Operationalization—Measurement

As you consider the selection of your research methods, it is important to refer back to your conceptual framework. Each of your variables should be individually conceptualized and then operationalized; that is, you need to decide exactly what you will measure and how. This requires that you define each of the concepts you are using in your study and the associated level of measurement (see Chapter 7). Operationalizing a variable requires you to explain how you are going to measure the concepts mentioned in your hypothesis. Typically, the variety of data collection approaches you employ is documented in the Methods section of your study. When your methods relate directly to the creation of a GIS data set, you need to be sure to record the data creation procedures in a metadata file that is included with each individual data layer.

In the example of the relationship between pollution and poverty, you might operationalize pollution as previously shown in Figure 4.1: low, medium, and high. In doing so, you would need to define exactly what is meant by these terms. Is "low pollution" something that is measured as a number of pounds or gallons released or as a medical definition, such as the odds of getting sick from exposure (e.g., 1 in 1,000,000 as low, 1 in 100,000 as medium, and 1 in 10,000 as high)? Of course, you could come up with a variety of definitions, each viewed as appropriate or inappropriate depending on the legal definitions, regulatory recommendations, expert opinions, or local experience, to name a few.

Coming up with a true definition is not necessarily as important (or possible) as explaining your definition so that others can understand and interpret your results. One advantage of the GIS is that, if you choose to change your definition or examine different scenarios, it is relatively easy to rerun your analysis with the adjusted definitions to determine how the results change.

Collect and Prepare Data

When using a GIS as a tool for your research, collecting and preparing the data for analysis can be significant tasks in the process. Although this is not an issue unique to GIS-based analysis, it is commonly expected that 75% to 80% of the time and effort in GIS-based projects will be used collecting, creating, or converting data to ensure everything is ready for the analysis. (Chapter 6 provides further discussion on data creation.) When we say creating data, we don't just mean making it up. Because GIS technology is fairly new, data may exist in a hard-copy format (paper maps, field notes, etc.) but not necessarily exist in a computerized, GIS-compatible format. For these reasons, researchers may have to be persistent and potentially a bit creative when seeking out potential sources of data. It is not uncommon to find multiple sources of what appear to be the same data, so it is essential to review and evaluate each prospective data set before settling on the perfect source of information for your particular study.

Of course, not all data you may need will exist, so it is quite likely you could be collecting your own data for use in a GIS analysis. For many social scientists, data collection is one of the most enjoyable components of the research process. Why? This is the part of the research process in which researchers actively implement ideas that, until then, have only existed in their minds (and, ideally, during the two previous stages of the research process have been put down on paper).

Data collection can come in a variety of forms. It may involve what social scientists call *going into the field*—face-to-face contact with the people in your study or detailed examinations of secondary data. This can involve distributing and collecting surveys or traveling to a faraway location to conduct a case study. Data collection is the part of the research process that motivated many of us to go into the social sciences in the first place and the part we have always found to be fun.

One should begin the data collection process with a good understanding of the type of data necessary for testing the hypothesis; an idea of where to find this information (agencies, corporations, universities, etc.); and clearly identified geographic components that best fit within the study. In this technological age and given security concerns, some organizations and agencies are somewhat guarded about sharing detailed geographic information. However, there is a wealth of free, preexisting geographic information available from a variety of data providers, libraries, government agencies, Internet resources, and others. Where you go looking for information depends on which geographic features you are looking for. (See Chapter 7 for a more detailed discussion of measurement and GIS.)

Ground Truth the Data

Because a GIS involves technology that can use data acquired entirely without ever leaving your office, it is theoretically possible to complete an entire analysis without ever leaving your desk. However, it would be foolish to believe such an analysis would be without flaws (especially considering the variable quality, scale, projections, data formats, and so on discussed throughout this book). Therefore, even if all of your data can be acquired without fieldwork, it is a good idea to ground truth at key points in the process. Whenever you use a GIS, you want to make sure that you ground truth, not only to ensure that the data you are using are appropriate to your question but also to validate that the results obtained in the GIS match what you find in the field. (Note: Ground truthing of results, by necessity, comes after the analysis described in Step 9, but we discuss it here because the issues are similar for both input data and results.)

In most cases, ground truth means actually traveling to the place where the study is located to get a visual on the data or results. In situations where physically visiting the site may be difficult, alternative sources might be used to cross-validate your data against a second, reliable source. For example, if you are studying urban development patterns, you might be able to use current aerial photography or satellite images to confirm that a particular location has or has not been developed. If you can go to the field, you would take along a map representing data to be used in your GIS analysis and make sure that your map is both valid and accurate. Of course, you cannot check everything, but simply spot-checking or sampling from the map can go a long way toward ensuring that you start with good data.

In our pollution example discussed earlier in the chapter, ground truthing could help to answer questions about the form of the pollution and where it travels. For example, observing a smoke plume from a factory may show that a prevailing wind carries the smoke in a particular direction most of the time. Or a drive through each census block could tell you if the residents are evenly distributed within the polygon or if they are clustered in specific portions.

Finally, ground truth is essential at the conclusion of an analysis when you are evaluating the results. Most GIS-based studies pinpoint certain locations as having met a set of criteria. Again, spot-checking in the field can go a long way toward telling you if the results look correct and if they make sense. If your study is large, you may want to spot-check a number of sites to assess the overall accuracy of the analysis (e.g., if 9 of 10 results are correct when checked on the ground, it would be reasonable to estimate accuracy at 90%). The topic of accuracy assessment in spatial data analysis is one that can fill an entire book, so we only mention it here and encourage those who are interested to pursue this topic independently.

Analyze the Data

In this step in the research process, you must again refer back to your primary research question and conceptual framework. The form of analysis you select will in part be determined by the type of data you have collected and prepared in the GIS. Some analysis tools work exclusively on vector data and others exclusively on raster data. Of course, many operations can be accomplished with either. Furthermore, if you collected quantitative data, chances are you will use a form of statistical analysis. Many of the common, descriptive statistics are available within GIS software. However, it is also common to enlist other statistical programs for some portions of the analysis. This is accomplished by extracting key information from the GIS using the spatial tools and exporting the raw numbers to a program such as SPSS® to analyze the information before returning it to the GIS to make maps of the results.

If you are working with qualitative data, you may require use of a data program designed specifically for qualitative analysis, such as NVIVO® or Atlas/ti®. In identifying your key variables, you can decide which type of contextual or geographic information might aid in studying the relationships between these variables. The geographic information that was collected as a part of your study can then be analyzed using a variety of methods.

Regardless of the type of data, the most important thing to keep in mind at this stage is to let your project dictate the analysis, rather than let the software drive the analysis simply because the software contains a menu option or button. Returning to your conceptual framework will be essential at this stage because the framework is your guide in the analysis. Chapter 9 provides a more detailed discussion of conceptualizing a project and completing the data analysis using GIS.

Share Results

For applied research, this is perhaps the most important step in the entire research process. Sharing one's results can occur through two basic avenues and for two different audiences: laypeople and members of the scientific community. If you are interested in sharing your findings with laypeople, you should package the results in a manner that will be both understandable and easy to decipher without a lot of jargon.

We've found that producing a report that discusses the methods and highlights the main findings of a study is most effective. You might also consider developing a visual presentation that can be given in a variety of settings and highlights both your research methods and your main findings.

If you plan to share your results with members of the scientific community, you will most likely want to write a paper for submission to a scientific journal or present your results at a professional conference.

Using a GIS can be very useful in sharing your results because it allows for the presentation of data in a visual format. Most commonly, the visual output is a map, but a GIS can also provide outputs as charts or graphs, or, if done as an interactive presentation, as animated or interactive maps. Not surprisingly, any of these visualizations can have wide-ranging applicability in a variety of contexts and support the old saying, "A picture is worth a thousand words."

The Role of Time

When designing research, one important element to consider is time. The nature of your hypothesis or issue under study typically dictates the role time plays. As you review your research question, consider if it focuses on a particular point in time, on a cross-sectional study, or on how things change through time (a longitudinal approach).

Cross-Sectional Studies

This type of research design is appropriate when you want to examine a research problem or issue at one point in time. Thus, when you are locating or collecting data for use in a cross-sectional study, it is best to acquire the data at a single point in time. Realistically, it is impossible to locate or collect all of the necessary data instantaneously. Any fieldwork will by necessity take several hours—and potentially months or years. Fortunately, time—much like space—can be measured at a variety of scales. (See Chapter 2 for a discussion on scale.) Therefore, as the researcher, you will want to consider a time scale that you can realistically use.

As a case in point, consider one cycle of the U.S. Census. Data for the census is collected once every 10 years and takes months to complete. Although the census is intended as a complete count of the U.S. population, it is clear that during the data collection period, changes occur—babies are born, people die, and individuals without traditional residences (migrant workers, homeless, etc.) may be missed or counted more than once as they move around. The last of these problems can also introduce spatial errors because the census is also concerned with where people are located. Nonetheless, the chosen time scale of the census allows for this data, collected over the course of many months, to represent a "single" point in time. We are willing to accept the small errors in the count because to avoid them would be very difficult and costly, even if there were means to accomplish it.

Because many studies draw data from a variety of sources, there are other time considerations to keep in mind. For example, if you were doing a study of a community, a variety of basic map information may be important. Perhaps you want to know locations of roads, parks, schools, neighborhoods, and businesses in a particular community. It is possible that all of this information is maintained in up-to-date form by a single entity (feel lucky if this is your situation). However, it is equally common to encounter data that are updated infrequently; perhaps the new subdivision or shopping mall that was built last year is not yet included on the map. What do you do? What if the "latest" map is many years old, as is common with many of the maps produced by the United States Geological Survey (USGS)? (In our hometown, the USGS quadrangle maps were last updated in the early 1970s!) In some cross-sectional studies, data that are a year old may be fine; in others, that data may be too old to be useful. You will need to decide on the time frame that meets your needs in representing a "single" point in time. If data that meet your definition do not exist, you may need to look to alternative sources, consider ways to collect the data yourself, or otherwise adjust your study to make the best of what is available.

Longitudinal Studies

A longitudinal research design examines data at two or more points in time. One important point to remember when designing a longitudinal study is that each point in time requires the same design considerations as used in defining a cross-sectional study. Of course, the U.S. Census example mentioned earlier holds true here because the census is actually a longitudinal study showing how the population has changed since the previous decade. Longitudinal studies are useful when researchers want to examine any type of change over time, be it physical, environmental, or social change.

As an example, let's consider a study in which we are interested in determining how proximity to particular types of natural or man-made environments influences individuals' level of exercise over time. We might be looking at access to exercise resources or opportunities to be active. Are recreational facilities located near where people live? Are there things that would discourage people from getting out and walking and exercising? The goal in this study would be the integration of data related to people and data related to places where they might participate in physical activities. To keep track of the social data, you could have residents keep a log of the type of physical activity they participate in, where they go to participate in it, and how often they participate in it. Using a GIS, you would then be able to plot locations of activity for each participant over time. You could use the GIS to examine where and when people exercise relative to the location of their home, workplace, or school and whether the activity correlates with proximity to certain types of facilities, including natural environments (such as parks or lakes) or human-constructed environments (such as a gym, tennis courts, or a track).

On its own, this example provides a temporal component regarding each participant's choices for being active (time of day, time of week, etc.), which might prove interesting on its own. More interesting, of course, would be to track this over longer time periods (seasons, years, etc.). For example, if you wanted to examine these phenomena by season, you might have residents keep exercise logs for a period of 2 weeks in the winter and 2 weeks in the summer. Therefore, you would have sequential sets of data from different time periods. The GIS could be used to physically measure distance between homes and natural exercise environments versus man-made exercise environments over time. Additionally, the GIS could be used to examine the role that weather plays in the winter versus the summer and how the weather affects people's degree of physical activity. Seasonal weather changes could be integrated as a variable in the GIS, and we might hypothesize people with access to nearby indoor recreation might have higher levels of activity in winter than those who must rely on outdoor options.

You could also distill data from a longitudinal study to develop a cross-sectional analysis as a separate component or study. A researcher might want to determine which of a series of sociodemographic factors influence a person's level of physical activity. There are certain fixed traits that could be included, such as age, income, level of education, occupation, and race. These are all predetermined factors (which can be individually controlled for) that might be examined using a cross-sectional research design.

Of course, it would not suffice to rely solely on GIS technology to investigate these relationships. A GIS would have to be used in conjunction with other measurement techniques, such as interviews or general observations of activity at the locations at different times. Using a GIS as a part of this longitudinal study allows for the incorporation of contextual data measures, such as temperature, weather conditions, general safety of the community (crime rate), degree of precipitation, and proximity to a place to exercise. (An area's crime rate may have a significant effect on people's willingness to go outside and exercise.)

A GIS is useful because it allows for a larger, contextual view of data in both cross-sectional and longitudinal studies. A GIS is diverse enough to fit into research designs that employ both approaches and can serve as both a means to organize and assemble data across space and time as appropriate to a particular study.

Errors in Human Inquiry

Engaging in social research is not a trivial matter. There are several things to be aware of in the early design stages of any social science research project. In his book *The Practice of Social Research*, Earl Babbie (2003) points out some common errors made in social research that should be addressed. These errors include inaccurate observation, overgeneralization, selective observation, and illogical reasoning.

With a little forethought, these pitfalls can be avoided. To ensure that you avoid inaccurate observations, it is important to have a well-defined plan for data collection. Most important, whenever possible, you should record data as it is observed, rather than rely on your memory to properly and precisely recollect what was observed. Data collection forms, tape-recording devices, and clear definitions of criteria or definitions relevant to your observations are essential.

If you have more than one person involved in data collection, it is essential that each person understands and uses the same definitions when making observations. If your study allows for it, get your data collection staff to record the same information through practice. Have them observe together in the same place for several data collection periods to ensure that all observers get acceptably similar results. Once you have everyone seeing the same things, the individual results from multiple observers will more likely be consistent across your study. Approaching a study with a defined plan for collecting information results in a higher likelihood of engaging in accurate observation.

Overgeneralization is another common error in research. This error is easy to commit because it results from the limitations (time, money, or other resources) common to most studies. Overgeneralization of study data occurs in two forms: It can occur when your sample size is too small or when an invalid sampling method is used, leaving you with results that do not accurately represent the intended study population, and it can result when the results of one study are inaccurately extended to other situations where they may not apply.

Suppose several houses on your street went up for sale in the same month. You might make an overgeneralization that the neighborhood is going downhill, and all the neighbors are fleeing. An even greater overgeneralization would be (without checking the status of any other neighborhoods) to assume the entire city is going downhill. It is entirely possible that this hypothesis is correct, but this is only one possible explanation. You would need to collect more information to determine the real reasons people are moving out of your neighborhood.

Following on the concept of overgeneralization is a natural inclination to see what we believe. Selective observation might be described as extending a pattern of observations that is likely to support previous findings, which, in effect, limits your ability to objectively observe. In other words, we see what we expect to see and miss things that do not fit our perspectives. Allowing preconceived notions to influence data collection can be a self-fulfilling prophecy and is an easy trap for researchers to fall into when they want to see their hypotheses or ideas supported.

To avoid this pitfall, it is important to develop your research design in advance, specifying the number and type of observations to be collected. For example, to understand why people decide to remain or leave various neighborhoods, you might survey a sample of houses from each neighborhood in the city, rather than only those whose houses are for sale in your own neighborhood. Stratifying your sample design by one or more sociodemographic or physiographic characteristics is one approach. Alternatively, you may prefer to do a random or systematic sample of the population. In any case, having a plan in advance, rather than allowing yourself to fall into assumptions about what you think is occurring, is the best way to avoid the problem of selective observation.

Finally, illogical reasoning is another potential pitfall to be aware of when engaging in good scientific research. Whenever you conduct research—especially research that is aided by computer analysis—it is essential to consider the logic behind the data and results of the analysis. If the results obtained in the study seem strange to you, there is a good chance they are! In the next section, we discuss the concept of ecological fallacy as the formal description of this problem. But in simple terms you always want to consider the logic of what you are doing rather than rushing blindly forward. Systems of logic can help you in this endeavor. For example, earlier in the chapter we presented the idea of a conceptual framework, a simple flowchart, as a means to begin developing your study. Chapter 9 presents a process for thinking through the logic of a GIS analysis in greater detail.

Ecological Fallacy

The ecological fallacy is an important concept to be aware of during any research study, especially when using a GIS. An ecological fallacy, also referred to as a spurious correlation, is simply an incorrect causal link that is born out statistically by the data. As an example, we might plot the locations of bars on a map along with a plot of educational achievement. If there seems to be a correlation between the number of bars and the level of education, one might wrongly conclude that greater access to alcohol makes people smarter. In fact, running a GIS-based analysis of the spatial correlations between these two data sets might show a highly significant relationship, whether or not it is a causal relationship. Of course, we might more correctly realize that in almost any town with a university there is likely to be a large number of bars, perhaps even a disproportionately large number.

It is easy for a researcher to make unfounded causal links between phenomena/variables that may not be related at all. This is more so the case when doing a computer-based analysis because you can easily lose sight of what the study variables actually represent in the midst of a computer-aided statistical analysis of large data sets. This can be especially true when the statistics become the focus as opposed to the meaning of the actual data.

To give a slightly less absurd example, consider the following: Assume you are studying an area that demographically has a high percentage of Blacks. This area may also have a high crime rate. It would be an ecological fallacy to assume that the high crime rate is caused by the large number of Blacks in the region. That two variables exist in the same geographic area does not necessitate a connection between the two. The ecological fallacy can be an easy trap to fall into, especially when coupled with the four errors of human inquiry described previously.

As data sets become larger and more complex, and more variables are included, the likelihood of a spurious correlation increases. When we add the spatial information provided with a GIS, we risk committing the ecological fallacy that because two variables coincide in geographic space they are correlated. It is worse yet to assume causality. Causality is another issue that is very difficult to prove and should be handled with a great deal of care so as not to produce erroneous results. Correlation and causality may, in fact, be real. However, it is essential to consider the logic and design of the study before jumping to such conclusions.

Ethics and GIS

As with any research tool, there are some ethical considerations worth mentioning at this point. Many studies in social science include information that is personal and thus must be treated with care and confidentiality. When we store data in a GIS, confidentiality is especially important because the information is linked to a specific location. In traditional data collection, it is relatively easy to decouple personal data from an individual respondent by assigning a random identification code to the person's responses. By simply removing identifying information, such as the name or address, privacy can be achieved. However, if this same data were linked to a map, one could simply look at where the data came from and determine the house or other location information that relates to that respondent.

Fortunately, there are a number of simple techniques that can be used at various points in the GIS process to decouple data from the true locations of the respondents while still maintaining the essential spatial relationships required for the data analysis. As with any study where privacy is an issue, it is essential that you take care to keep data secure during the course of the study and to remove any identifying information as soon as possible in the process.

Privacy and Data Aggregation

In considering research ethics, the first topic addressed is one of privacy and confidentiality. When researchers collect information, they should ask, "At what level of detail do I want to collect data for my project?" Of course, the answer to this question will be determined by the research question to some degree. Do you need to know the specific location of each respondent's home, or would the neighborhood, zip code, or city of residence be sufficient to meet the needs of the study? The decision you make about the level of individual detail to maintain during data collection needs to be weighed in the context of the ethical use of GIS data so as to protect the privacy of individual respondents.

Using a geographic variable that relates people's responses to within a specified geographic area could raise many questions, particularly about the level of detail associated with the data. For example, say that you are studying individuals' responses to political questions by street. A GIS could be used to locate responses to specific houses. For instance, from the data, you would be able to tell which neighbor supports gun control and which neighbor does not. Because of the emotional nature of this topic, it would be preferable to mask responses at the household level to protect the privacy of individual respondents.

One common way researchers deal with this is through data aggregation. Data aggregation is one potential solution to dealing with some of the privacy issues that inevitably arise as a result of mapping social variables. In this process, the researcher simply chooses another, more general spatial level at which to view the data. Although he or she may have the capability to connect individual responses with specific households, by aggregating data, the researcher may elect to analyze the data at the neighborhood or community level (Figure 4.3). This would ensure the privacy of responses related to individuals.

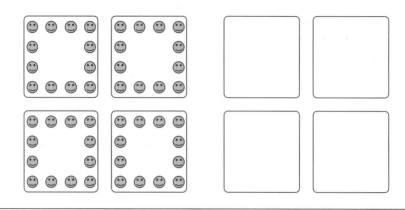

Figure 4.3   Data may be collected by individual households, as shown on the left. Although it is possible, and perhaps important, to retain the household-level information, many studies do not require this detail. If not, it might be preferable to aggregate data into larger units of analysis. The map on the right would be an example of aggregating data to each block or neighborhood. Other units of aggregation might also be used, for example, street, census block, zip code, phone prefix, city, or county, to name a few.

Other creative methods can be used to decouple individuals from data, depending on the specific requirements of the study. For example, if you need to maintain individual responses, you can map the data to a false coordinate system so that the true geographic location on the ground is not stored in the GIS. This would be accomplished by mapping locations relative to a false origin located someplace in or near the study area. By using a false origin, it is possible to maintain spatial information, such as distances and directions, without producing a map that could be used to navigate back to a specific respondent's home.

For example, a true geographic location might be described in Universal Transverse Mercator (UTM) coordinates as (479688, 4600488). UTM coordinates for the northern hemisphere are based on an origin located to the west of the UTM zone (for the X values) and at the equator (for Y values), measured in meters. You can simply alter the coordinate values by a set amount. In other words, by simply adding or subtracting a fixed value to all of the X and Y geographic coordinates in the study, the true locations are no longer known, but the spatial positions are maintained. In your GIS software, this sort of adjustment can be accomplished en masse for an entire data set by setting the values to be applied with the tools designed for the reprojection of data.

Figure 4.4 shows the calculations necessary to adjust the UTM coordinates mentioned previously, as well as a simplified example of adjusted numbers, which shows that the spatial relationships of distance and direction are maintained.

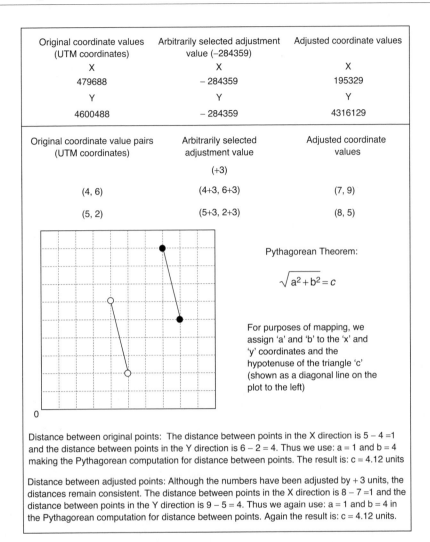

Original coordinate values (UTM coordinates)	Arbitrarily selected adjustment value (–284359)	Adjusted coordinate values
X	X	X
479688	– 284359	195329
Y	Y	Y
4600488	– 284359	4316129

Original coordinate value pairs (UTM coordinates)	Arbitrarily selected adjustment value (+3)	Adjusted coordinate values
(4, 6)	(4+3, 6+3)	(7, 9)
(5, 2)	(5+3, 2+3)	(8, 5)

Pythagorean Theorem:

$$\sqrt{a^2 + b^2} = c$$

For purposes of mapping, we assign 'a' and 'b' to the 'x' and 'y' coordinates and the hypotenuse of the triangle 'c' (shown as a diagonal line on the plot to the left)

Distance between original points: The distance between points in the X direction is 5 – 4 =1 and the distance between points in the Y direction is 6 – 2 = 4. Thus we use: a = 1 and b = 4 making the Pythagorean computation for distance between points. The result is: c = 4.12 units

Distance between adjusted points: Although the numbers have been adjusted by + 3 units, the distances remain consistent. The distance between points in the X direction is 8 – 7 =1 and the distance between points in the Y direction is 9 – 5 = 4. Thus we again use: a = 1 and b = 4 in the Pythagorean computation for distance between points. Again the result is: c = 4.12 units.

Figure 4.4   The adjustment of a true UTM coordinate using an arbitrary adjustment value to be added or subtracted from the true coordinates. The first calculation shows the adjustment of a true UTM coordinate using an arbitrary adjustment value to be added or subtracted from the true coordinates. The second set of calculations uses smaller values to make the example easier to follow. This calculation and the associated plot show that the mapped (Euclidian) distance between points, as calculated by the Pythagorean theorem, does not change when these adjustments are made. The original points are shown in white, and the altered points in black. It is important to note that when mapping geographic locations with latitude and longitude (which are spherical coordinates), this process is not valid. You must first project your map data into a planar coordinate system, such as UTM.

One other consideration when masking spatial data is to remember that, even if you do adjust values so that mapped coordinates are no longer apparent, you must be careful about the information included on printed

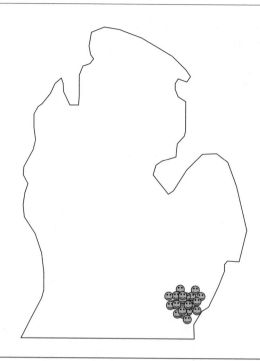

Figure 4.5 With basic contextual information, people with a general knowledge of the geography would find it simple to determine several things about the location of this study. Ask yourself the following: Can you determine what country this study was completed in? What about the part of the country? Can you make an educated guess about the city that was the focus?

Odds are you could answer most or all of these questions correctly given a simplistic map that only gives an outline of the major region where the study occurred.

What if the outline had been left off? Of course, in that case you would be hard-pressed to determine where the study was done. Leaving out even basic details can go a long way in providing confidentiality in a study.

maps related to your study. For example, inclusion of common cultural features, such as roads and political boundaries, or natural features, such as rivers or lakes, may provide an informed viewer enough information to recognize the location in which the study was conducted (Figure 4.5). For studies that require confidentiality, you should use map figures that provide minimal information.

Primary and Secondary Data

Data aggregation is also a consideration when deciding whether to use existing data (secondary data) or to collect your own, new data (primary data). Sometimes, the detail provided in available data is insufficient to serve the needs of your particular research. For example, if you are interested in conducting a study at the small-town level and the data for your study are only available at the county level, it would be difficult to draw any conclusions about the small towns, or even to separate the small-town data from that of the large towns that exist within the county. If the information you require is not available, your only option is to create your own data at the appropriate level of detail to conduct your research.

Keep in mind that others also aggregate data. Before going through the trouble of collecting new, more detailed data for a study, contact the agency or institution that produced the data you are interested in to determine if more detailed information was retained and can be obtained for use in your research. For example, the U.S. Census publishes only aggregated data for official release. However, the individual records are maintained and do become available after 72 years. Thus, at the present time, census data from individual respondents collected in 1930 or earlier can be accessed, providing an incredibility rich data set compared to the aggregated census data.

Of course, a variety of factors may influence access to any particular data set. If your research requires more detail than is readily available, it may be worthwhile to look into the possibility of obtaining the extra detail. This is also worth keeping in mind when you collect and create your own data sets. If the policies and procedures of your organization allow for the unaltered, individual data to be retained for future researchers to use, then the original data may be worth maintaining, even if it will not be distributed to the general public as part of the final report. All issues related to procedures used for data collection, input, aggregation, or other processes should be documented in a metadata file (data about the data) so that others who consider the data in the future are clear about what the data are.

Accuracy Considerations

In Chapter 2, we discussed a number of accuracy issues related to mapping. Scale, projection, coordinates, and datums can all contribute errors to the mapping process. Additionally, when data-processing operations are carried out in GIS software, there are sometimes computational issues that affect the overall accuracy of the result (most often due to rounding or other tolerance settings in the GIS software). For the most part, social science research does not require detail to the order of inches, or even a few meters, so these errors will often be irrelevant.

It is worth remembering that even though GIS is based on computer analysis, there are always a variety of assumptions behind the processing methods and algorithms in these programs. Human errors, discussed earlier in the chapter, may affect data collection and quality when the data are entered into the computer. Be careful not to trust the computer too much! Be logical in the conclusions you draw and be clear about your assumptions and potential error when you report your results (see Figure 4.6).

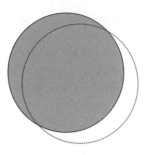

Figure 4.6   Consider what appears as a visually small error in the alignment of the two circles to the right. If these circles represent the overlap between two variables in your study, it might suggest that they are highly correlated. Is this correlation statistically significant?

If your study required 95% correlation and the computer gave a value of 94.3%, what would you say? What if there was 95.2% correlation?

These differences, especially when small, may just as likely come from errors in mapping or other places in the data collection process. It might be unethical to cancel a new project or program to assist this community if it falls just short of some predetermined cutoff value, especially if the shortfall is just as likely an artifact of the analysis process itself.

Relevant Web Sites

> *"The Influence of Data Aggregation on the Stability of Location Model Solutions":* This article, by Alan T. Murray and Jonathan Gottesgen, discusses the influence of data aggregation on census block group data. www.ncgia.ucsb.edu/~jgotts/murray/ murray.html

> *"Primary Data Collection Methods":* This article is from the Thames Valley University dissertation. http://brent.tvu.ac.uk/dissguide/hm1u3/ hm1u3text3.htm

Suggested Reading

> Creswell, J. W. (1998). *Qualitative inquiry and research design: Choosing among five traditions.* Thousand Oaks, CA: Sage.
> Creswell, J. W. (2003). *Research design: Qualitative, quantitative, and mixed methods approaches* (2nd ed.). Thousand Oaks, CA: Sage.

5 Qualitative Research Methods and GIS

Chapter Description

This chapter offers a discussion of how GIS can be integrated with various forms of qualitative research. Some of the specific forms of qualitative research that are addressed include grounded theory, participant observation, ethnography, and oral histories. This chapter provides a concrete discussion of sociospatial grounded theory research, including seven specific steps for the integration of GIS into one's research. Coding and analysis of spatial qualitative data are also discussed.

Chapter Objectives

- Introduce methods for the integration of social science theory and research methods into a GIS-based analysis approach.
- Present an example of how GIS can be integrated into a public participation planning approach.

After reading this chapter, you should be able to perform the following tasks:

- Select data collection methods and approaches that facilitate integration of data into a GIS.
- Differentiate between an inductive, grounded theory and deductive, scientific method approaches to data collection and analysis.
- Develop an approach to using GIS in a public meeting or focus group to enhance the end result or decision arrived at through an analysis.

Introduction

For those researchers who plan to collect qualitative data, the notion of using a GIS as a part of the research process may be somewhat daunting.

Have no fear, however, because a GIS can be just as useful to the researcher who collects qualitative data as it is to the scientist who collects quantitative data. In fact, a GIS provides an excellent opportunity to integrate both types of data into one comprehensive database.

Grounded Theory: GIS Using an Inductive Approach

As a researcher, you also have the option of employing an inductive model in your research design. This type of approach begins with a different series of steps than those traditionally followed when using a deductive approach. An inductive approach begins with the data and proceeds to glean an understanding of themes and patterns. From this information, theory is then generated, thus the term grounded theory. It is called grounded because of its strong connection to the reality represented by the data. This inductive research approach is qualitative in nature. Grounded theory is a very appropriate research method that can be used to assess case studies, transcripts, oral histories, and archival data.

Grounded Theory and GIS

The key to determining whether or not you will use grounded theory is to consider the purpose of your research. Grounded theory is an inductive research approach that is characterized by its sequencing: data collection followed by theory generation. Glaser and Strauss (1967) first coined the term grounded theory in the late 1960s in their seminal book titled *The Discovery of Grounded Theory: Strategies for Qualitative Research.* Since that time, many other qualitative researchers have adopted and written about grounded theory. Grounded theory has become a popular approach that has been embraced by a variety of disciplines, including public health, business, and criminology, just to name a few.

One of the primary attractions of grounded theory is that it provides the opportunity to "generate theory that will be relevant to [scientists'] research" (Glaser & Strauss, 1967, p. vii), unlike verifying theory, which one uses when following the traditional scientific method, which is a deductive approach. Grounded theory is a good approach to employ when you are interested in the discovery phase of gathering information because it is more appropriate for researchers whose goal is to generate information, themes, and patterns, not to prove theory.

The main premise of grounded theory is that theory emerges from an examination of the data. Rather than the researcher dictating themes and ideas that will be investigated, the data dictate what is relevant and important to study further. "Grounded Theory is based on the systematic generating of theory from data that itself is systematically obtained from social research" (Glaser, 1978, p. 2). Thus, the grounded theory approach views research methods as a part of the theory-generating process. The process is very iterative; the researcher is constantly conducting analyses, looking for themes, and then conducting more analyses. It is a very hands-on approach to sorting through one's data.

The core of grounded theory is in the analysis and search for patterns in the data. In the analysis, the researcher attempts to reach a point of "theoretical saturation" (Dey, 1999). This means that there are no additional themes or concepts, categories or relationships that emerge from the data. This can only be achieved after the researcher has made a series of run-throughs with the data: identifying themes and looking for data that support the themes. This process is continually repeated until no new themes emerge. When this occurs, one is said to have achieved theoretical saturation.

Bernard (2000, p. 443) summarizes how grounded theory can be accomplished using the following series of steps:

1. Begin with a set of information (e.g., interviews, transcripts, newspaper articles).

2. Identify potential themes in the data.

3. Pull data together as categories emerge.

4. Think about links between categories.

5. Construct theoretical models based on the links.

6. Present the results using exemplars.

Following these steps, you begin with whatever set of data or information you want to analyze. This information will most likely be of a qualitative nature. Identifying potential themes in your data can be done by hand or with the help of a qualitative computer data-analysis program. As you sift through the data, certain words or phrases begin to emerge consistently. You can then use the themes that you identify to develop a coding scheme (see Strauss & Corbin, 1998) to complete the analysis of the themes. Step 3 calls for grouping, or categorizing, your information. In essence, you look for similarities, differences, and repetitions that occur in what has been stated. This is an iterative process that evolves as you analyze the data using your own specific coding process. (See Dey, 1999, for more specifics on coding your data.)

Step 4 calls for thinking about the links between the grouped categories that you have seen emerge. In essence, it is akin to developing a conceptual framework or model, as described in Chapter 4 (see "Stages of Sociospatial Research," Step 5). This leads to the next natural step, which is to construct a theoretical model based on the links that you observed. This is your best model of the relationships that you saw emerge between themes that you identified in the data. Finally, in Step 6, you present the data using exemplars. These are nothing more than quotes or snippets from the data that illustrate the themes, concepts, and relationships that you are discussing. One can think of exemplars as examples (shared words, quotes, etc.) of concepts or themes that emerge from the data analysis process.

Sociospatial Grounded Theory Using GIS

To date, a GIS has rarely been incorporated into analyses that explicitly use grounded theory. We believe that the spatial information provided by GIS can provide an important additional component to research that adopts an inductive approach. The visual patterns that are often visible in spatial data can provide a powerful indicator when exploring emergent themes drawn from existing data to develop theory. We've developed a series of steps that you could follow when using GIS as part of this approach to social research:

1. Determine a topic of interest.

2. Determine a geographic location of interest.

3. Collect the data (qualitative, spatially linked social data).

4. Geocode the data.

5. Ground truth the data.

6. Analyze the data and look for spatial and social patterns.

7. Generate theory (spatial and social).

Determine a Topic of Interest

This step is almost exactly the same step that was mentioned in Chapter 4, which explains the 10 steps in the deductive research process. The same basic advice applies here. In choosing your topic, you want to make sure that you pick one that you find interesting. That way you will enjoy the process more and actually be more energetic throughout the research process. In considering your topic, you should also consider what might be a feasible area of study, considering time, money, and interest. Having a lot of time, money, or resources substantially influences your research method selection—for example, you might select detailed interviews. If you have less time, money, or resources, then you may need to rely more heavily on available data.

Determine a Geographic Location of Interest

Determining the geographic location of interest means that you identify a study location that is associated with your topic. This could be a neighborhood or county or something less defined, such as former residents of a community that no longer exists. In New Mexico there was one such community called Santa Rita. It was located next to an open pit mine, and when the mine expanded, the town site became part of a giant hole that was the mining pit. Many of the town's homes were moved to other surrounding towns, and ex–Santa Rita residents moved into them. A study today of these residents' perceptions of the town would be conducted about a place (the town of Santa Rita) that no loner physically exists.

Assuming you can track down the former residents of this town, you could conduct your interviews with these individuals regarding their perceptions of the town. You would also want to note where these individuals now live. Why? Because the geographic locations where former Santa Rita residents currently reside may be a factor that corresponds to their individual perceptions about the former town. For instance, questions you might ask would be, "Do residents who live within 5 to 10 miles of the old mining pit (Santa Rita town site) share different perceptions of the community than individuals who moved farther away from the town? Or do all residents, regardless of current geographic location, share the same perceptions of the town?" The point that we want to make is that the physical location of a place can play an important role in the analytical process when using grounded theory.

Collect the Data

When you collect your data, even when using a grounded theory approach, you can simultaneously collect information about the spatial surroundings. Why do we advocate this? Our reason for collecting both types of data comes from a philosophical belief that the social and physical environments interact with and affect one another. The degree to which a researcher employs a dual data collection process will be determined only by the researcher and her or his preferences.

It makes sense when employing a grounded theory approach to collect information on the geographic location and the natural environment related to your data. Why? The inclusion of this type of information could greatly enhance the emergence of themes, ideas, and relationships that exist in your model. In fact, it may lead to the inclusion of physical, social, and environmental features into your theoretical model, features you had not previously considered. That is where grounded theory and GIS are quite compatible. Grounded theory is flexible enough to allow for the inclusion and identification of a variety of different data types, including geographic information.

Geocode the Data

When you spatially code the data, you are assigning a code that reflects the geographic location of your data. For example, let's say you are interested in analyzing different newspapers' coverage of the issue of immigration. In your content analysis, you choose to analyze newspaper articles from various locations around the country. As a part of your grounded theory analysis, you could code the location of each newspaper, note other attributes about the community in which it is published, and see what kinds of patterns emerge in your data analysis. This would enable you to determine if the physical environment and population are related to perceptions of immigrants. If you fail to collect this information and treat all of the newspapers the same, you may be missing a key explanatory element for your theoretical model. In conducting your analysis, it would be interesting to observe if differences in attitude toward immigration emerged between various newspapers' coverage of these issues. A content analysis of the data mentioned would reveal some themes and patterns that could then be crafted into a theoretical model.

Ground Truth the Data

What do we mean by ground truth? Ground truthing involves checking to ensure that the computerized data that you have are representative of what exists on the ground. How do you ground truth data? Most often, ground truthing is accomplished by physically visiting the location under study and field checking a subset of the data. In cases where this is not possible (inaccessible or unsafe location, historic data), alternative sources may be used as surrogate ground truth (e.g., phone books, property tax listings, historic records, aerial photography). Ground truthing data is perhaps one of the most important steps of integrating GIS into social science research. Why? Anytime you are dealing with GIS data, although it may be tempting, you must not accept data at face value. You should check (at least a sample of the data, if not all of the data) to ensure that the data are without major errors and represent the information required and to the level of detail necessary for your analysis. Most problematic are data sets that are not current or that were originally collected for a different purpose. For example, you might have a data set from several years ago detailing the location of soup kitchens in a city. It would be wise to visit these locations to ensure they are still active or, if this isn't possible, to check the locations in a current phone book. Errors may also arise when data from multiple sources, scales, or projections are combined in your data analysis. Successfully employing grounded theory requires that the data informing the theory are free of major errors because reliance on flawed observations or data can produce a theory that does not accurately fit the situation under study. If your observations do not reflect reality as defined for your specific analysis, you risk a serious problem, especially when it comes to geographical data (e.g., the location of something).

Analyze Data and Look for Spatial and Social Patterns

As mentioned earlier, a major part of the grounded theory approach is the search for patterns in your data. Ideally, if you want to integrate a GIS into your information-gathering process, you connect each piece of data or information with its geographic location.

For example, let's say that you have a collection of historic diaries from the 1940s. As a researcher, you might be interested in understanding how World War II influenced people from that time period. You could employ grounded theory in your analysis of the diaries and simultaneously develop a coding system that notes the geographic locations of where the diaries were recorded. For instance, individuals living in different parts of the United States may have had very different experiences during the war, depending on a myriad of factors. For example, were military bases located nearby? Did the diaries' authors live in a region populated by particular ethnic groups from parts of the world viewed either positively or negatively because of the war?

Keeping track of the geographic information as you conduct your qualitative data analysis may reveal geographic patterns in the data indicating that location plays a role in the attitudes expressed by people in their diaries. Certain geographic areas may have been harder hit by rationing, may have had a greater number of local men and women who went off to war, and so on. None of this would be obvious at the outset of a grounded theory analysis. However, if you keep track geographically of where the diaries were recorded, your analysis could produce some interesting results.

One might ask the logical question: How do you know when you have sufficiently analyzed the data? Dey (1999) provided a clear summary of the analysis process using grounded theory. He noted that researchers should conclude their research when they reach theoretical saturation, identify a core category or main story line, integrate the analysis around the main story line, and then use the coded information to modify the results, stopping the process with the emergence of a useful theoretical model (Dey, 1999).

Generate Theory (Spatial and Social)

This is the most creative part of the grounded theory approach. At this stage, you get to generate a theoretical model that reflects the patterns you observed in your data. As mentioned in the previous step, the geography—or, rather, spatial location—associated with of a piece of data may factor significantly into the theoretical model that you generate. In any of the examples provided in this section, the variable geography could potentially play an important role in the analysis. When you construct your model, you should indicate whether the physical, social, or environmental context, or all three, factored into the grounded theory that was generated through the research process. Figure 5.1 is an example of a model that does just that. The

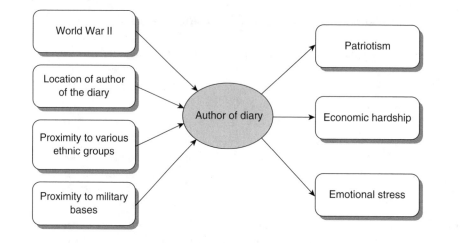

Figure 5.1   A variety of variables, including environmental, geographic, and social, are believed to affect the author of the diaries assembled for an analysis using a grounded theory approach. In some combination, these might influence the themes that emerge from the diaries and help to inform the eventual theory that is suggested from this research.

figure illustrates how geographic location can play a role in people's perceptions of World War II, as evidenced in their diaries.

Figure 5.1 illustrates some patterns that might be observed through an analysis of data from wartime diaries. Conducting a grounded theory analysis generates the following emergent themes: economic hardship, emotional stress, and patriotism. Perhaps those living in the heartland felt less stressed than those on the coasts fearing attack from German submarines or Japanese kamikaze planes. Those near bases might have felt a greater sense of stress because many of their friends and loved ones were directly involved in the war effort. Areas of the country with concentrations of ethnic groups tied to the Allies may have felt a greater sense of hardship or stress. This figure illustrates grounded theory in action from a historic perspective.

Questions to Guide Integration of GIS Into Field Research

You should consider the following questions before going into the field to use a GIS as part of the data collection process:

1. Will you bring a laptop with GIS software to the field location under study?

2. Do you have a base map of your research area or other map data that represent one or more of the key variables? What format are the map(s) in?

3. Have you verified or ground truthed the source map(s)?

4. What are the cultural perceptions of technology (including computers) at your study site?

5. What will happen to the results of your study once you are finished? Who will have access to this information?

6. Are there any written sources of local, traditional knowledge and information?

The following sections provide detailed answers to these questions to help explain how to incorporate a GIS into various types of qualitative research.

GIS Software in the Field

Although it can sometimes be convenient to enter data directly into the computer, it is not always the best choice. Consider factors such as the climate and conditions where you will be conducting your research. If it is going to be rainy and damp all of the time, it may not be advisable to bring a computer to your site, especially if your lodging accommodations are primitive. Will you have access to power the computer or recharge the batteries? Can you reliably store and back up your data while you are in the field? What would you do if your hard drive crashed? Will your computer be secure? If you have a safe place to store your computer and a power source, it might be worthwhile to bring a GIS to the field.

You may also want to consider the process of recording data directly into your computer. If you will be interviewing respondents, will you be able to type responses at an adequate pace to keep up? Will the computer distract them? Would it help to have the GIS map available for respondents to mark information on and to interact with and assist in data collection? In many situations, it may be preferable to gather data using some other means (e.g., a tape recorder, a camera, or even paper and pencil) and then transfer this data to the computer later. When you transcribe interview data, it is especially useful to transcribe the interviews as soon as possible after completing them and while they are fresh in your mind. Any of these alternative methods can always be incorporated into a GIS at a later time.

Maps of Your Research Area

Obtaining a base map of your study site could be easy or extremely difficult depending on the location and whether or not it has been previously or recently mapped. Even in locations where you would expect maps to be available, they may not be up to date enough to be useful for your study. There is also no guarantee that the maps will be available in digital form.

You can work with a hard-copy map (hard-copy meaning a map that exists in a physical form). Most often maps are available on paper, although maps may be made of other materials, from stone to papyrus (if you are doing research on ancient societies) to photographic paper, microfilm, plastic, acetate, and other materials.

Chances are that a map of your research site exists in some form. However, this map may not be in the level of detail that you require for your study. If that is the case, we advise starting with the best map that you can find. You can then add additional detail as you visit the field and gain more information on the region.

As with any other data collection process, it may be safer to mark all of your data points or features on a hard-copy map. This information can then be transferred into a GIS at a later date. Computers do occasionally have technical problems, get dropped, or run out of power. Paper and pencil do a much better job of surviving a fall than the average laptop computer, not to mention your pencil is unlikely to run out of batteries and need to be recharged. Sometimes a low-tech data collection methodology is better for fieldwork; that way if a glitch happens with the technology, you are safe-guarded against data loss.

Ground Truth of Map Data

If you are planning to conduct fieldwork, you may not always have the ability to ground truth some features of the map until you are physically on site. You might find that the map you have is several years old, but what may be less apparent is how much things have, or have not, changed since the time the map was made. An old map is not necessarily bad; sometimes little has changed and the data are perfectly appropriate.

Regardless of the age of your map sources, it is a good idea to engage in some amount of verification or ground truthing. If you have access to the site, you might do spot checks of the map, especially if you have a sense of features that might be new or different since the map's creation. If you are unable to visit the site in person, you can compare the map to an alternative source. Often there are more recent aerial images from an airplane or satellite that can be used as a comparison; this is sometimes referred to as surrogate ground truth because the photo acts as a surrogate for an actual field visit. Furthermore, imagery can provide additional detail necessary to locate sites in the field that are not depicted on standard maps. For example, a map might not show each individual house, barn, or shed, but these features may be clearly visible in an aerial photograph of the same location.

To use surrogate ground truth, you do not have to go physically in the field, but you need to get a sense of appropriate indicator variables that are visible in the alternative data sources used. An indicator variable is something that can substitute for the real variable of interest. For example, using the imagery you might be able to infer particular land uses observed in aerial photos. In an American agricultural region, one might observe large expanses of crops, often organized in regular geometric patterns with a few buildings and roads intermixed, showing a low population density. This looks very different from a rural region dominated by other industries, such as forestry or mining, and certainly has very little in common with the land use for a large urban area.

Therefore, one could infer by observing aerial photos of various regions which particular communities might be termed agricultural communities, based on the observable land use. Similarly, aerial photographs of an urban area with high population density that indicate the presence of many factories might indicate the presence of an industrialized or manufacturing-based community. In both examples, the aerial photographs assisted in helping to determine the classification of these communities based on land use. The indicator variable for these two conditions is land use. Although it is not directly related to ground truth per se, it is worthwhile to note that this same process might be useful in selecting sampling locations when designing your study.

If you want to ground truth a map that illustrates different population distributions by ethnicity, an image may not serve you well. You may be able to see houses, but you cannot see the ethnicity of the people who live there! Instead, you might opt to ground truth the data against other sources of data for population, such as the U.S. Census. The goal of ground truthing is to determine if the data you are using for your study are reasonably current, accurate, and appropriate to your goals.

Of course, you need not rely solely on existing data; you can gain invaluable ground truth by eliciting help of some local experts—people who are familiar with the lay of the land and local social and geographic features. This is part of the notion of public participation and GIS, which is discussed later in this chapter. Of course, you want to be clear about your plans to conduct research in the area prior to soliciting the help of local people. A clear communication of your stated research objectives should occur early in the data-gathering process. This is to ensure that locals are aware that the ultimate goal of your presence at the site is to collect data about their community. There may be some cases in which the research method being employed precludes total openness about your purpose in being on-site (e.g., participant observation), but as in any research it is important to follow protocols appropriate to the study.

Cultural Perceptions of Technology

Prior to collecting data of any sort or using any technology (even a tape recorder), it is a good idea to investigate how that technology is viewed by people living in the local area. Does it make them uncomfortable? Are they afraid of it? Do they embrace it? For example, if researchers were to conduct a field study of the Amish, researchers would need to realize that the Amish religion forbids them from having their picture taken because a picture is considered a graven image. Any researcher who goes into the area to "study" the Amish needs to be aware of this and use alternative methods. It is no wonder, with the significant presence of tourists and researchers, that Amish children are taught to run when they see a car slowing down near their fields! If you are conducting a study in a part of the world that is largely unfamiliar with modern technology, it may be better to avoid using such tools than to risk your study by assuming the technology will be embraced by those you are studying.

Access to Results

When you begin a study, it is important to consider who will have access to the data when you are through with your study. This is an important question to consider because the answer could affect the type of data that you will collect. For example, if you are going to collect data on individuals participating in some type of illegal or socially unpopular behavior, you need to be particularly careful about the data you collect and how you collect it. Divulging such information could get your respondents in trouble with the law and could put you in danger for simply trying to collect it. Always consider the need to protect both yourself and your study subjects to the degree that is possible and appropriate.

When researchers conduct their research, they are aware of their own proximate purposes for the data. Wherever you collect data, it is very important to consider who else might at some point read your report or see your data. It is essential that whenever you conduct a research project that you carefully select the information to include in the final report and realize that once information is out of your hands others may have access to it. Of course, you should also consider how data will be kept secure and confidential during the course of the study, especially when that data may contain additional details that are not planned for public distribution in the final report.

Local Sources of Data

For the social researcher, local knowledge is always an important data source. Sometimes, local groups preserve their knowledge about features important to their group, such as oral histories. Other communities commit such information to written form. Local sources of data might appear in the form of stories, dances, rituals, and ceremonies, none of which may be officially recorded, except for in the heads of community members or in some cases specific community members (community elders, healers, religious leaders, or others, depending on the culture). An exciting part of your research might be to try to record this information in a form that is accessible to researchers as well as to other members of the community or future generations or simply for the preservation of knowledge.

The advantage of finding any form of data, especially if it is not recorded in a form that is already accessible, is that it can then be incorporated into your study. For instance, let's say that you are interested in documenting the geographic location and relevant social information concerning the sacred sites of an indigenous group of people in Latin America. The maps that you have access to may be rough, but they give a good working picture of your study site. Sacred sites important to the local indigenous people—places that the local people consider to be important—are probably missing from these maps. When you are in the field collecting data, a GIS could be useful for matching your field notes with geographic locations of these sites. As mentioned earlier, your starting point would be a base map of your area.

Oral History Interviews

Oral histories are an important way to collect data from people who don't necessarily conceptualize their lives as data. The stories that people tell about significant events in their lives can be very informative to a researcher who wishes to gain an understanding of a particular time and place. Oral histories can be collected in a written form, where the researcher conducts an interview and takes copious notes. They could also be recorded on tape or digitally as long as the person being interviewed does not object. Using a combination of both written and recorded interviews offers an opportunity to capture the story as told by the respondent. Digital recordings can be stored on the computer as part of the GIS database and linked to the location the respondent is being interviewed about. Written notes and transcriptions of the recording are also useful in conducting qualitative analysis and for linking the interview information in the GIS database using key words or concepts.

GIS and Oral History

How would a GIS be integrated into the oral history method? There are several ways. First, the GIS can be used as a data organization and visualization tool. Imagine you are conducting oral histories about how people perceive the Mississippi River. You plan to interview people who live at different locations along the river. A main goal of your study is to determine if people's locations on the river affect their perceptions of the river. For instance, people living close to a busy commercial port might have a different view of the river than those who live in peaceful, remote locations along the river.

As you collect your data, you can incorporate contextual factors about the environment, such as the number of people who live in the community where the informant was surveyed, the number and locations of ports and industry, the presence or absence of oil spills in the region, and the presence or absence of nature preserves along the river. You could then create files for the different geographic locations on the map and attach coded data regarding the environmental and social contexts that are important to your study. This would help you find patterns in potential factors affecting people's perceptions of the Mississippi River.

The second way to incorporate a GIS as part of the data collection process for oral histories is to use maps portrayed with the GIS to display information about particular issues or problems for research subjects. The oral history method is useful for studying the social and environmental context. For instance, you might be interested in researching the social and physical transformation of a particular neighborhood over time. You could use the GIS in the course of interviewing longtime residents of the community to interactively gather an environmental and social history of the neighborhood under study. Respondents could be shown various historical maps of the neighborhood and could point out relevant and important features or buildings (e.g., local town square, parks, neighborhood gathering spots where people interacted or gossiped), which could then be marked on the GIS map. In this way, the GIS becomes an interactive data recorder as well as a technology to assist people in relating their oral histories and remembering stories and important events from a time gone by.

The GIS is perfect for both the portrayal and recording of historic information. Such information may exist in people's heads or on old maps and historic photographs. This information could be integrated into a working GIS that then interactively produces stories, photographs, or historic documents related to locations on the map that can be viewed by others in the research process.

Most social scientists are familiar with a data analysis method called content analysis. A GIS could be used as part of environmental and social history content analyses over time. One could conduct a geographic content analysis of particular variables in a spatial context. For example, you might identify patterns of particular variables and attributes across the study space: Do they cluster or are they dispersed? Do certain variables seem to relate to particular locations or physical or environmental features on the map? Such patterns can be assessed as part of the GIS analysis.

Participant Observation

Participant observation is a research method in which researchers actively participate in whatever issue or topic they are studying. Researchers make observations of the group they are participating with. At the same time, researchers record their own experiences in a field journal. This journal reflects social and environmental observations about the group being inter-acted with as well as some of the researchers' sentiments about participating in the group. So how could GIS become a part of this process?

An example of participant observation might be as follows. Say that you are interested in recreational activities of people of different social classes. Your hypothesis is that people of different social classes engage in different forms of recreation. Participant observation would necessitate you going into the field and participating in recreational activities with the people in these groups and interacting with these people. To integrate into a group of higher-social-class individuals, you might temporarily join the local country club and participate in activities such as golfing and tennis. Because the elite sometimes maintain barriers to unknown individuals participating in their circles, perhaps you would take a job as a waiter or waitress at a country club. In both cases, the goal is for you to place yourself in a role where you can simultaneously participate and observe. Similarly, if you were seeking to research the recreational activities of the middle class, you might spend your time in the city park playing pick-up basketball games or participating in a community softball league.

So where does GIS fit into the study? You can integrate GIS by geo-graphically locating these different recreational activity sites into a GIS and coding them by social class. It would be interesting to see if the higher- and middle-class people recreate in different sorts of geographic locales and how these locations relate to where they live and work. Is there any overlap between classes and, if so, at which sorts of recreational facilities do these interactions occur?

As a part of maintaining your detailed field journal, you could actively record observations about the context of these recreational locations and the people who frequent them, using the following questions: What types of facilities are present? Are there tennis or basketball courts? What about a golf course or swimming pool? What are the conditions of the facilities? Where are these facilities located relative to where the people live? Do these facilities charge a fee for use and if so how much? Are these facilities limited-access, members-only facilities, or are they open to the public? What ameni-ties are located near the facility? Are they secure and well lit? Do the facilities exist in natural or man-made environments? All of the data would then be combined with base maps of sociodemographic data and other relevant information for the analysis.

News as a Source of Data

News is an excellent source of data. In addition to being a good source of background data for your research, the news may actually be the data you are studying. Some researchers may choose to investigate a research question that involves the news as a data source. The news has a lot of information that could be useful to a researcher who is interested in conducting content analyses within a GIS. Almost all articles in a newspaper list the location of the story in the opening line. This alone can be the basis for linking stories to geographic locations. It might also be important to know the location associated with the newspaper or the author of the article. Similar spatial information is included in some form in magazine, television, and online news formats.

News analysis might be done using a content analysis approach as one approach. In this approach, a researcher would search through the news stories in an attempt to find patterns related to a particular topic or subject. Let's say for instance that you are interested in conducting a content analysis of newspaper articles related to immigrants. To incorporate a GIS into your study, you could note the location where the newspaper is produced and see if that relates to the type of immigrants being discussed. For instance, would the articles referring to immigrants from Canada be published from locations in the northern United States? Or would the articles that focus on Latino immigrants occur in newspapers located on the West Coast? To extend this analysis further, using a GIS you could investigate if there was a difference in focus on immigrants between rural and urban areas? For instance, do newspapers located in rural areas present a more negative portrayal of immigrants than newspapers located in more urban areas, where there are more diverse populations and higher percentages of immigrants?

Another example of using a news source and integrating a GIS is identifying patterns of car chases for a transportation agency or the highway patrol. Over the last few years, car chases have become a regularly reported event in the media. You could integrate the GIS to help identify patterns in your analysis. For example, you might be interested in determining whether there are differences based on the police jurisdiction in which the chases occur. Let's say in your analysis you were going to go back through a review of TV news segments over the last 10 years for various parts of the country. You could find the date that the car chase occurred, the time that it occurred, what type of road it occurred on (freeway or city street), this street's geographic location, and whether the drivers were charged with another crime in addition to the car chase. The GIS would be an important part of the process of identifying patterns of car chases. Ideally, identifying these patterns would provide information to the authorities about how to better intercept and prevent such chases from occurring in the future.

Ethnography and GIS

If researchers are interested in conducting an ethnographic study, they are interested in providing a detailed description of their problem or issue, rather than attempting to provide an explanation. Earl Babbie (2003) notes that an important part of conducting an ethnography is telling people's stories the way the people want the stories told. This does not involve the researcher coming in and critiquing or changing what people have told you but rather recording what they said and the exact way that they said it.

A GIS could be integrated into this type of research by having people contextualize or environmentally situate their stories for you over time. For instance, let's say that you are studying the homeless population of San Francisco, and you want to engage in an ethnographic approach. Part of your study might involve collecting the perceptions and stories from home-less people about what it's like to be homeless. You may interview homeless people who have been on the street for at least 20 years and record their sto-ries about being homeless over time. For example, you might map locations described as having been good for sleeping, getting meals, or panhandling at different times, perhaps 20 and 10 years ago as well as at the present time. Key elements or variables that arise from these stories could then be exam-ined in the context of where current homeless shelters are. Such a study might elicit support for the location of new or relocated services for the homeless to better meet their needs.

Case Studies and GIS

In a case study, a researcher seeks to record in great detail a multitude of fac-tors related to a specific geographic or social location. A sociological exam-ple of a case study could focus on a particular organizational situation or place, or both. The researcher spends time in the community gaining an understanding of the people, places, and interactions that occur there. A case study is an excellent method when using the grounded theory approach. A case study may occur in a single location or in conjunction with other com-munities (in such a case, it would be a comparative case study).

Case studies are useful when you have an idea about a particular place or event that could potentially serve as a model for other, similar places. You as the researcher can conduct a case study with the idea that a particular community is a model example of a successful community because it has a thriving economy, local residents appear happy, and health is a major focus for residents. To prove or disprove this hypothesis, you could carry out a case study. The information that you discover in the process of conducting your case study may or may not confirm your initial ideas.

So what role would a GIS play? Let's say that you are interested in con-ducting a case study not of a particular place but of a particular organiza-tion: a local senior citizens' center. The center has a good reputation of providing food to seniors who are shut-ins in a city. To conduct a case study of this particular organization, you would need to gather as much informa-tion as you could about its outreach programs: Where do the older adults served by the center live? How does the center organize its food distribution efforts? Does the senior center get food donations from these older residents' home communities? Are there times of day when the traffic is congested on the streets near the seniors' homes? How does the senior center avoid that? Obviously, the senior center has been successful in keeping its constituents happy and has found a way to accomplish this on a limited budget.

Using a GIS to help document and tell the success story of this organization within its particular spatial context could be very helpful to organizations that have similar goals and to other types of social service outreach organizations. Case studies provide extensive information about successes (and possibly failures) to others so that they do not need to reinvent the wheel or attempt numerous different approaches before finding one that works.

A GIS is useful to those who use grounded theory. In using a grounded theory approach, researchers do not go into the field with a traditional hypothesis or idea about what they are going to find. Instead, they allow the concepts or ideas to arise from the fieldwork itself. In the previous example, researchers would begin the investigation with no preconceived notions about what it is that makes the center successful, but rather they would simply collect the data and see what patterns emerge.

Public Participation and GIS

Public participation is often a major part of the planning process. As GIS technology becomes more prevalent in the field of planning so too has its incorporation into the public participation process, so much so that there is an entire developing subdiscipline known as public participation GIS (PPGIS). What does this mean? Public participation in the planning process means that local people's ideas, thoughts, and actions are solicited to be a part of the process. Public participation is something that has been mandated by many state and federal agencies to become a permanent component of the planning process.

One form of public participation is to hold community meetings or to stage hearings to solicit community input about what is going to happen in a particular situation. Whichever agency has jurisdiction over the issue in question is the agency responsible for soliciting the input. Other important forms of public participation in the planning process include focus groups, surveys, key-informant interviews, and needs assessments, just to name a few.

When soliciting public input, a GIS can play an important role. As different methods of soliciting public input have evolved along with the recognition that this is an important and valuable thing to do, GIS has become part of the process. One drawback of having GIS as a part of the public participation process is that not all members of the general public have an understanding of GIS. However, this can be solved by having trained staff familiar

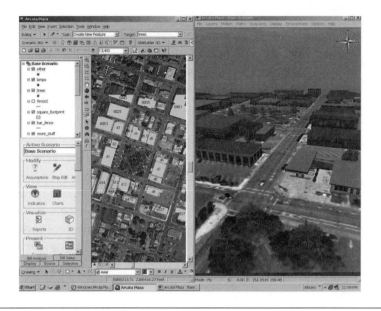

Figure 5.2 An example of a three-dimensional visualization for community planning, using ESRI ArcGIS® with CommunityViz Scenario 360® software. The GIS is used to establish the base data, including a terrain model, a high-resolution aerial photograph, and ground-based photographs of key features, including building facades. Prospective alterations to the city can be placed into the model to assist community members in visualizing how these changes would appear when complete. In the lower left of the image, the red lines show the point of view selected in generating the view of the right. After all of the data have been prepared, it is possible to actually move through the data in a fly-through mode, allowing a variety of perspectives on the proposed project.

with both GIS and the issue under discussion available to assist with the technological aspects of using a GIS in an interactive fashion with the general public.

For example, participants at a public comment session could be asked for questions about their vision for the local community, and GIS professionals could chart different development scenarios using the GIS software. With the proper software, it is even possible to generate a three-dimensional model of how different scenarios look, portraying different options on a screen or using printed maps that are further marked up with comments or input from the community. Figure 5.2 provides an example of a three-dimensional visualization generated in a GIS.

The main advantage of using GIS as a part of participatory planning is that it allows people to visually see the data and its physical, environmental, or social context as it is now and perhaps could be in the future. For instance, what if you were interested in soliciting input about what should happen to a local bay located in a seaside community? Different proposed scenarios might call for further industrial development of the bay, more tourist development, and more recreational opportunities for local people in and around the bay. Using a GIS as a part of the public participation process allows for management professionals to portray different scenarios immediately so that an interested public can actually see the suggestions put forth as part of the planning process. Having the ability to see options in a realistic way provides a very powerful experience and lets members of a local community know that their suggestions are being heard (Figure 5.2).

Similarly, using the GIS as a means of idea portrayal can also give local planners an idea of what the public desires from a planning perspective. It should be stated here that use of the GIS is not for everybody. There are some people who don't like technology and computers and who might reject the use of a GIS because they feel it's too technologically oriented and complex for the layperson. This is a field that is evolving even as we write this book. We look forward to seeing the new developments that arise in this area as GIS become a more commonly used part of planning efforts at local, state, national, and international levels.

Relevant Web Sites

CommunityViz: This is the Web site for CommunityViz, a program of The Orton Family Foundation, the Vermont-based, nonprofit operating foundation dedicated to helping communities make better, more responsible land use planning decisions. http://www.communityviz.com/

The Grounded Theory Institute: This entire Web site is devoted to the methodology of grounded theory. www.groundedtheory.com

"Grounded Theory: A Thumbnail Sketch": This site provides a nice overview of grounded theory from the Resource Papers in Action Research Web site. www.scu.edu.au/schools/gcm/ar/arp/grounded.html

Oral History Association: The Oral History Association, established in 1966, seeks to bring together all persons interested in oral history as a way of collecting human memories. http://omega.dickinson.edu/organizations/oha/

Oral History Society: The Oral History Society is a national and international organization dedicated to the collection and preservation of oral history. http://www.oralhistory.org.uk/

PPgis.net: This site is the electronic forum on participatory use of geospatial information systems and technologies. http://ppgis.iapad.org/

"Public Participation GIS (PPGIS) Guiding Principles": This site contains an article about PPGIS by Doug Aberley and Renee Sieber. http://www.urisa.org/PPGIS/2003/papers/PPGIS%20Principles2.pdf

6

GIS Data Collection and Development (Sources, Input, and Output)

Chapter Description

This chapter is about GIS data sources, including data from existing sources, which includes the Internet, as well as one's own data. We also discuss the integration of other data types, including those not explicitly formatted for GIS. We introduce fundamental concepts related to locating and organizing data for use in GIS. A section on database fundamentals and organization is provided to assist readers who are not familiar with these concepts as they relate to GIS. Because GIS may be used both for data development and storage as well as an analysis tool, it will often be used in conjunction with other familiar tools, techniques, and software packages. A discussion of formatting and data transfer between sources is included. Finally, a section discussing the various outputs GIS offers is provided in the context of visual, variable, and statistical data outputs that are relevant to the analysis.

Chapter Objectives

- Provide guidance on parameterization of research with appropriate data sources.
- Consider factors for establishing a base map to which to tie your research data.
- Introduce fundamentals of database organization for GIS.
- Offer suggestions for data collection that can be easily incorporated into a GIS, including the use of global positioning system (GPS) technology.
- Discuss options for importing and exporting data between a GIS database and other sources.
- Expand on the discussion of GIS data outputs, visualization, and statistics.

> After reading this chapter, you should be able to perform the following tasks:
> - Identify, locate, and evaluate the relevance of online sources for GIS base maps and data for your research.
> - Develop GIS-compatible database tables.
> - Import and export data between GIS and other software programs, including statistical software, spreadsheets, and others.
> - Develop a means for geocoding or spatially linking nonspatial data into a spatial structure for GIS.
> - Choose the best output formats for communicating research results.

Introduction

In the previous chapter, we discussed a variety of common data collection methods used in social science research and the ways these may be integrated with GIS. Examples provided with each method presented a general concept of how you might use GIS in various situations. In this chapter, we extend those general concepts to a variety of specific issues related to GIS data acquisition. Data come in two major forms: primary data (data you collect yourself for your specific research project) and secondary data (data collected for another purpose appropriate to your research).

Important concepts and practical advice related to finding and incorporating existing, secondary data are presented. We offer a variety of suggestions to help you in locating data and evaluating data quality and appropriateness for your own research. Additionally, we highlight important considerations related to developing your own primary data sets for use in a GIS. Issues relevant to importing data from other software applications as well as exporting GIS data into such programs are also included.

Data Acquisition

Of course, to carry out a GIS analysis one must have spatial data—that is, data that are somehow linked to a real location on the ground or in a user-defined hypothetical space. This chapter addresses a variety of data sources that currently exist, approaches to collecting your own data, new data that incorporate a spatial context, and the linking of nonspatial data to map locations to facilitate its use in a GIS.

Countless sources of data exist, and we can in no way cover them all here. Many useful data sets are available via the Internet, especially those distributed by government agencies in the United States and around the world.

Such data are often provided in formats compatible with popular GIS software packages. As one searches for data at the local level, the Internet tends to be less helpful. Although many local organizations and agencies use GIS and produce data, they may not have the need or the resources to provide online access to their data. Many smaller local organizations do not have the legal mandate to make their data available. It is just as likely that you will find yourself visiting local organizational or agency offices or making phone calls to find out whom, if anyone, has the data you need.

In other words, searching for data to use in a GIS analysis is no different from searching for any type of data necessary in conducting a research project. It would be foolhardy to assume that all of the data you require for a GIS-based study will be ready and waiting for you to download from the Internet. This may seem obvious, but surprisingly the majority of people we interact with regarding the issue of data make this assumption. Getting out on the ground, talking to people who have the data, and collecting the data yourself are still essential components of the process, components that should not be discounted. In fact, for a typical GIS project, as in any study, a substantial portion of time and effort goes into data collection and entry prior to carrying out the actual data analysis.

There is one other item of note we should mention at this point. A good amount of data is not readily available, even data considered public and collected by government agencies. There are a variety of reasons for this, many of which are often related to data incompatibilities, budgets, individual personalities, or agency rivalries. Regardless of the reasons, you may find that it takes some effort to acquire data from some organizations.

Evaluating Data Suitability

In any of the previous cases, finding existing data online or through direct contact with an organization or individual can be time-consuming, and there is no guarantee that when you do locate such data it will precisely meet your needs. Careful evaluation of available data is important to any research project. Because many existing GIS data sets tend to be of coarse resolution, you may find it better to collect new, detailed data specific to your study rather than trying to make existing, and potentially out-of-date information, fit your needs. Spending time and effort securing an existing data set aggregated at a county level will not serve the requirements of a neighborhood-level study. Similarly, obtaining a data set that is poorly documented (e.g., doesn't include information on how and when it was collected and entered into the computer) may not serve you well and is time better spent locating or collecting data of appropriate quality. In short, this is where the computer acronym GIGO (garbage in, garbage out) comes into play.

When considering data from any existing source, you must answer five key questions:

1. Do the data contain the information I need for my study?

2. Is the data appropriately documented (metadata) so that I understand how and why it was collected and coded in the way provided?

3. Is the format of the data appropriate for my study, and, if not, will I be able to convert it?

4. Do the data contain a geographic element to link it to the GIS, or, if not, could one be added easily?

5. If there are multiple versions, is this the best one for my purpose?

Obtaining GIS Data From the Internet

Vast amounts of GIS data are now available via the Internet. A search on the World Wide Web for "GIS data" returns over 600,000 sites! The issue of locating data online is not so much one of finding data but rather one of finding appropriate data for your project. To this end, there are several important considerations when searching for data online.

Perhaps the most important issue relates to the source or provider of data. With thousands of providers online, it is not unusual to locate multiple versions of a data set that appear to meet your needs. In very broad terms, data is available from four unique types of providers: government agencies, universities and research organizations, nonprofit organizations, and private firms. What may be less apparent is that in many instances these varied data sources may all be based on the same original government data.

Much of the existing, available GIS data originate in government agencies, such as the U.S. Census Bureau, the U.S. Geological Survey (USGS), the Environmental Protection Agency (EPA), the National Aeronautics and Space Administration (NASA), and others. In many cases, data you obtain from private firms fall into the category of value-added data. In simple terms, this refers to government data that have been somehow enhanced by a private firm and packaged in a user-friendly manner. For example, the USGS quadrangle maps, a commonly used data source, are a publicly available data source. However, a number of private companies have taken the time to collect and organize these maps on CD-ROM or Web site interfaces to facilitate their easy use. Some include additional information for specific purposes, such as planning a backpacking trip, navigating with a GPS unit in your car, and so on.

Of course, these companies charge a fee for these products. When you purchase such products, you are not paying for the data per se but rather for the convenient access and interface. The advantages of preprocessed data are that the data tend to be easier for novice users to access and the data may already be packaged for a popular GIS software package, among other benefits.

Similarly, nonprofits, especially those with limited budgets, may obtain freely available government data and add value to the information as well. Where we live there are a number of environmental organizations that monitor natural resource issues related to logging and salmon. These organizations tend to be suspicious of the private industries they are monitoring, so they obtain the public data and supplement it with their own field data. Because these nonprofits tend to run on very limited budgets, they often share and rely on volunteer labor to compile the GIS data.

In situations where similar data are available from multiple sources, the value of one version over another may come through the added information, through the time and effort saved by using data someone else has packaged, or a variety of other perceived benefits. The question for you, the researcher, is, "Which data meet my needs the best?" If time is of the essence, the cost of commercial data may well be worthwhile compared to the time and cost of in-house data preparation and processing. If, however, time and processing are less significant concerns (perhaps you have student interns from the local university), obtaining original data directly from the agency that produced it could be preferable.

This all sounds great, but what are some specific issues to look at when searching for data? Everything we discussed in Chapter 2 is a consideration. That is, once you think through your project, you should have a sense of the scale of the analysis, the data model that is most appropriate (vector or raster), and the map coordinates and datum you wish to work with. All else being equal, avoiding conversions in any of these four areas reduces the potential for error in the spatial component of the data. If you must make conversions, changes to the coordinate system or datum are generally reliable in the GIS software.

Conversions of scale or data model (raster to vector, vector to raster) should be done with care, making sure to respect the level of accuracy of the original data collection. The scale issue is fairly straightforward. A map collected as small scale (e.g., 1:100,000) would be a poor choice for use in a GIS analysis in which you need to know on which side of a road something is located. Although you can zoom in on the screen and see this detail, the error associated with the lines on a map of 1:100,000 scale permits the line representing the road to be misplaced by well over 100 ft, more than enough for a particular object to appear on the wrong side of the street. A good rule of thumb is to obtain maps at a larger scale than necessary; it is fine for you to zoom out. The opposite is not true: Zooming in can lead to errors in your analysis.

When converting data models, a similar scale problem can occur. For example, if analyzing a data set derived from raster pixels that were originally collected at 30 m × 30 m (900 m2) and subsequently converted into a vector map, you should be careful not to analyze the resulting vector map at accuracies greater than the original 30 m accuracy. Figure 6.1 shows the origins of this conversion problem and how an unknowing end-user of the data might not have the detail he or she anticipates.

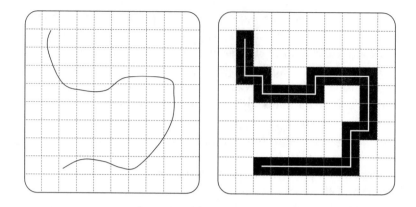

Figure 6.1   A comparison of the true shape and position of a linear feature in space as it would appear in raster format and as converted back to vector format. The graphic on the left represents the true shape and position of a linear feature in space. On the right we see the pixels (represented as black squares) that would be mapped in a raster format, for example, a land use, land cover map provided by the USGS. If you were to take the raster map and convert it into a vector data set, the resulting line (in white) would be placed at the center of the raster pixels and would no longer accurately represent the original feature particularly well.

At some mapping scales, and for some analyses, this loss of detail may be perfectly fine. The risk comes to the end-user who doesn't know the origins of the data and obtains the vector data on the right (the white line) without the accompanying understanding of the data's accuracy and fitness for use in the particular analysis.

A second and equally important issue relates to the data attributes. The attributes are the information about features represented on the map and contained in a database that accompanies the map information. If you were looking at the attributes for a data set showing local businesses, there might be information about the number of employees, type of industry, gross sales, and so on. As in any data collection process, there will be a predetermined level of measurement (nominal, ordinal, interval, or ratio) incorporated into the data coding process. Regardless of the spatial accuracy of GIS data, if the information you require for your study is not present in the attribute database, your analysis won't get very far.

In some cases, the data attributes may be decoupled from the map information. That is, you may locate some of the data sets you require as plain database files, which must be connected to the spatial component of the map. For example, you might have a postal service map showing the location of the zip codes in a community. Separately, you could obtain membership lists (these being databases in some form) from a variety of organizations of interest in your study. Although these data sets may not have originally been associated with, or even created by, a single organization, they can be linked together to create a spatial data set. We discuss this process in detail later in this chapter.

Of course, it is entirely possible that the data you need will not be found on the Internet, or the data you find online are insufficiently documented or from an unknown source that you are uncomfortable including in your study. It is important to remember that just because data are available on the Internet does not necessarily mean it is quality data. In many cases, you may find that searching for data elsewhere or creating your own new data is preferable.

Obtaining Data From Offline Sources

Quite often the data you require will come from sources that do not have an online presence. Examples include local agencies and organizations, professionals, students, or archival sources. The same data quality considerations hold true for data obtained through offline channels; however, when obtaining data from offline sources, several additional issues are worth considering.

In the case of historic or archival data, it is highly likely that the data only exist in printed or other physical formats rather than as digital computer files. Examples of such sources include anything from a printed map sheet, a figure in a text or journal, or even the actual data sheets or notes residing in someone's file cabinet. Other sources of data might include photographs, audiotape-recorded interviews, or video footage.

Any data that exist in one of these physical formats require conversion to a digital format to be integrated into a GIS. When we refer to a digital format, we simply mean the data are in a format a computer can directly manipulate; in contrast, when we obtain data in physical formats, the first step in the data development process is data entry into the computer. Therefore, if there is an option to obtain similar data in digital form, a substantial amount of data entry can be avoided. The time and cost of entering nondigital data into the computer for integration into the GIS analysis should be weighed against the benefit of doing so.

For many questions, the inclusion of data sources collected in the past is obvious. The primary consideration should lie in the reliability and consistency of the data, especially if it will be used as baseline information for determining trends or changes. Data collected in the same way (both spatial and nonspatial) by the same organization over time—for example, the U.S. Census—can prove extremely valuable in an analysis. However, data collected using a variety of different methods, mapping scales, and technologies may simply lead to an erroneous analysis.

Let's illustrate this point with a simple example. Imagine using a map of North America drawn by explorers in the 1500s in conjunction with one collected using satellite imaging to determine changes in the locations and extent of populated places in the eastern United States. Of course, we would expect that the accuracy of maps made in the 1500s would be substantially different from those made today. Thus, differences observed between these two data sets are just as, if not more, likely due to differences in the data quality, not because there are actual differences in the size and locations of the places under study.

Although this example presents an obvious difference in data types, there are often more subtle differences. For example, what differences in data quality, accuracy, or methodology would you expect to be present in data collected just a few decades apart? What about data collected a few years apart? What about data collected on a single topic but by different organizations? What about other information that may not be included in a particular data set?

Consider data on occurrences of lung cancer. Would you feel confident that lung cancer is decreasing if you were to see a drop in the number of cases between 1970 and 1990? What if you knew that the 1970 data came from a government public health agency, and the 1990 data came from an industry report? The more likely explanation would be that the differences are not due to a real decrease but rather to a difference in data sources and method of analysis. What if all the data came from a single, reliable source, but then you discovered that a large, polluting industrial facility in the study area closed down in 1975?

One of the great benefits of a GIS is its ability to integrate data from a variety of sources. In the previous example, even if you didn't know the relevance of pollution, socioeconomic factors, medical care, and so on, if data are available, the GIS is an effective tool for the exploration of potential relationships between and among various data sets, often from different disciplines and sources. So long as the data you incorporate are of similar mapping quality and scale, it can be integrated with other sources using location as a common link. However, when the detail of one or more data sets is of substantially lower resolution (i.e., one data set is state level and another is county level), meaningful spatial analysis may only be possible at the level of the least detailed data.

Statistical interpolation methods (discussed further in Chapter 9), used to estimate data values in unsampled locations, can sometimes provide a workaround but may not be optimal. Deciding when data are appropriate to include in an analysis and when new or different data may be required depends on the kinds of questions and answers you require. If local detail is necessary, estimating from state or national data may be inappropriate; however, for broad-based studies, that same national data set may be perfectly acceptable.

How Can I Use My Own Data?

Quite often you will want to develop your own data for use in a GIS. Whether this is due to a lack of appropriate, preexisting data or simply a requirement for new data, creating new data is a common step in a GIS analysis.

The fundamental issue in creating your own data for GIS is to have a spatial component, preferably in the projection, datum, and coordinate format you will use for your GIS analysis. Several approaches are available in creating new data:

1. Collect information in a digital format (database, spreadsheet, statistical, or similar software package) that can be directly linked to an identifier contained in an existing GIS map.

2. Create digital data that contain inherent spatial information, most commonly via the use of a GPS receiver carried into the field.

3. Manually input the data into the GIS by creating the necessary map data along with the other information collected for your study. We review each of these options in greater detail later in this chapter.

Approaching the Use of GIS With and Without a Computer in the Field

GIS Without a Field Computer

One common question that may come up for the social scientist interested in using GIS is "Do I need a computer to gather data that could be analyzed using a GIS?" The answer is no, not necessarily. Your data gathering in the field may involve administering surveys, collecting oral histories, or conducting ethnographies. If you do not have a computerized GIS database in the field, it is important that you observe and take careful notes about the geographic locations that pertain to your key variables. This might be as simple as marking data collection locations on a map or noting a geographically identifiable attribute, such as the street address or the name of the town or watershed that the respondent was located in when the particular data were collected. Of course, if there are issues of confidentiality in your study, you need to be careful to only record at a level of detail consistent with the needs of the study and according to whatever institutional human-subjects research process is appropriate given your organization and funding source.

GIS With a Field Computer

If you are fortunate enough to have a laptop computer with a GIS system on it, you can code and enter your data into the GIS system as you go, minimizing the need for later data entry and transcription. Of course, having GIS technology in the field can afford you, the researcher, an evolving look at the geographic relationships being explored in your study as you go. Of course, in some research settings, this type of data exploration in the midst of a study may be considered inappropriate; however, in many applied situations the ability to obtain preliminary results as the data are collected and entered can be extremely valuable. Immediate and evolving data visualization can be particularly useful when analyzing issues that are time sensitive and related to safety, security, and health. Even if you cannot take the GIS into the field, data can be entered each time you return to the office or another place where the GIS is accessible to begin the process of data entry, coding, and preliminary visualization.

Data Collection Considerations

Optimally, when you collect your own data, it can be linked to an existing base map. A base map is a map layer that has basic geographic information appropriate to your study, including a coordinate system, projection, and scale. Some common feature types present on many base maps include political boundaries, census tracts, zip or area code boundaries, or major landscape features, such as roads and water bodies. Depending on the level of detail required for your study, some common base maps might include national or state maps containing several of these key features. For more detailed studies, base maps might include the address ranges along streets by block, census block groups, or other detailed location information.

When your study can be tied directly to an existing base map of this sort, the process of getting your own data into the GIS is greatly simplified. It will not be necessary to collect detailed spatial information for your sample units; instead, you can simply record the common spatial identifier along with the other information required for your study. For example, you could use a phone company map to link respondents in a phone survey to a geographic location based on their phone number. Thus, simply recording which area code or prefix was dialed would be sufficient to map a respondent to an appropriate location on the map, while still retaining an appropriate level of aggregation necessary to ensure privacy.

So long as you are able to directly tie study data to an existing base map, the process of linking your data to the GIS requires that you know the coding scheme used on the base map. In many cases, the codes used for units of analysis are a one-to-one correlation to the map units (e.g., area codes on the GIS map would be the actual area code). However, in some data sets, the coding scheme used for the GIS map may be less apparent (e.g., county names might be coded with numbers or abbreviations in the GIS).

When there is not a direct or obvious coding scheme, you have two options. Optimally, you will be able to determine the coding scheme that was used on your base maps in advance of your data collection and use those same codes as you assemble your new data. If the codes used on the base map cannot be obtained in advance, or are not readily available, you may still go forward with data collection, but you will need to plan on adding the appropriate coding information before linking the data to a GIS map. In some cases, these codes may already be incorporated into an existing GIS data layer; in others there may be a separate document, or data dictionary, that defines codes used by the organization or agency.

Address Matching

Address matching is another popular method for linking data to a geographic location on the map. This process uses a map layer with street names and addresses coded into the data. When you provide an address, the GIS attempts to match the street name and street addresses to the proper location on the map. This is accomplished in much the same way as locating an address by driving around your neighborhood. Once you locate the street, addresses can be located by determining which address ranges fall in a given block and on which side of the street the odd- or even-numbered addresses fall. This process works fairly well in a GIS so long as the underlying street and address information is properly stored within the database (some problems in this regard are discussed in the section on database concepts later in this chapter). The benefit of address matching is that data are mapped to a relatively specific location without the need to collect ground coordinates in the field with a GPS receiver.

Using a GPS

The GPS is becoming a readily available and inexpensive technology that complements GIS quite well. A handheld consumer-grade GPS unit can be purchased for less than $200, and in many research applications it is very sufficient. Using a GPS receiver, either a model mounted in a vehicle or a handheld model, you can determine your location on the globe in a matter of just a few seconds. The GPS receiver obtains a signal from a set of satellites in orbit high above the earth. These satellites constantly transmit the information necessary for the calculation of position in a variety of coordinate systems and datums. With the touch of a button, the GPS unit stores these locations in memory, and these data can be downloaded to your computer for mapping in the GIS, along with whatever additional data you collected at that location.

In the context of data collection for a GIS-based study, simply taking along a GPS receiver to acquire location information at each sample site provides the additional data required to link any of your other field-based data to the map. Of course, there may be some issues of privacy that must be considered. For instance, a survey respondent may not take kindly to you recording a GPS location on his or her front porch while asking a series of questions. However, GPS data may be especially useful in getting location information for environmental data—for example, the locations of vacant lots, city parks, or illegal roadside dump locations. It can be especially useful in contexts in which data may be difficult to obtain through formal channels.

The two most important concepts and considerations when using GPS for location information are that GPS is not as accurate as it appears but is accurate enough to be useful and that GPS data, like any data source for your study, must be in the same coordinates and datum as your other data. Let's look at each of these concepts in turn.

The issue of accuracy is initially addressed by reviewing the specifications of the GPS receiver you are using. In the product manual, there is typically a statement of spatial accuracy for both the horizontal (X, Y) plane and the elevation (Z axis). Also note that specifications typically state that these levels of accuracy are achieved 90% of the time, which allows room for larger error 5% of the time. Oddly, most GPS units report your location to within 1 m in all directions, even though it is unlikely you would get a location reading that is truly that accurate.

Most current consumer-grade GPS units, such as those available in new vehicles or at outdoor stores, provide accuracy to about 5 to 10 m on the (X, Y) plane. This should be more than sufficient to locate your data in a particular neighborhood and street but might present some difficulty if you need to locate which side of the street you were on. Of course, given the need to maintain confidentiality of personal information, the errors in GPS are not likely to be of great concern. If being off 10 m is problematic, much more accurate (and expensive!) GPS systems and techniques are available to obtain accuracy down to a few inches.

Although there is a great deal of math and physics behind the function of the GPS system, the end-user can learn most of the necessary methods by simply reviewing the manual that comes with the unit and practicing for a day or two. Getting the location information out of the GPS receiver and into the data set in the GIS is the final step. At a minimum, all GPS units record a location ID (typically starting with 1 and counting up, although the user can also assign IDs as they wish) along with X, Y, and Z coordinates as well as the date and time. In conjunction with a survey or data collection sheet, all information collected in the field can be easily linked to its proper location on the map.

Data stored in the GPS receiver's memory can be downloaded to your computer. Some GPS units include software tools that may allow you to link to a laptop to record all of the information directly into a database or other software program. Other GPS software may require that you export the data and then bring it into the GIS as a separate step. This later process is addressed in the section on database concepts later in this chapter.

Creating Base Maps From Scratch

Perhaps the least desirable option for generating data necessary for a study is doing so from scratch because it is tedious and time consuming. However, in some studies, especially those requiring historic data, this may be the only option. Data created from scratch are most commonly based on either maps or aerial images (photo or satellite). The actual map or image may be used in its printed physical form or scanned into the computer as a digital image.

Regardless of the format, the basic process of creating the base map is the same. The map or image is interpreted by the analyst, and individual features of interest are traced one by one into the computer through a process referred to as digitizing. For each object digitized in this manner, descriptive information (attributes) must be entered into the computer. For example, if we were to digitize a map of county roads from 1950 for comparison to roads in 1990, each road name from the 1950 map would need to be individually entered into the computer.

Of course, maps show only the information deemed relevant by the mapmaker, so to get an unbiased picture of the past it is often preferable to work from aerial photographs. This is because an aerial photograph provides a complete and unbiased view of the data as they were at the time the photo was acquired. By contrast, when a map is drawn, much of the detail is intentionally left out to avoid clutter on the printed map.

Mapping-quality aerial photographs are collected in many parts of the United States on a regular basis and in some parts of the country go back to the 1920s. The process of delineating, tracing, and naming individual features in the photograph is the same as described for a map, with one added complication. Maps generally show some type of location information (e.g., latitude and longitude), whereas photographs often do not. Thus, to make data digitized from a photograph useful, it must first be correlated to the actual locations on the ground. If you are fortunate, a sufficient number of fixed locations will be identifiable in the historic photograph, perhaps key road intersections, buildings, or other features known to be in the same location. With several such locations identified, you may then match these to a map with marked coordinates or perhaps physically visit those locations with a GPS receiver in hand.

Without more in-depth knowledge of map projections, coordinates, and datums; map and image analysis techniques; and related issues, GIS data creation such as described earlier may best be referred to someone with this specific expertise, especially if this map is to become the base map for your entire analysis. For completeness, it is important to realize that creation of your own base data is an option, albeit not the easiest or quickest of the options available.

Unit of Analysis

A statistical concept that is relevant to any analysis and potentially imposed by the data when conducting a spatial study is the unit of analysis, introduced in Chapter 4. The unit of analysis refers to the sample unit being analyzed. For example, when surveying people about their smoking habits, the individual could be the unit of analysis; however, if your work is focused on differences in smoking rates by county, your unit of analysis might better be each county. In the latter example, individual responses are aggregated at the county level, which simplifies the data substantially (see Figure 4.3). Selecting and altering the unit of analysis can have important implications in your analysis depending on the area of the spatial unit selected. This is discussed in the section about the modifiable area unit problem in Chapter 7.

One important point to consider in any statistical analysis of data is independence of the observations. When looking for data sets or preparing to collect new data, it is important to understand if the individual observations are independent, or unrelated to one another. There are a variety of causes of nonindependence in data, which are discussed in most introductory texts in statistics. The unique consideration in spatial analysis is that of spatial autocorrelation, which refers to a situation where observations taken close together in space are similar (positive autocorrelation). For example, people who live in the same neighborhood may be more likely to be of a similar socioeconomic class than people from different neighborhoods. Sometimes spatial autocorrelation is useful in pointing you to the presence of an underlying factor that influences the observed characteristics. If the relationship is negative (observations near one another are different), then a greater diversity of data in space exists. Many GIS software packages provide tools to examine spatial autocorrelation. Two of the most popular statistics are Moran's I and Geary's C. It is beyond the scope of this text to provide the details of these statistics; however, numerous resources are available in both the statistical and the GIS literature.

The bottom line in considering the unit of analysis is to select an appropriate level of analysis considering both the variables to be measured and the level at which those variables actually operate. Measuring data at the individual level may not be relevant if the data actually function at a higher level. For example, in electing the president of the United States, individuals vote, but for most states all of the electoral college votes are cast for the candidate with the majority vote for the state. This is what makes it possible for one candidate to win the popular vote, while another wins the electoral college vote. Thus, using individuals as the unit of analysis is not particularly useful given the selection of the president operates at the state level.

Sometimes when seeking data for use in a study, you need to be especially careful. Just because a data set is available at a particular level of detail does not mean that level is the appropriate unit for your analysis. Consider your own question and the level at which the variables operate, and then (if appropriate) aggregate the data at an appropriate level. Of course, it is not possible to obtain additional detail in data that were previously collected and aggregated by someone else. You can, however, aggregate detailed data to a larger unit of analysis, for example, group individual responses to the county level. There is always a risk that you may commit an ecological fallacy (Chapter 4) if you do not conduct your analysis at the same level as the generalizations you intend to draw from the data.

Database Concepts and GIS

Some basic database concepts are important to introduce at this point. In simple terms, a database is a collection of organized information. Of course, modern databases are computerized, but in the past many databases existed in a physical form, residing in filing cabinets, library card catalogs, and bound volumes. Many of these older data sets are of great value in modern analyses, and when this is true, coding the relevant information into the computer is necessary. Databases that already exist in the computer or that are being newly collected must follow some simple rules to ensure they blend well with the GIS.

The software used to store database information is, at some level, irrelevant. Using a formal database software program can streamline the process, especially for complex data sets; however, for simpler data, you may prefer readily available spreadsheet software, such as Microsoft Excel®. In fact, even a typical word processor or text editor can be used as a simple database so long as the basic rules are followed.

Rules for GIS Database Development

What are these basic rules? First, let's consider the layout of the information on the computer screen. A database is typically organized in rows and columns. The rows represent individual records in the database; perhaps these are survey respondents. Table 6.1 shows the individual respondents: A, B, and C are represented in rows. In GIS jargon, we often refer to these as entities in the database.

Columns in the database represent the information collected about each record, for example, the answer given by the respondent for each question on the survey. These are often called the attributes in GIS. Table 6.1 provides an example of a small database. There are three entities: A, B, and C—in this case the respondents. For each entity in the database, we recorded four attributes: in this example, the individuals' numeric answers to each of four questions, perhaps using a Likert scale ranging from 1 to 5.

Table 6.1   An example of a simple database table with three entities, A, B, and C. Each entity is represented by a row in the database. For each entity, the answers to four questions are recorded as attributes; each question is represented as its own column in the data table

Respondent	Question_1	Question_2	Question_3	Question_4
A	4	3	5	5
B	2	4	3	3
C	5	4	4	5

Table 6.2   An example of a database table that incorporates a spatial identifier that can be associated with a map, in this case a postal service zip code map

Zip_Code	Respondent	Question_1	Question_2	Question_3	Question_4
55113	A	4	3	5	5
55401	B	2	4	3	3
55112	C	5	4	4	5

Two other terms that are useful to introduce here are cell and field name. A cell is an individual box on the table. In the example, a cell might store information representing an entity (e.g., respondent B), an attribute (e.g., 2 being respondent B's answer to the first question), or a column heading, such as "Question_1." The cells at the top of each column are referred to as field names.

One item is missing from Table 6.1 to easily link it to a GIS map: a spatial component or identifier. If you have a base map that you would like to tie this to, add one additional column. Assume you are collecting data for a large urban area with the intent of analyzing results by zip code. Adding a zip code column to Table 6.1 allows your information to be linked to a postal service zip code map. The key to accomplishing this link is to incorporate one attribute—in this example, the zip code—in common with the base map. Thus, the more effective database that includes a spatial identifier might appear as shown in Table 6.2.

Creating GIS-Friendly Data Tables

As long as you follow the basic format described previously, you will be well on your way to developing data that are readily compatible with a GIS. However, to facilitate an even smoother transition, a number of additional formatting considerations are relevant when determining how easily your database will link to the GIS:

1. Consistent use of space and case

2. The format and coding of the data

3. The structure of the file saved by your software

Space and Case

First, let's look at some issues related to space and case. Although the Microsoft Windows® operating system and many of the programs that run on it allow you to put spaces into file names, it is not generally good practice. This is because some computers and software, including some GIS software, do not recognize spaces in file names. Another thing Windows ignores is the distinction between upper case and lowercase characters. Although these appear not to be problems in the Windows® computing environment where many of us do our work, use of spaces is generally a bad practice when working with databases in GIS; similarly, variations in case can cause problems with GIS software.

The reason these two issues cause problems relates to the fact that a significant amount of GIS data, and particularly base data coming from large government agencies, was developed on Unix-based computers where case matters. That is, a Unix-based computer considers "E" and "e" to be different letters, whereas a Windows®-based computer views these as identical. A related concept is that of punctuation. For most computer databases, the use of punctuation is also good to avoid because these characters often have special meaning.

Although issues of space and case might not cause problems in every situation, given the realities of data sharing, information downloading from the Internet, and variety of software and hardware platforms, it is best to avoid the use of punctuation and spaces. You may notice that in Tables 6.1 and 6.2, in those places where a space might normally be expected, an underscore was used instead. Similarly, it is important to be consistent in the use of character case.

At this point, you might ask, "What about when I need to store somebody's first and last name?" Although it might seem appropriate to place the name all in one field, from a database perspective it is preferable to place the first and last names into their own individual fields, rather than placing the names in the same column with a space between the names or with a comma between the last and first names. Of course, in many social science research applications, you may need to protect your respondents' privacy by coding information as numbers instead of names. There are situations where use of spaces or punctuation may be appropriate; for example, a city name such as Los Angeles can reasonably be coded in a single attribute column. However, it would be less appropriate to include the state name, separated with a comma, in the same cell (e.g., Los Angeles, California).

The reason for splitting city and state into separate columns is to facilitate sorting and analysis later in the process. This is no different than you might do when entering data into Excel® or SPSS® formats. By using separate columns for city and state, you can select only those cities in a particular state for an analysis comparing different states. Later, the same database might be used for a more detailed analysis comparing different cities done via use of the city name column. In short, the more you can differentiate attribute components into separate columns, the more options you will have in the data analysis phase later in the process.

Table 6.3   Although most individuals would interpret any of the following codes as referring to the same location, a computer takes the data literally and views some, or all, of these codes as unique values.

San Francisco
SAN FRANCISCO
S.F.
san francisco
s.f.
Sna Francisco
SanFrancisco
Frisco
The City by the Bay

Data Format and Coding Considerations

When preparing to code data into the computer, be it your own, new data or the transcription of existing data, there are several important considerations. As mentioned in the previous section, many computer programs take the data very literally, so differences in spacing, case, or coding can cause significant problems when creating and combining data sets for an analysis. Humans have an uncanny ability to understand that all of the codes in Table 6.3 refer to the same real-world location, even though there are substantial variations in how the coding has been done (including the possibility of typographic errors).

Unfortunately, a computer database would consider each of the codes for San Francisco as unique. This would result in an analysis that requested all data for San Francisco excluding any of the data records coded differently than the analyst requested. This is an important consideration when developing a coding scheme. Of course, if you are planning to link your data to an existing base map, it is preferable to use the same codes used in that existing data set. Similarly, when working with multiple data sets from multiple sources, it is important to verify that coding is consistent. If coding is not consistent between data sets, one or more may require editing or updating to facilitate interoperability.

It is not unusual for differences in coding to occur at political or jurisdictional boundaries between organizations, for example, two adjoining counties. For example, if you were attempting to conduct a regional planning exercise in a large metropolitan area made up of several counties, it would not be unusual to find that each county in the region uses different zoning codes. Just as the variations in spelling or abbreviations in Table 6.3 would cause you problems, so too would having data from several different counties each using their own zoning designation codes.

Of course, if there are opportunities to develop consistent coding schemes between organizations, often recorded in a data dictionary, many of these issues can be preempted prior to any individual or organization attempting to create databases of their information. Data dictionaries are used to set out the specific codes and definitions to be used when entering data into the database so that the codes are clearly understood by anyone who uses the database.

One additional, computer-specific issue in coding is the difference between a number field and a character field (or string). Many software programs used for data entry, especially database, GIS, and even spreadsheet programs, differentiate data by the type of information being entered into the computer. Although it may seem obvious that numbers are numbers, a computer also can treat a number as a character. However, letters and words are always treated as characters and thus cannot be inadvertently stored as numbers. Data tied to a GIS ultimately reside in a database, and databases treat these two data types differently.

In short, what this means is that your computer will not view a number stored in a character field in the same way as a number stored in a number field, and furthermore, mathematical operations will not work on character data in the same manner as they will on numeric data. Therefore, it is important to consider, in advance, the format your data should take before coding occurs. If your data values represent a real measurement (interval or ratio data) for a quantitative analysis, the numbers should be coded as number fields in the database. If you are using a qualitative approach (nominal or ordinal data), you may find that either numeric or character fields are appropriate.

One final comment on data entry and coding relates to the choice of software to use. Many of us are limited by two realities when it comes to software: what we have available or can afford and what we know how to use or have time to learn. Of course, if you are reading this book, you are most likely contemplating the use of GIS software even if you have not yet acquired it. GIS software packages include a database component as one part of their functionality; however, many people find it preferable to use an external software program for the data entry and management of the nonspatial data. If you are already using another software package for data entry, you may decide to continue using it.

The major advantage of using a true database program, be it the one built into the GIS or a stand-alone product such as Microsoft Access®, is that it allows a high degree of control during data input. That is, when developing a database, each individual field or cell can be programmed in advance to accept only appropriate data. Using these techniques can significantly reduce data entry errors by only allowing acceptable data to be placed into the database. This may not be a major concern if you have a small amount of data, and, in fact, programming a database may take more time than simply entering the data. However, in large projects involving multiple individuals or staff in the data entry process, the ability to preprogram automatic checks to ensure proper coding can be very advantageous.

For example, if using a Likert scale with a range of 1 through 5, the database could be programmed to allow only the digits 1 through 5, rejecting any letter or number other than those specifically allowed under the predetermined coding scheme. Similarly, databases can offer lists of possible answers, which in the case of textual responses can reduce misspellings or other typographic errors.

Software Output Formats

Regardless of the software used to enter your data into the computer, you will eventually have to find a way to make the data work with your GIS software. Of course, file compatibility can be problematic, and there are too many possible variations to discuss in detail here; however, we discuss two of the most common formats. One or both of these are available in most of the major software programs and are generally applicable to all GIS and database packages.

Most of the mainstream GIS software packages are able to directly read or import files in delimited text formats. Delimited text refers to a simple plain text data format readable by all popular computer programs. However, it is also worthwhile to review the specific documentation to determine if your GIS can read formatted database files, thus circumventing this step. One of the most common database file formats is dBASE®. These files are typically named using a .DBF file extension. This format originated in the early days of the PC and became quite popular as a database format in the 1980s. Due to widespread use in the database market for over 20 years, the .DBF file format has been integrated into many other software packages, including SPSS® and Microsoft Excel®, used to create and manage data. When you can use common formats such as dBASE to import and export between the software you use to create data and your GIS, you will inevitably avoid some of the more common errors associated with data sharing.

If using dBASE files is not appropriate for the particular software you plan to use, files saved in plain or ASCII delimited text are another excellent choice. Typically, you will find options to save your data to a text format in the Save As menu or Export menu in your software. The "delimited" descriptor indicates that the file will be saved with simple formatting that indicates where one data value ends and the next begins, most commonly using a comma or space. Figure 6.2 shows a repeat of Table 6.2—a small database we viewed earlier in the chapter followed by the comma delimited version that would result from saving this table in your choice of software.

Zip_Code	Respondent	Question_1	Question_2	Question_3	Question_4
55113	A	4	3	5	5
55401	B	2	4	3	3
55112	C	5	4	4	5

Zip_Code, Respondent, Question_1, Question_2, Question_3, Question_4

55113, A, 4, 3, 5, 5

55401, B, 2, 4, 3, 3

55112, C, 5, 4, 4, 5

Figure 6.2   An example of a database table (top) exported into a comma delimited format. Notice that the columns are separated by commas (bottom). Had any commas been included as part of the data values, they would present problems. Column headings are retained in the first row with each subsequent row in the list corresponding to an individual record in the database.

Notice that the comma delimited file simply puts the data from a given row all together using a comma to indicate the end of one cell and the beginning of the next. With this in mind, it should be easier to understand why use of commas within the database (e.g., names entered as last, first) could be problematic when saved to a comma delimited format. The comma between the names would be confused with a comma used to indicate the cells of the original database table.

The dBASE and comma delimited text formats are two of the most common methods for importing or exporting data between a software package you are familiar with and the geographic data in a GIS. If your preferred software does not offer one of these options, you may need to explore alternative import and export formats (although to be honest, if your software cannot work with one of these formats, we would recommend finding new software!). In addition to the data conversion tools included with each individual software package, countless stand-alone data conversion tools are available both for free and commercially.

Integrating Other Types of Data

To this point we have discussed tying what might be considered typical survey or census types of databases to a location on the map. In many cases, these will be the primary data types used for analysis purposes. However, in some cases, especially those where the final output of a study will be communicated using an interactive, multimedia format, the GIS can also link to databases containing other information. Most commonly, these other data types include image, sound, and video files.

By linking data of these types, a significant amount of additional information can be stored within the GIS context. For example, if you are conducting fieldwork, digital photographs or even video shot at various key locations can then be linked to the map for later review. Similarly, recorded interviews can be linked to the location where the interview was conducted or to the location that the interview is about (e.g., a historic location that no longer exists on the map).

These concepts can be extended further by capturing other forms of information, such as scans or photographs of artwork, artifacts, or other information, that are related to the map and study in some way. Beyond the immediate value of these additional data types to the goals of a particular study, they can provide a greatly enhanced database for future work. Imagine how much information is lost when a recorded interview or field visit is filtered by an individual collecting the data and transcribed or coded for analysis or to find major themes related to a particular analysis. If the raw data contained in that interview are stored in a readily available computerized database, particularly one linked to geographic points of interest, there is suddenly a rich archive of information that can be applied to future studies, not only on the particular topic but also on any study seeking information for a particular region or location.

As computer technology and data-capture techniques continue to improve in quality and decrease in cost, archiving these rich spatially and topically oriented databases will become easier, and even more of the data that once were trapped in individual filing cabinets can be made readily available for cross-disciplinary research and analysis.

GIS Output

Although it may seem a bit premature for a discussion of output from a GIS, we want to introduce some of the possibilities at this point. Having some sense of the desired outputs from a GIS analysis can provide important direction to the data collection and analytical procedures incorporated early in the process. Two broad categories of output are discussed in the following sections: (1) data visualization, the graphic output of the GIS, most commonly in the form of a map, and (2) statistical output, which may take on the form of numbers, graphs, or mathematical models. Last, we discuss exporting the results of your GIS analysis to other applications, both to facilitate analysis and to communicate the final results.

Data Visualization

The saying goes, "A picture is worth a thousand words," and this is certainly true in the world of maps. Perhaps the most obvious output from a GIS is the map, a graphic form that has a long history. Open any atlas and you will find maps that communicate information about demographics, economics, cultures, languages, history, politics, and a host of other information related to the social sciences. The GIS provides a tool for generating these maps in an efficient manner. GIS can provide many and sometimes all of the software tools necessary for data collection, organization, storage, analysis, and output.

Static maps are the most common of the graphic outputs from GIS. That is, maps that are drawn to display the relationship and distribution of a limited number of variables for a particular geographic extent (study area) and usually for a particular time. By getting a bit more creative with cartographic design, a single map might effectively show change over time or a larger number of variables in combination; however, in most cases, the more information placed on a single map, the more difficult and confusing it becomes for the end-user to interpret the information. A simple rule of thumb when considering output from an analysis is to limit maps to just a few variables and, if necessary, to use multiple maps, much like an atlas, when you are attempting to communicate lots of information resulting from an analysis.

Static maps can be enhanced when working in an interactive environment. If the end-users of your analysis have the ability to select the data layers they wish to view and the geographic area they want to look at, perhaps via a Web site, the appropriate map data can be presented. Countless interactive GIS Web sites are now available for the interactive exploration of data. The national atlases for a number of different countries are now provided in Web-based format rather than in print. For example, the National Atlas of the United States (http://nationalatlas.gov/) provides a variety of static and animated maps along with the underlying map data available for use in your own GIS software (Figure 6.3). Other examples include the Atlas of Canada (http://atlas.gc.ca) and the Atlas of Sweden (http://www.sna.se), which provide similar services for those nations.

Animated maps provide an alternative that allows for the communication of more complex information, particularly the change of information across time. Animation is an effective tool if the results of your study will be communicated using video formats on a computer using the Web or even traditional video. The animated radar maps shown on your local news' nightly weather reports are a common example. Most current GIS software is somewhat limited in providing tools to generate animated maps, so an external software product may be necessary to produce high-quality animation.

Three-dimensional visualization is yet another powerful means for communication of data. The GIS can be used to create realistic perspective views from anywhere on the landscape, such as that shown in Figure 5.2 in the previous chapter. Often, when attempting to show a proposed project or outcome, providing a picture that shows how things will look at completion can make the difference at a community meeting. For example, how will the

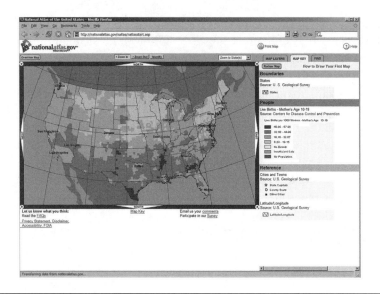

Figure 6.3   An example screen from the U.S. National Atlas Web site (http://nationalatlas.gov/). The site allows visitors to view data in a wide range of categories for the entire United States or any portion. This view shows the number of live births per 1,000 women, ages 10 to 19 years. Each data set is linked to the source agency, in this case, the Centers for Disease Control and Prevention (http://www.cdc.gov/). Interactive maps may be produced on either an individual computer with your own GIS software and data or via publicly available Web sites. The advantage of these interactive GIS maps is that the user can explore variations and combinations of data much more effectively than would be achieved via static maps on paper or as scanned computer graphics.

construction of a new building on a vacant lot affect the appearance of the neighborhood? How will it alter the skyline of the city?

Even more dramatic, three-dimensional images can be animated to create a fly-through of the landscape, thus providing a variety of realistic views and perspectives in an animated movie format. A fly through allows users to interactively navigate a three-dimensional landscape, giving them a feel for how things would appear if people actually walked in, drove through, or flew over the landscape. This is also sometimes referred to as virtual reality.

Statistical Output

Perhaps less apparent to a newcomer to GIS are the nongraphic outputs. It surprises many students taking an introductory GIS course to discover that the first GIS systems were developed before computers were capable of any graphic output at all. In fact, the first GIS systems did not even produce maps, and typically the computers used for the analysis also lacked a monitor to display the data. Having grown out of a nongraphical heritage, one of the most valuable outputs of a GIS analysis is the statistical or numeric output. For example, if you were using a GIS to determine how many new housing units could be built in a particular community by redeveloping vacant and abandoned parcels within a certain distance of the city center, a number is the desired result of the analysis. In such a situation, the map is secondary to answering the question at hand and may not be necessary at all.

In answering many questions, the value of the map or visualization may be outweighed by the need for the numbers. This is especially true in decision-making applications where knowing the percentages, risks, and likelihoods or dollars and cents are more compelling data to the researcher than obtaining a map. A typical GIS software package includes a variety of basic statistical tools. At a minimum, descriptive statistics can be generated, along with charts and graphs of the results, much like in a typical statistical analysis software package. Of course, the major strength of GIS in these analytical situations is the ability to carry out spatial operations on the data.

When the GIS does not offer the required statistical analysis, the database of both spatial and nonspatial data contained within the GIS can be readily queried for the appropriate information to export into a statistical software application. In fact, several of the major GIS and statistical software tools provide add-on tools or utilities to facilitate the direct transport of data between applications.

Exporting Data to Other Applications

Just as data tables can be imported into the GIS, the GIS can be used to analyze spatial relationships to generate new tables of information to export back into other software packages. Imagine you have a GIS database of public health statistics for the entire United States, but you are doing a study of one particular region. The spatial analysis tools of the GIS can select only those records associated with the region in question and create a new, smaller database table with only the information you require for your study. In this way, the GIS is used as a data extraction tool that allows you to select and extract data needed to run statistical tests or other analytical processes.

Of course, you might think, "I could do that in a database by querying the state or county names I require, so why use the GIS?" This is a valid point. If the database contains that information, you wouldn't need a GIS, but what if your study region consisted of households located within 1 mile of an industrial facility registered with the EPA for release of registered toxins? Or, if you were doing a study of the spread of West Nile virus, you might want to locate all residential areas within 2 km of lakes and ponds (bodies of water where mosquitoes could breed). Spatial analysis such as this is not as simple to do with a standard database query but is readily accomplished in a GIS.

Conclusions

As stated earlier in the chapter, a GIS acts as an integrator for a wide array of different data and information. The strength of the GIS is in its ability to analyze and explore this information in a spatial context. Data can be tied to base maps at any geographic scale, and in many cases to analysis at multiple scales. For example, data analyzed at the local level in a countywide study could later be aggregated at county level for the purpose of a regional or statewide analysis. Spatial patterns and distributions in data across space may help to explain relationships that would not otherwise be apparent in the data.

In addition to the ability to integrate existing information, the GIS offers us a platform to create and store new information collected through any of the traditional methods as well as to synthesize new data through combinations and queries of data already in the system. In combination, these provide a powerful set of tools for analysis.

Lastly, GIS offers a variety of options for both visual and numeric output. These may include final products such as maps, tables, and graphs as well as exported data that are used for further analysis in statistical software or discipline-specific modeling. These techniques may output information that is returned to the GIS as new data sets for use in additional analyses in the future.

Relevant Web Sites

Atlas of Canada: This site is an example of an interactive GIS Web site. http://atlas.gc.ca/

Atlas of Sweden: This site is an example of an interactive GIS Web site. http://www.sna.se/

Centers for Disease Control and Prevention: This agency provides an array of national databases related to public health, disease, births, and deaths. http://www.cdc.gov/

National Aeronautics and Space Administration: This site provides a variety of imagery and monitoring data for the world or portions thereof. http://www.nasa.gov

National Atlas of the United States: This site provides a wide variety of mapping data for the United States, including agricultural, biological, social, governmental, historical, and many others. http://nationalatlas. gov/

National Map of the United States: This is the Web version of the USGS topographic base maps. However, in addition to traditional topographic information, this site offers a variety of additional mapping layers from federal, state, and local partners across the country. http://nationalmap. usgs.gov/

Natural Resources Canada: This site provides a variety of national data sets, including aerial images, geographic places, maps, and topographic information. http://www.nrcan-rncan.gc.ca/inter/index_e.html (Natural Resources Canada also provides information on multivariate statistics and spatial autocorrelation. http://www.pfc.forestry.ca/profiles/wulder/mvstats/spatial_e.html)

U.S. Census Bureau: The is the official site for the U.S. Census demographic data, TIGER files, and other related data. http://www.census.gov

U.S. Environmental Protection Agency: The EPA provides a variety of national databases related to environmental quality. http://www.epa.gov

U.S. Geological Survey: This site provides a variety of national data sets, including aerial images, geographic places, maps, and topographic information. http://www.usgs.gov

7

Measurement

Chapter Description

This chapter explores issues of data collection that may influence the selection of data variables for an analysis. This includes methods for the collection of both social and geographic parameters within the context of their appropriateness for analysis in a GIS. The chapter also examines data selection and level of measurement as they relate to the GIS database. Sampling approaches and the unit of analysis in data development and analysis are also discussed in the context of the selection of appropriate variables to best work within a spatial analysis. When choosing variables in GIS, the social scientist must always be cognizant of the geographical links between spatial and social variables.

Chapter Objectives

- Introduce types of data you might incorporate into your GIS analysis.
- Discuss the operationalization of research into measurable variables for analysis.
- Review levels of measurement, their structure, and the analytical options each type offers for your research.
- Present issues related to data reliability and validity in both the attribute and spatial domains.
- Review approaches to sampling and the influence of your spatial sample units when conducting analysis in GIS.

After reading this chapter, you should be able to perform the following tasks:

- Differentiate between primary and secondary data sources and list the advantages and disadvantages of each.

- Understand the implications of measuring your variables at various levels of detail and select an appropriate level of measurement for each variable in your own research.
- Explain how and why study boundaries can influence the results of your analysis.
- Contrast various sampling methods you might use in collecting data and suggest which would be appropriate for particular variables and attributes.

Introduction

This chapter establishes the connection between social and spatial conceptualizations of space. People have different conceptualizations of space depending on a variety of characteristics, including social class and culture. We discuss different boundary systems, their appropriateness, and the various values given to space and spatial interpretations. Additionally, the role of GIS in helping communities, neighborhoods, counties, and nations to define and further develop is discussed. The issue of boundary determination from various social and analytical perspectives is also explored. GIS have an important role to play in the determination of boundaries, including political, social, economic, and environmental boundaries.

Type of Data Source: Primary or Secondary

When beginning a study in GIS, it is important to select and understand the data to be used in the analysis. Generally speaking, we refer to data collected directly by the research staff for the specific project as primary data. By contrast, data collected by someone else for a different purpose is referred to as secondary data. Although both data types have their place in any study, there are pros and cons to using each type.

The advantage of primary data is that you know exactly what it is you are working with, and you have complete control over the data creation process. This can be extremely beneficial in obtaining an end result that meets the specific goals of the study. However, collecting all of your data from scratch for every analysis you do can be quite time consuming and costly. Herein lies the value of secondary data sources.

Secondary data, though not collected with your specific research question in mind, are often quite appropriate and certainly can save a lot of time, money, and effort when you need to get your analysis done quickly and efficiently. As discussed in Chapter 6, a wide variety of GIS data sources is available from various government agencies, private firms, and other sources. Many of these secondary data sources are well documented, including metadata meeting the Federal Geographic Data Committee (FGDC) standards and specific criteria for accuracy and completeness. When data are well documented with FGDC metadata, a determination of its appropriateness to your study is easier to make. In short, consider the source and purpose for the data.

Generally, we assume that when data are collected for research purposes, care will be taken to ensure it is unbiased and complete, but this is not necessarily so. Every data set is collected with a purpose in mind and, potentially, a bias based on this intended use. This is not to imply that data are intentionally biased but rather that data collected for a purpose other than the purpose of your study may have built-in bias. For example, you may obtain a data set that was collected by surveying shoppers in a local mall. Although that data may have been perfectly appropriate for a study of the shopping behavior of people in that specific mall, it may not be appropriate for a study of the purchasing habits of the entire community. Therefore, it is important to be sure that secondary data are appropriate for your purposes and to your specific research needs.

Secondary data can raise concerns in two general situations: when it is similar to but not exactly what you need and when it is unclear how and why the data were originally collected, raising questions about how and why particular variables were selected and measured. In many cases, using secondary data requires effort on your part to prepare it for use in your analysis. In the case of existing GIS data, this could range from a simple map reprojection, which takes only a few moments, to a more extensive reorganization of the database attributes to facilitate links to the base map or other spatial information. (Refer to Chapter 6 for a discussion of database structure and compatibility of attributes.)

Some considerations that will influence your decision to either create your own data or rely on secondary data include the following:

1. *Your study question:* What is your study question? Your data selection should serve the needs of your analysis. If existing secondary data can do this, you may be able to save the time and effort of collecting new data.

2. *Data requirements:* What type of data are you looking at? Is the available data up to date? If you are looking for base data (infrastructure, built environments, etc.), it may not have changed significantly since available secondary sources were collected. However, if the data involve people or natural environments that can change rapidly, then the available secondary sources may not be at all appropriate.

3. *Combined approaches:* Sometimes a hybrid approach can be used. Perhaps you can work with an existing source and make updates to bring it up-to-date or to add the missing attributes that you require.

In the end, realities of time and money typically limit how much new data you collect and how much existing data you include or edit to use. In the remaining sections of this chapter, we focus on how data are measured in the preparation of your GIS database. Even though you may use secondary sources exclusively, it is important to understand how and why those data sets were collected and organized in the way they were. Without that knowledge, you run the risk of incorporating inappropriate data into your analysis. This can lead to incorrect or misleading results.

As you evaluate the fitness of any data for use in a particular analysis, it is essential that you have a firm understanding on the goals and design of your study. The following sections detail the process of conceptualizing your project, measuring variables, and designing the analysis framework. With these things in mind, you will be better prepared to evaluate when secondary data fit the needs of your analysis and, if not, how to best go about collecting your own data.

Concepts, Variables, and Attributes

A concept refers to a body of ideas taken together as a unit. In the research process, we go through a process called conceptualization, in which the researcher clearly identifies and names the main ideas that are a part of his or her theoretical model. The primary tasks of conceptualization are to develop a definition of your concept and to determine a label or name for it. Examples of concepts include poverty, community strength, and environmentalism. Each of these concepts reflects an area that could be studied in great detail. It is important to recognize that one simple concept may be composed of multiple attributes.

Operationalization of Concepts in GIS

Once you define the concepts that will inform your analysis, you must determine how to measure each one, a process termed operationalization. This is typically accomplished by identifying the specific variable or variables to measure. A variable can be described as an indicator for the measurement of your concepts. Very often in the GIS context, these variables are physical entities, such as a person, a facility, or another feature that can be located in space and about which data can be collected for use in the analysis.

For example, if you were going to identify variables related to the concept of poverty, one indicator you could measure is income. Of course, there are other variables that could be measured as components of the concept of poverty, for example, nutrition, education, number of children, and employment. A variable can be anything that provides an indication or measurement of your concept. Depending on the concept being measured, you may

One of the fundamental issues when mapping information, whether for use in a GIS or else-where, is the form of the data relative to the tools used to map it. Traditional maps and their computerized counterparts typically use lines to define borders. Consider the lefthand sketch in this figure. If you are told the areas defined on the map represent parcel bound-aries, those are a discreet data type. Property boundaries can be precisely surveyed and mapped so that the map accurately represents them.

However, if you were told this was a map of annual rainfall in millimeters, you would right-fully assume that the borders on the lefthand figure must be generalized. That is, the amount of rain falling on the land does not change abruptly as you cross a line from one mapped polygon to another. More realistically, you would expect rain to vary gradually across the region of the map, with some areas getting more and others less.

The figure on the right is a more realistic rendition of a nondiscreet variable changing grad-ually across the map. Although raster mapping can reasonably simulate nondiscreet data, many existing data sources are structured in discreet, vector formats. The trick for the ana-lyst is to accept this simplification of reality and treat these variables as though they are dis-creet, or alternatively find ways to compensate for maps made in this way by converting the data to a raster format.

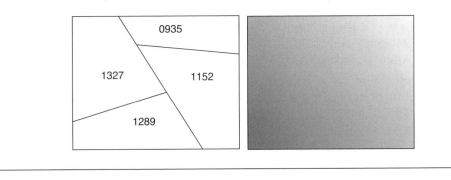

Figure 7.1   Discreet and Nondiscreet Data.

choose to use just one or perhaps several variables as indicators. Each of these variables may include one or more attributes. When choosing variables to include in your study, you should consider variables that relate to the main concepts you are studying. In other words, the concept behind the research question must always drive the selection of variables and attributes.

The database structure behind a GIS dovetails well with this approach. As discussed in Chapter 6, a GIS organizes the data in database tables, which are linked to geographic locations. In this structure, individual variables are often stored in the first or second column of the table, using a user-defined naming system (these may be real names or codes assigned to the individual items). The attributes, or specific descriptive characteristics of the variables, exist in subsequent columns with as many columns as necessary being cre-ated to hold all of the attribute data, as shown in Table 7.1.

Table 7.1   An example of a simple data table containing entity and attribute data collected about four individual study subjects. The first column labeled ID may be assigned automatically by your GIS or database software

ID	Variable/Entity	Attribute_1	Attribute_2	Attribute_3	Attribute_4	...	Attribute_n
1	Jane	53	Female	Hispanic	College	...	$45,000
2	Chris	27	Male	Caucasian	High School	...	$35,000
3	Bob	61	Male	Asian	College	...	$55,000
4	Sue	36	Female	Caucasian	Graduate	...	$65,000

Attributes of a variable can exist in numeric or nonnumeric form. The GIS can account for both numeric and nonnumeric data. (See Chapter 6 for further discussion of this concept.) For instance, if you are interested in the concept of rural community wellness, what are some variables that could be examined as indicators of this concept? A starting point might be to examine the health facilities that are available in these rural areas. Some questions to consider would include the following: What type of facility is available? Is it a clinic or a hospital? During what hours is the facility available? Is it a 24-hour facility or is it open only during business hours? Is it located in a rural or an urban area? What is the bed capacity of the facility? Given these questions, using a GIS our primary variable would be "health facility." Attributes might include names such as "type," "hours," "location," "beds," and so on, which would be identified and used to develop the actual data table within the GIS software or another data entry package.

These are all descriptive characteristics of the variable "facility," which could be integrated into a GIS to help investigate your hypothesis. As a result, one of the main variables or entity types in your study would be "health facility." All of the descriptive attributes that accompany your variable could be classified as attributes. How these entities are ultimately represented in the GIS is another consideration. Will you represent them as point locations, or is it more useful to measure and map the actual shape of the building footprint? In this example, the former would likely be sufficient, whereas the latter would create a significant amount of additional work with very little analytical payoff because the physical shape of the facility is unlikely to have much to do with the level of care provided.

Different Data Types: Matching Geographic and Social Variables?

Data come in a variety of formats, often including variables of different types. Variables are typically categorized as being nominal, ordinal, interval, or ratio.

Table 7.2   An example of a simple data table containing entity and attribute data collected about four individual study subjects. Columns are marked according to the level of measurement the data was collected at (nominal, ordinal, interval, or ratio)

ID	Variable/Entity	Attribute_1	Attribute_2	Attribute_3	Attribute_4	. . .	Attribute_n
1	Jane	53	Female	Hispanic	College	. . .	$45,000
2	Chris	27	Male	Caucasian	High School	. . .	$35,000
3	Bob	61	Male	Asian	College	. . .	$55,000
4	Sue	36	Female	Caucasian	Graduate	. . .	$65,000

Nominal	Ratio	Nominal	Nominal	Ordinal	Interval

Nominal Data

Nominal variables typically are used to name data without giving the data any numeric value. For example, if we reconsider Table 7.2 (now with the columns labeled according to their data type), we can see that for the nominal attributes shown the data contain nothing inherent to use to judge quantitative information based on the attributes' names.

Because nominal data have no associated quantity, we cannot make quantitative judgments about relationships between them. For example, it would make no sense to make statements such as the following:

Chris > Bob

Hispanic = Caucasian

$2 \times Male < Female \div 7$

For simplicity in data entry, you might opt to assign a numeric code to nominal data. For example, in a study of communities, you might choose to describe a location as urban, suburban, or rural. These three categories, or attributes of the variable location, tell us something about the variable but do not have an inherent quantitative basis. Even if you choose to code them as *city* = 1, *suburban* = 2, and *rural* = 3, the numbers assigned are simply nominal and hold no meaning in a quantitative sense.

A dichotomous nominal variable (e.g., male/female) might also be coded using numbers to allow for quantitative analysis using a system called dummy coding. In this situation, the values are assigned values of 0 and 1. You could use a system of dummy coding to highlight the difference of the variable "gender," between male and female. The number 1 = *female* and

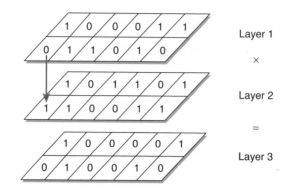

Figure 7.2   Coding raster layers with only 0 (unacceptable) and 1 (acceptable) provides a means to mathematically identify pixel locations in the resulting data layer, meeting all of your desired analysis criteria. By multiplying these two layers (Layer 1 × Layer 2) using map algebra (see Chapter 9), we obtain a new dataset (Layer 3) where 0 indicates locations where one or both criteria were unacceptable and where 1 indicates locations where both criteria were met. This same approach works equally well for studies with any number of layers coded in this manner.

0 = *male* can then be employed in a quantitative analysis to differentiate between two categories for a particular variable. Dummy codes can provide a means to use variables in an analysis that requires numbers.

In a GIS context, the process of coding 0 and 1 can be especially useful when conducting an analysis with yes/no or acceptable/not acceptable data. By using dummy coding where 0 = *not acceptable* and 1 = *acceptable,* raster data layers can be multiplied to ensure that any location that is unacceptable for one of the criteria results in a 0 in the output. Similarly, if all criteria are acceptable, the result of a multiplication of raster layers is 1 (see Figure 7.2).

Ordinal Data

Ordinal variables are best described as variables or attributes that can be logically rank ordered but whose actual quantity is still not defined. These variables are the type that can be measured along an ordered scale. The Likert scale (Table 7.3) commonly used in survey research presents an excellent example of an ordered scale in which the specific quantity between each level is undefined.

Although data on such a scale are clearly ordered, there is not a defined spacing between categories. In other words, we know a respondent who selects 2 has shown a lower level of agreement than a respondent who selects 4, but we cannot state that the difference of 2 has any real meaning in a quantitative sense, nor can we say that the gap between these individuals is identical to the gap between individuals selecting 1 and 3, respectively.

You could measure the variable "education" (Attribute_4 in Table 7.2) as follows: 1 = *less than high school,* 2 = *high school graduate,* 3 = *some*

Table 7.3   An example of a 5-point Likert scale. The numbers indicate a respondent's level of agreement. Using an ordinal variable of this type leaves the relative distance between values undefined. It is up to each respondent to interpret his or her meaning

Strongly Disagree	Somewhat Disagree	Neutral	Somewhat Agree	Strongly Agree
1	2	3	4	5

college, 4 = *college graduate*, and 5 = *graduate or professional degree*. Again, in this example the numbers indicate something in terms of the rank order of these variables (a level of education, where a higher number indicates more years of formal education), but the distances between the measures do not have specific quantitative meaning. The goal in using ordinal values is to obtain a rank order of responses.

In a GIS context, the process of coding ordinal data is again useful in some quantitative analysis applications. Because there is an order to data of this type, queries of the GIS data can appropriately incorporate mathematical statements that would not have been sensible for nominal data. For example, statements such as "college > high school" or "neutral < somewhat agree" make logical sense. When presented in word form, they may be more difficult to code in the GIS. Therefore, it is helpful to code ordinal data with numbers rather than character strings for the purpose of analysis in GIS.

Interval Data

An interval variable incorporates a true distance between the recorded measures; therefore, quantitative analysis becomes much more practical. Table 7.2 shows that Attribute_n represents annual income in dollars. We can examine these numbers and determine that Chris makes $10,000 less than Jane and that Bob makes $10,000 less than Sue. In both cases, the difference of $10,000 is exactly the same, even though the locations along the income scale where each of these salaries falls are different. Interval data can be thought of in terms of a number line, where the distances along the line are at a fixed scale, much as the scale on a map would be expected to remain consistent for the entire map.

In the GIS context, interval data offer an analyst the ability to conduct detailed quantitative analysis of the data because typical mathematical and statistical operations are valid and meaningful with these numbers. Distances between values are meaningful including geographic intervals (e.g., distance between locations) or intervals of other attributes as in the example of income in Table 7.2.

Ratio Data

The last of the four variable types used in data collection is the ratio measurement. The distinct feature of a ratio value is the presence of a true zero. This concept is sometimes confusing because some uses of zero are arbitrary. A good example of the use of a false zero is the description of time. Year 0 on most any calendar you choose to refer to is not truly the beginning of time. It is widely accepted that regardless of the human calendar used, time existed before the point selected as Year 0. Many cultures through time have devised calendars to meet their own needs, each one having a different 0 point (e.g., Roman, Mayan, Hebrew, or Hindu).

In Table 7.2, Attribute_1 refers to age. As individuals are concerned, before they are born, they have no age. Zero in this case is an absolute, or true, zero. One cannot be a negative number of years old. This might raise the question of why we classify income as an interval variable rather than an ordinal variable. The simple answer is that it is possible to have negative income. Anyone who has a home loan or a credit card realizes that dollars can be positive or negative. Having zero dollars at any particular point in time will not necessarily get you out of paying your bills.

The reason the distinction in the zero is so important is because in quantitative analyses where the zero is arbitrary, things can get confused, especially if the zeros end up causing other data to incorrectly zero out in a multiplicative process or, perhaps worse, if the zero causes your computer to crash due to a division by zero error.

Validity and Reliability

When preparing to collect data for a study, two important considerations related to your measurement of the variables and their attributes are validity and reliability. A good empirical study cannot proceed forward without valid and reliable data. Validity means making sure that there is congruency between the concepts you want to measure and your measurement techniques. In other words does your study really measure what you are setting out to measure?

For instance, let's say that you are interested in studying the popularity of cigarette smoking in a community. One way to do this would be to employ unobtrusive measures, such as observing how many people purchase cigarettes at a local store at different times during the day. This information could be recorded in an unobtrusive manner. Another approach might be to go to different public places—for example, restaurants and bars—to observe how crowded the smoking sections are. Both of these approaches would be reasonable methods for getting a sense of smoking in that community.

However, it would be invalid to measure cigarette smoking by studying people's consumption of pickles. That would not be a valid measure of the concept you are interested in studying. There may be some concepts that are strongly correlated, in which case it may be easier to observe one over the other. For example, assume there is reliable information regarding the relationship between the annual number of medical visits per capita and cigarette use. If this were true, perhaps medical data from a secondary source would serve as a reasonable surrogate for cigarette use and could save time and effort in the field.

Validity and GIS

In the GIS context, validity is also important to accurate analysis. In addition to measuring the concept of interest, we also need to measure the location where it occurs. For example, let's say that you are interested in studying urbanization of a rural area. You are interested in studying the amount of land in a county that has been converted from a natural or agricultural designation to a developed designation. Developed land is a category that would include houses, roads, and other built features. These features indicate human development via the presence of man-made structures.

Assuming that you had historical land use data over a specified time period, this proposed project would be fairly easy to accomplish in a GIS. To conduct a valid study, you would choose variables and employ methods that reflect the actual concept that you are studying—urbanization. This can be accomplished by looking at land use data from one of any number of sources. Using historic maps or aerial photos, you could interpret features visible on the older sources and compare them to features on more recent maps or photos. A review of the county assessor's records might show zoning designations and ownership changes that indicate when and how land was converted from one use to another.

A simple way to accomplish this would be to overlay data sets (discussed in detail in Chapter 9) using a GIS to determine the percentage of land in the county that has been converted from natural categories to the category of developed land. It might be invalid to make assumptions about the phenomenon of urbanization by looking at the amount of agricultural land that has been converted to something called idle, which might indicate fallow fields, parks, or other nondeveloped uses.

Reliability and GIS

Reliability is the second major consideration in the process of measurement. Reliability is the quality and consistency of measurement: Does the research method you employ in your study provide an accurate and consistent measure over time? The best example of this would be a scale. If you were to step on a scale in the morning and it gave your weight as 130 pounds, and then in the evening it gave your weight as 160 pounds, chances are there is something wrong with the measurement ability of your scale. In other words, your scale is not reliable. It is up to the researcher to determine the reliability of the measurement devices that he or she is using in the field.

In theory, if the same entity is measured several times, it should remain consistent. This should be true if the same item is measured with different instruments (e.g., all thermometers should give the same air temperature) or by different people (e.g., two researchers should both obtain the same air temperature when each is using a given thermometer). In studies involving multiple staff, there can be differences in how the staff members measure the same item.

It is a good idea to be certain that all procedures related to data collection, measurement, and entry are well defined and consistent so that there will not be variation caused by the people doing the work. Any instruments used to collect and manage the data should be calibrated to ensure consistent, accurate reads. Simply put, it is a good idea to check your methods and equipment to anticipate and correct, in advance, any issues that could affect the reliability of the data.

The California redwood forests are an environmental feature that attract many different natural recreationists and preservationists who all enjoy interacting with the forest in various ways. Let's say, for example, that you are interested in measuring the contribution people have had in the erosion of trails in the forests. How would you measure this in a GIS? One possibility would be to take a map of the trails and walk them, marking the map as you notice any erosion you observe. This data could then be digitized into a GIS data layer. Alternatively, you could use a global positioning system (GPS) receiver to record locations along the trail where erosion is present and download the data directly into the GIS.

If after review of these two data sets you notice significant differences in the amount and location of the erosion recorded along the trail, you should question the reliability of your GPS unit or your recording accuracy; perhaps you didn't correctly mark locations on the map while hand-recording the data. Sometimes it is best to use more than one measurement technique to ensure that data collection is reliable and, when discrepancies occur, to determine which technique is best in your particular application.

When data are entered into the GIS, reliability of this process should also be assessed. Field data marked on a map or collected via a GPS receiver need to accurately line up to the proper locations on the base map being used. Mismatches of datum, projection, coordinate system, and so forth can all lead to minor and sometimes major misalignments in the geographic position of the data. If these mismatches are severe, they can seriously corrupt or invalidate your study results.

Furthermore, it is important to note that as spatial data are entered into GIS software, in particular when entered by hand, each package will have a different set of tolerances or settings related to positional accuracy.

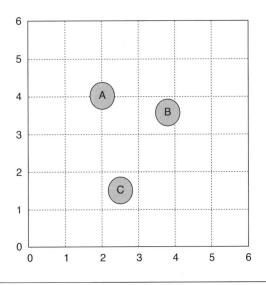

Figure 7.3   Points that should, in reality, fall in between grid intersections are recorded in the computer's memory in whichever grid intersection is closest. Point A falls at intersection (4, 2) and would be properly mapped at that location. Point B lies off of any intersection, but clearly lies nearest to (4, 4) and would snap to that location. Point C presents the most complex case. Because it lies equidistant from four different intersections, the software may map it to any one of them, and, as the end-user, you probably do not have an easy means to control this decision.

Regardless of the specific technique used (scanning, digitizing, etc.), most data entry processes for maps and images involve a rasterization process (even when creating vector data).

Figure 7.3 illustrates why this is the case. All computer screens, scanners, and digitizing tablets are composed of a set of pixels, charge coupled devices, or gridded wires. When a mapped location is entered into the computer, there is a good chance that the actual coordinate on the ground will not align perfectly to the grid system used internally by the computer for data storage and display. This results in the point being shifted to the nearest grid intersection when stored in the computer. Although these shifts are typically extremely small and do not significantly affect map accuracy, they do exist. In most cases this issue can be ignored; we mention it here for completeness and, if you see minor shifts in spatial data you have entered carefully, you will know where these originate and can adjust tolerance settings to minimize the shifts observed.

In most GIS and other computer drawing programs, a snap distance is defined, which describes how close two points entered into the computer must be to be considered unique (see Figure 7.4). Conversely, if two points are within the defined snap distance, they are automatically connected together by the computer. Of course, if the spacing used for the grid is large, these errors will increase proportionately. Therefore, choices made for

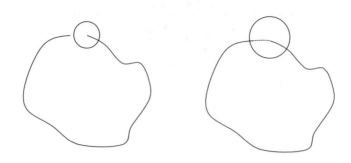

Figure 7.4   Snap distance is best viewed as a circle of a given radius. In the left-hand figure, with a smaller snap distance set, the gap in the polygon remains open. However, the same figure prepared with a larger snap distance setting results in the GIS automatically closing the gap. Depending on the type of data and the accuracy of entry, errors can exist in two forms: (1) Gaps exist where they should not, and (2) gaps are closed inappropriately where they should remain open. Neither is desirable, so finding an appropriate balance for these tolerance settings is important.

scanning resolution, the megapixel rating of a digital camera or sensor, and snap distance or other data tolerance settings can have significant effects on data quality. It is important to keep in mind that although you can adjust software settings to some degree, these errors cannot be completely eliminated and are a normal part of the data development process in GIS. What is important is that you have a basic understanding of how the computer stores data on a grid so that you can minimize the errors to a point that they will not affect your study results.

Data Sampling and GIS

Sample design is of course a substantial area of inquiry that we can only briefly cover in this text. We present an overview of commonly used sampling approaches and suggestions for their implementation in a geographic context. If you are unfamiliar with sample design, you might want to explore this topic in more detail by referring to sources specifically related to sample design referenced at the end of this chapter.

Probability and Nonprobability Sampling

Sampling is an important part of the research process. The type of sampling that you engage in is dictated by your research question. Sampling can be divided into two basic categories: probability and nonprobability sampling. The type of sampling that you choose will be based on the question you are trying to answer as part of your research project as well as the resources you have available. Generally speaking, probability sampling approaches take more time and effort than nonprobability approaches, especially when working in a GIS with a geographic component to the study.

When working with spatial data, your sampling frame is the entire area of the study, and you must be prepared to collect data at any randomly selected location on the landscape. For some studies, the ability to physically access a randomly selected location may raise concerns of cost, safety, or privacy that can make random sampling in a geographic context a bit more complex.

Probability sampling can best be described as sampling that incorporates some form of random sampling. In these sample designs, every element that is part of your study has the same chance of being included in the sample. The sample is merely a subset of the entire population that is used in an analysis when collecting data for the entire population (census) is not possible. The population is defined as the entire group of elements you are interested in studying. For instance, the opinion polls that rank public attitudes of the president cannot sample the entire population of the United States. Instead, pollsters randomly select individuals throughout the country and question them about their opinion of the president. This group of people is representative of the larger U.S. population. We can say that the opinions of this smaller group of people reflect the opinions of the entire U.S. population because these individuals were randomly selected.

The advantage of probability sampling is that it allows you to generalize findings to a larger population. It is a more representative sample type because it avoids biases inherent to other forms of sampling. The disadvantage of conducting a probability sample is that it sometimes is difficult to get a sampling frame that is complete enough to include all of the potential elements.

Nonprobability Sampling

Nonprobability sampling can be explained as sampling that is not based on the random selection of elements to be a part of the study. There are certain instances in social research when a nonprobability sample would be preferred over a random sample, such as when a researcher has targeted a population to interview as part of the research process. For example, let's say that you want to study what it is like to be a member of the Hell's Angels; you could not take a random sample of the general population but rather must target individuals who are known members of that particular population. Studying such a group involves taking a nonprobability sampling approach. There are four types of nonprobability sampling: purposive sampling, reliance on available subjects, snowball sampling, and quota sampling (Babbie, 2003).

Purposive Sampling

Purposive sampling means that there are specific characteristics that are integral to your study to justify sampling a population from a specific and perhaps somewhat limited group. Purposive sampling is a type of nonprobability sampling that occurs when researchers deliberately choose the population that they want to include as part of a study. It is a type of sampling that is often employed by people who have a clear idea about whom they want to interview, based on the research question. Earl Babbie (2003) notes one characteristic of purposive sampling is that it can be difficult to enumerate the entire population you wish to study. There is a reason for choosing the type of people that you choose to interview. You may become aware of who these people are through contacts, their outward visibility, or their membership in a particular organization.

For instance, if you are interested in studying successful entrepreneurship in your hometown, you first need to identify the business entrepreneurs who have been successful, perhaps by reviewing the local business section of the newspaper. To carry out your study, you would select and interview a number of business leaders who fit your definition of success. Even if you don't successfully identify every successful entrepreneur in the community, a purposive sample could provide an appropriate set of individuals to give you a sense of what it takes to be successful in the community.

Available Subjects

This type of sampling can be problematic but is commonly employed in the social sciences. When collecting data from available subjects, individuals are interviewed at a particular location. This can be very useful if the locations are spatially relevant to the study question. For example, if available subjects are sampled to find out why they visit a particular location at a particular time, the data set tied to a point in space can be powerful. However, if sampling of available subjects is done for a study unrelated to the location—for example, to determine presidential favorability ratings—the location may introduce an unanticipated bias into the sample. For example, if your sampling location is an upscale shopping mall, you may find very different responses than had you sampled outside the local ballpark.

In other words, this approach severely limits the representativeness of the sample to the overall population. An advantage of available subjects is that they provide a means for rapid data collection without going through the difficulty of first defining the population and then developing a sampling frame from which to randomly select respondents. This method would also be appropriate in instances when you are interested in studying people's perceptions of a local or one-time event.

Snowball Sampling

In this type of sampling, you rely on already interviewed subjects to provide information on further potential research subjects. An example of sampling is key-informant interviews. Let's say that you are interested in interviewing military veterans who are opposed to war. You might easily obtain a list of veterans in your hometown, but you would not necessarily have knowledge about the political feelings of these individuals until you interview them. Therefore, you might engage in a type of sampling called snowball sampling.

In snowball sampling, you first interview people in the community who are knowledgeable about a topic. You can usually identify interview subjects by asking community members for names of people who might be good to talk to about the subject of interest. Alternatively, you could begin your snowball sample by talking to individuals who have been featured in the local newspaper as being related to your topic. As the initial interviews are completed, the subjects are asked if they can recommend other individuals to be interviewed for this process. In this way, you benefit from the individual knowledge of the respondents, who are more likely to be aware of other individuals who fall into your target population.

Over time, this technique builds a list of potential research subjects, using information that early respondents provide along the way. To double-check and make sure that you are on the right track, determine which names appear repeatedly as numerous interviews are conducted. If certain individuals are recommended repeatedly, then you are interviewing the appropriate people, given that others in the community recognize and confirm the recommended individuals' expertise in the particular area that you are researching.

Quota Sampling

Quota sampling is a stratified sampling approach in which the researcher selects the sample based on characteristics that are defined in advance. These are typically characteristics that exist in the larger population that the researcher wishes to study. Quotas can be used to identify respondents based on information obtained as part of the sampling frame. In a social science context, you may determine that you want to sample equal or proportionately relevant numbers of individuals from different community service organizations. If this were your objective, you might obtain membership lists from each club (e.g., Rotary, Lions, Elks, Kiwanis) and from each of these randomly select a certain number of individuals to survey. In a geographically based study, the criteria for stratification might be spatial—for example, a certain quota of respondents might be desired from each neighborhood in the city.

Random Sampling

In random sampling, all elements or individuals in the study population have an equal chance of being selected. If random sampling is to be used, there are a number of methods for accomplishing this task. For example, if you were developing a sampling frame for a community, the sample might be generated from a list of addresses, phone numbers, membership lists, and so forth. When sampling spatially, a random list of (X, Y) locations can be generated for the study region, or subregion if taking a stratified sample. Using coordinates with GIS is particularly convenient for spatial studies because the coordinates can be easily generated using random number tools in a spreadsheet, statistical package, or the GIS. Armed with (X, Y) positions and a handheld GPS receiver, it is a relatively simple process to navigate to the selected locations for the purpose of collecting physical, environmental, or sociodemographic data. For instance, this method could be useful as a means to select locations to visit for the purpose of survey data collection.

Study Area and Sample Unit Boundaries _____

We have alluded to the need to define study and sample unit areas geographically when conducting a study with GIS. On the surface, this might seem straightforward; however, there are a number of considerations to review before assuming you know the proper boundaries to use for your analysis. Before discussing the methods of boundary selection, we should point out two important considerations related to the eventual GIS analysis: edge effects and the modifiable area unit problem (MAUP).

Edge Effects

In any spatially defined study, there is often a problem in the analysis of data near the edge of the study boundary, especially when the analysis involves quantitative procedures. Consider the simple analysis question of population density in a city full of happy people, as illustrated in Figure 7.5.

The upper and lower halves of the figure show the same population in space. The placement of the study boundary, represented by the box, varies. In the upper portion, we obtain twice the population density (10 people per unit area) as we obtain in the lower portion of the figure (5 people per unit area). Of course, there are infinite possible placements of this study boundary, each potentially giving us a different result.

Without seeing the map or knowing something about the placement of the sample boundary, we have no way of knowing what is occurring just beyond the edge of the study area. For example, in the lower portion of Figure 7.5, we may not capture information about the community that is common to the large number of individuals on the left side of the figure.

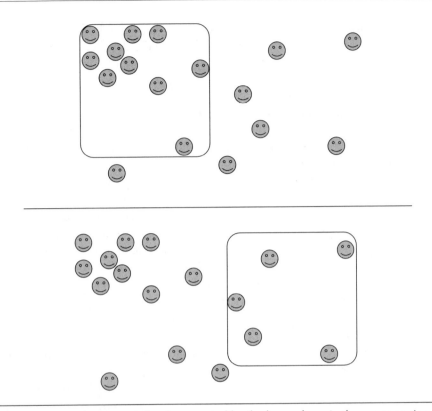

Figure 7.5   For a given population (represented by the happy faces in the upper portion of the figure), a study boundary can be placed in an infinite number of locations. The upper and lower portions of the figure represent just two of these possibilities. Each placement of the study boundary provides a potentially different result for whatever attribute or variable is to be measured based on the selected population (or sample from this population).

Thoughtful selection of your study boundary is an important step in study design, whether or not a GIS is used.

Of course, one advantage of the GIS is that if we have data about all of the people in this town, we can run the analysis multiple times (multiple realizations) using a Monte Carlo simulation approach. For example, if we were to run the analysis 100 times, with 100 random placements of the boundary, we could determine what the most common (and thus most likely) result is, as well as obtain statistics regarding the distribution and standard deviation of those results.

Another example might be if we were looking at cancer rates in a particular population without knowing about an important source of pollution upriver or upwind of the study site. Knowing something about the relative geographic positions of important variables is essential to determining where and what to include within your study boundary. Conversely, having a sense of these issues can improve your ability to critically assess the meaning of the results in your own work and the work of others. You can think of a study boundary much like a cookie cutter: Whatever falls outside the boundary gets thrown out and is no longer part of the data (or potential data in the case of a sample).

The Modifiable Area Unit Problem

A related issue is the actual size of the sampling frame or study boundary used. As we alter the geographic area of the study boundary, the results obtained from the analysis can change. Again, consider the happy residents shown in Figure 7.6. The area of the lower sample boundary is exactly twice the area of the original upper boundary. This results in a population density of 10 people per unit area in the upper figure, and 14 people per unit area in the lower boundary. Because the lower boundary is twice as large, the resulting density is actually $14 \div 2$, or 7 people per unit area.

Of course, the placement of the boundary also influences the results. Thus, these two issues work in concert with one another, either offsetting or potentially compounding the variability in the results. As mentioned previously, if you have the ability to run multiple realizations in a Monte Carlo simulation, you can determine the answer with the highest probability resulting from the data.

Unfortunately, much of the spatial data that are collected do not take these issues into account. Being careful to consider how and why your study boundaries are defined can be essential to getting results that will be accepted as valid. Interestingly, this concept is fairly new to the analysis of spatial data, having only been identified in the last 25 years. Most notably, Openshaw and Taylor (1979) started much of the work on this issue, and its relevance to the social sciences began to be recognized in the last decade or so.

Selecting Boundaries

In the earlier examples, the boundaries were selected artificially by the researcher by simply dropping a square frame onto the landscape. This is a valid approach and may be done randomly or systematically by using a grid of sample areas. However, in many studies, other types of boundaries may be associated with the data. For example, you might select from census tracts, zip codes, county or state borders, or a wide variety of other options. As you consider one or more of these as potential study boundaries, give due consideration to the goals of your research and the influence your choice of boundary might have on the resulting sample design and analysis.

One approach is to consider your study from a geographic standpoint, that is, consider the geographic scale. At what level does your research question focus? Perhaps you are interested in local-level differences between blocks or neighborhoods. If so, use of census blocks might be an excellent choice for stratification, sampling, and analysis. If you are doing a statewide

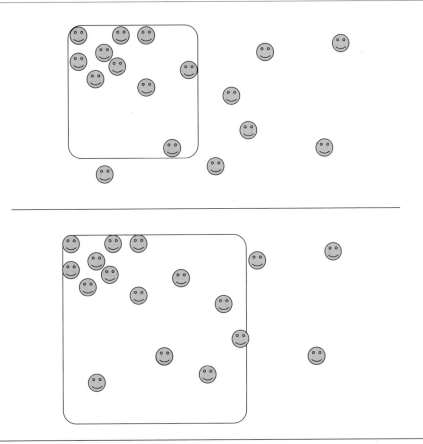

Figure 7.6   An example of the modifiable area unit problem. For a given population, represented by the happy faces, the size of the sample unit, represented by the box, can significantly alter the results obtained. In the lower portion of the figure, the area of the sample unit is exactly twice that of the sample unit in the upper portion. With identical populations, this change results in two distinct population density measures: 10 people per unit area in the upper figure and 14 people per unit area in the lower figure.

or national study, it may be more appropriate to use county or state boundaries. Are there important features that would influence the data just outside one of these boundaries (e.g., a large industrial facility or a military base)? How was boundary placement determined and for what purpose?

If your study is longitudinal and involves time series data about a particular place, you will need to determine how that place is defined. Where are you going to draw the boundaries? Presumably, you would choose to draw the boundaries with consideration of the research question being investigated. However, this can be a bit complicated because often the boundaries change over time—cities expand, political districts are redefined, and so on. If you are you interested in looking at the same geographic area over time, you may need to establish a fixed study boundary, especially if the other boundaries are inconsistent over time.

Conversely, it may be the change in the boundary itself that you are interested in. If that is the case, your study data will need to allow for the largest geographic area necessitated by the input data in your analysis. Possibly this will require you to have access to or create geographic data for the same location over different time periods, so you can determine the outer limits, or geographic extent, of your overall analysis. Examples of boundaries that may change over time include almost any politically or jurisdictionally defined boundary (e.g., school districts, voting precincts, city limits, and so on). Boundaries based on sociodemographic factors can also change over time. For example, a lower-income neighborhood may be gentrified and become an upper-income neighborhood.

If you are comparing data at one time for different locations, you may need to address consistency between areas. Are there geographical commonalities or differences that exist between your research locations? If so, this may inform decisions about the stratification of study areas. You may choose to weight or compute ratios of the data for each location to normalize for the differences. For example, a comparison of population between a large city and a rural town would be better achieved by taking a census of the entire population and determining a density for the entire area of each location, as opposed to using a fixed sampling frame, as shown in Figure 7.6. If you sample fixed areas of each community, it is possible that the placement of the samples could produce biased, misleading results.

Finally, there is the issue of how boundaries are conceptualized. If you are using political or legal boundaries, they are typically well defined. However, if we consider a concept such as *wilderness*, different individuals will have different conceptualizations of what that term means, even though a legal definition may exist. Similarly, even the definition of a city varies by individual. Consider how people refer to their hometown when visiting another place. Although you may be from a suburb of a major urban area—for example Naperville, Illinois—you might say you are from Chicago when visiting Europe or even Los Angeles. Conversely, if you are in downtown Chicago, you would more likely specify your hometown as Naperville. How an individual defines space is a rather personal and often contextual issue. In defining boundaries, you want to do two things: (1) clearly define the concept being studied, and (2) clearly define the boundaries of your study area based on the concepts you are examining. Thus, when analyzing data geographically, it is essential to clearly define your boundaries or to define them based on local knowledge or spatial conceptualization as appropriate to your study.

In some studies, you may be interested in examining a social or physical system. If that is the case, you might prefer an ecological or structural approach to boundary definition. Many systems have boundaries associated with their definition, which would be appropriate in developing a geographic extent for your data in the GIS.

Factors Affecting Choice of GIS Variables

As you consider forms of measurement for use in your study, you can simultaneously think about how to integrate a GIS into your study and relate a GIS to your chosen variables.

The following guiding questions will assist in the decision-making process about whether or not to include a GIS as a part of your study:

1. What is the main goal of your study? Is it predictive? Comparative? Descriptive?

2. Does your study involve a variety of variables? Does their location matter?

3. What kinds of data exist for your study location and variables?

4. Does your study involve comparison of different locations?

5. Does distance play a role in your study?

6. What are your project resources?

One of the most powerful benefits of using a GIS as part of the measurement process is that the GIS allows for the study of a holistic context. We can describe the use of a GIS as providing a socioecological model of whatever issue or problem you are interested in studying. Why do we say this? We note this because a GIS allows for the simultaneous integration of many different variables into a study, thus integrating information from a variety of sources and disciplines.

As mentioned earlier, the GIS could be part of the data collection process or part of the analysis, or both. A GIS gives the researcher the option to communicate with the research subjects on another, visual level. This could be invaluable in a study or culture where people are illiterate or don't speak the same language and where a visual representation of data could make more sense to the subjects of the study. Beyond this, a GIS allows for the creation of models that mirror real life. By that we mean that a GIS allows the researcher to contextualize both the social and the physical environments and elements into a study. It provides what we define as a holistic systems approach, which is very socioecological in nature. The social scientist who studies almost any social problem or issue could find such a tool useful.

Relevant Web Sites

Electronic Statistics Textbook: This site, from StatSoft, is a complete introductory statistics textbook online, including sections on measurement scales, sampling, and analysis. http://www.statsoft.com/textbook/stathome.html

Housing Patterns: This U.S. Census Bureau site details choice of units of analysis for census data analysis. http://www.census.gov/hhes/www/housing/resseg/unitofanalysis.html

Suggested Reading

Openshaw, S., & Taylor, P. J. (1979). A million or so correlation coefficients: Three experiments on the modifiable real unit problem. In N. Wrigley (Ed.), *Statistical applications in the spatial sciences* (pp. 127–144). London: Pion.

8 Data Documentation and Model Development

Chapter Description

This chapter provides a discussion of the ethical and practical reasons to ground truth data—an important research practice of checking the relevance and accuracy of data that are created, analyzed, or output from a GIS to minimize error. An introduction to data documentation standards (metadata) is also included here. Approaches to planning your GIS analysis and techniques for doing so (phases of abstraction) are included using realistic examples that benefit via the addition of a spatial component. Examples are provided showing how researchers might enhance their view of data as having a valuable geographic element.

Chapter Objectives

- Discuss the importance of understanding the quality of data used in analyses.
- Provide an overview of the data documentation process, including metadata standards and core components (Content Standard for Digital Geospatial Metadata; Federal Geographic Data Committee, 2000).
- Introduce the abstraction process by which researchers convert their conceptualized study and operationalize it in a specific GIS software analysis framework.
- Provide an overview of commonly available statistics in GIS software.

After reading this chapter, you should be able to perform the following tasks:

- Explain the importance of understanding the quality of your data and the methods by which you might determine this.

- List core items that should be documented about your data layers
  when creating metadata files to accompany them.
- Discuss each of the four stages of the process for the abstraction of
  your analysis from reality to GIS.

The Importance of Ground Truthing Data

Earlier in the book, we discussed approaches for the location and creation
of data for use in GIS. Depending on where your data come from, it is
important to reiterate that ground truthing is an essential component of
assessing data quality. This is especially true when using data that you did
not collect yourself. The difficulty in assessing data accuracy is that data can
be highly accurate at one scale of analysis but wildly inaccurate at another.
Therefore, data accuracy is not so much a question of "Did the organization
or individual that created the data set do a good job?" but rather "Is the data
I located appropriate to my study?" In other words, determining the inherent quality of data is not as important as determining the data's fitness for
a particular use. As the researcher, you want to determine if the data are
indicative of the concept or concepts that you want to study. It is a question
of validly of the data in your specific situation.

As a simple example, assume you are doing a study that examines the life
span of populations of individuals who live at different elevations around the
world. You may notice from your own experience that as you enter many
cities, a sign states the elevation of the city as well as the population. Does
this mean the entire city is at exactly the stated elevation? Of course not!
Does this mean you will need to spend time mapping the elevation of each
household in every town for your study? Probably not, unless you have reason to believe that differences of a few feet higher or lower than the average
elevation are likely to be relevant.

Consider this same concept as it relates to percentages of a city's population that are likely to be seriously affected by a flood. A few feet could be
the difference between remaining safe versus watching your house float
downstream. Although these are simple examples, the point should be obvious: A specific data source may be completely appropriate in one study and
completely inappropriate in the next. In the latter study, very accurate mapping may be necessary.

Documenting Data Accuracy and Quality (Metadata)

If you are generating your own data for inclusion in an analysis, it is important to clearly note the data characteristics that relate to data quality and

intended use in a metadata file that goes with your GIS data layer. Metadata, simply put, are data about the data or, in simpler terms, information that describes the lineage of a data set from how it is collected or sampled through how it is coded into a GIS database. There are a variety of characteristics you might want to record about data you create, and in many situations there are actually standards for doing this.

The United States Federal Geographic Data Committee (FGDC) sets metadata content standards that are to be followed by federal agencies and contractors. If you work for a federal agency or collaborate with one, you may be required to follow these standards when you create spatial data in a GIS. Even if you are not legally or contractually obligated to follow FGDC metadata standards, it is typically worthwhile to do so. There is nothing more frustrating than neglecting to record the lineage of an important data set only to discover that a few months or years down the line nobody in the office can recall how it was made.

Because these standards were developed over a long period of time (and in some cases are still not finished), not all spatial data you obtain will include a complete metadata file. When data are not well documented, it can make using the data in an analysis questionable. However, because more organizations begin to adopt these standards, metadata are typically better for data sets created more recently.

The FGDC maintains a Web site (http://www.fgdc.gov/) that offers a wide range of information about these standards, software tools for creating metadata for your GIS data sets, training and grant opportunities for creating metadata, and other related links. An executive order signed by President Clinton in 1994 and amended in 2003 by President Bush establishes a National Spatial Data Infrastructure (NSDI) by which federal agencies are to make public their geospatial data. The NSDI, in conjunction with FGDC metadata standards, will build a framework for efficient searching and sharing of spatial data in the United States. This framework is well underway, and a large amount of data can already be located via the NSDI. Organizations that wish to include their own data sets as part of this searchable framework may do so by following the standards and procedures outlined on the FGDC Web site.

Core metadata components include information such as the following:

- Who collected the data
- When it was collected
- By what means
- For what purpose/intent

Additionally, there is information about projection, coordinate system, datum, and the geographic extent of the data as well as the GIS software and file format used. In total, the FGDC lists several dozen metadata elements as mandatory information. Approximately 100 elements are listed as mandatory if applicable, but it is left up to the individual researcher to determine which, if any, of these are needed for their particular data set. In total, there are more than 300 metadata elements that may be included in a complete metadata file, depending on the specific type of data and standards that are associated with it. Many of the GIS software packages offer metadata tools as part of the program, streamlining much of the data documentation process.

As you complete your own data layers or create layers through analytical processes in the GIS, it is important to keep track of which processes you used and how they may have affected the accuracy or quality of the resulting data. Just as it is important that you understand the data that go into your analysis, anyone reviewing your results incorporating your data set into their own study will appreciate a metadata file that clearly documents and explains the data you created.

Even if you do not expect or intend your data to go beyond your own organization, it is important to develop metadata standards that meet your own organizational needs and that will make sense to future members of that organization. There is nothing more frustrating to someone entering an organization that relies on GIS than to find vast amounts of poorly documented or undocumented data. Although it is possible to do background research to determine the source and quality of such data, doing so can mean hours of time wasted in attempting to track down former employees, original paper files, or other archival information that can attest to the value of that data in ongoing longitudinal or historic studies that would benefit from such data.

Analytical Approach

When preparing an analysis in GIS, there are four distinct phases of abstraction, or modeling, that you must go through in sequence:

1. Evaluation of the real-world situation that you intend to analyze

2. Conceptualization in terms appropriate to a computer-based analytical approach

3. Organization of the logical approach to the analysis

4. The specific software implementation

Although many people conducting a GIS analysis tend to address the first three of these informally, taking the time to write these out in some form can greatly reduce missteps and dead ends as you carry out your analysis. In other words, taking a little extra time up front to plan the analysis process typically pays off in the long run. We address each of these phases in the following sections.

Before getting to these four phases, keep in mind that at this point we are only considering the GIS aspects of the analysis, our assumption being that, through topics and examples discussed in earlier chapters, you have already determined the general nature of your study and that incorporation of a spatial component through the use of GIS will benefit your overall process.

Phases of Abstraction

Reality

Before initiating an analysis with GIS, it is essential that a GIS provides us with a computer model of reality—the computer does not understand reality! Although this may seem obvious, all too often as people start to consider how they will work with their project inside a GIS environment, they allow their GIS environment and data to dictate the approach. Of course, it is the knowledge of the data, the project, the disciplinary expertise, and the local knowledge that should drive the approach to the study.

Although it can be quite enticing to allow the capabilities of a particular GIS software program or available data to dictate the analytic process, this is something to be cautious about, especially when the realities of time, money, and personnel available to conduct an analysis are limited. Unfortunately, there is no simple solution we can offer you. Every project requires finding a balance between the real world that you are analyzing and the abstraction required to make that reality fit into a GIS. It is important to recognize that there is a distinction between reality as it truly is and reality as represented in the model. When assessing a GIS model or its result, be sure to keep yourself firmly planted in the true reality, where your results and decisions affect real people.

Beyond the issues of how the reality fits into the GIS, you also will need to consider (as a precursor to this) what reality is for your study. We don't intend our discussion of reality to be in a philosophical sense but rather a practical sense. Defining reality is not always quite as simple as it may seem. For example, if you are doing a survey of household income, where is the breaking point between economic classes? How might this vary in different geographic regions? Are only dollars and cents relevant? What about bartered services? What about work performed in the home by a member of the household for no pay? As you can see, there are numerous possible components to how income might be assessed and analyzed.

As the analyst who is going to locate, collect, or use this data, how do you define your variables and classes? When looking for archival data, referring to the data dictionary and the metadata may help, if they exist. When collecting your own data, these are the kinds of issues you need to ponder and, in many cases, need to debate with colleagues, community members, or stakeholders. In short, defining reality is no small task, but it is by far one of the most important.

Conceptual Data Model: Incorporating GIS

The second phase of abstraction is to form a conceptual model. The conceptual model does not consider any GIS issues but rather takes the analysis goals from reality to a spatially conceptualized analysis. In accomplishing this task, the key components of the analysis are determined and the appropriate data identified. To illustrate the process of conceptualization, let's consider as an example the accessibility of prenatal care for low-income families at public health clinics.

There are a number of data sets that would be useful in an analysis of this sort. The conceptualization phase is the point at which you begin to identify appropriate data by working through the thought problem of your analysis. Identifying data layers is not simply stating, "I need a layer X for my study." It includes specifications regarding what must be in the database to complete your analysis.

So, in our example, what data would be necessary? We clearly require some demographic information, perhaps from the most recent U.S. Census, that will give us some sense of socioeconomic characteristics as well as locations (to the census block level). A map of clinic locations is also essential. If no such map already exists in a GIS format, other options for creating this layer should be explored (e.g., geocoding an existing map by street address). If there is detailed information about clinics, perhaps it will be possible to more specifically identify clinics in the database that provide prenatal care services. Perhaps the data on clinics do not exist at all; then you will need to do some field research to create your own database.

Don't forget a base map of some sort; you'll need to determine an appropriate scale for the analysis. Are you studying clinics in one city, an entire region, or an entire nation? For this example, let's assume a local-level study, so perhaps a city street map from a local city or county planning department would be most appropriate and up to date.

Last, and likely the most conceptually difficult, you'll need to develop a working definition of accessibility that can be used throughout your study. We propose a few possibilities here, but in all likelihood there are additional conceptualizations that you could include in your analysis. One aspect of accessibility is related to transportation. You might expect a significant number of individuals in this study to rely on public transportation to get to the clinic, so route maps and schedules could be important data. Additionally, there may be time-related accessibility issues, such as work schedules, time taken off work, school start and release times, and so on. How do these time and transportation issues relate to where the clinics are located and when they are open? All of these issues have a social-psychological component related to an individual's willingness to go to the trouble of getting to the clinic. How far are prospective clients willing to travel and how much time are they willing or able to spend in actually going to the clinic?

The list could go on to consider accessibility related to knowledge. Do the prospective clients of the clinics know they are available? Is clinic staff fluent in appropriate languages for the populations they serve? Are printed materials at an accessible reading level for the clients? What about funding for the clinic? Can the clinic handle the demand? How long are people kept in the waiting room? Do clients know what health coverage is available to them and can they navigate the paperwork to get it? Suddenly, what at first may seem like a simple concept rapidly balloons into something very complicated; of course, this is the very nature of social science research.

In this laundry list of concepts, a number are spatial, particularly those related to where the client base is located and how people will get to the clinic. Are people likely to be coming from their homes or from their workplaces? When looking at the willingness to travel component, it might be possible to develop some values that make sense. For example, if we determine that a person would be willing to travel for 1 hour on public transportation, we can convert that time into a map of bus routes that are within 1 hr of clinics. In this way, the concept of willingness (with a series of variables that inform that concept) is operationalized into a map with a distinct spatial component. In other words, the GIS is used to integrate a set of concepts into something we can more easily analyze.

When actually going through this thought exercise, it is sometimes helpful to sketch it out as a figure (Figure 8.1) or to write it out in outline form. Having a picture of your concept provides a framework for other important information, such as the source of the data (if known) or the data that need to be created for the completion of the study. If the conceptualizations of your analysis result in data sets that cannot be located from an existing source, you will have a better sense of how much new data collection will be required. This is also a good time to assess the feasibility of the study.

Taking time to reevaluate each component of your developing model early can save a significant amount of time, money, and energy later in the analysis. After all, there is no sense in incorporating data that provide only minimally to the overall model or that present significant uncertainty in the final results. As in any study, relationships between variables should make sense, not just conceptually but also in a practical sense. Some possible questions you might consider at this point are as follows:

- Will the results of the model be useful?
- Can actual, on-the-ground decisions be implemented based on results of the model?
- Are the relationships in the data statistically significant?

Once you have considered each component, data availability or your ability to create data, and the overall use of the model, you are ready to move beyond thought problems. But remember, until you complete the thought problem, it is probably not a good idea to go rushing forward with a GIS

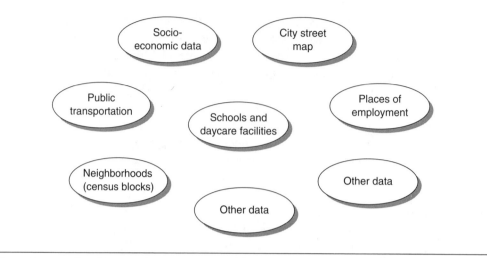

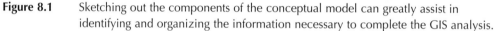

Figure 8.1   Sketching out the components of the conceptual model can greatly assist in identifying and organizing the information necessary to complete the GIS analysis.

analysis. As mentioned earlier, many people gloss over this stage of the GIS process and end up going down dead-end analysis pathways that result in wasted time, money, and effort. Once you are content with your conceptual model, then you are ready to move on to the third phase of abstraction, the logical data model.

Logical Data Model

The logical data model adds specific processing steps to the conceptual model developed in the previous step, thus specifying the analytical procedures necessary to complete the analysis. That is, we want to add a workflow to the conceptual figure. This step can be represented graphically by creating a flowchart that specifies each step in specific detail. One unique characteristic about the logical model is that it does not include software-specific processing steps, only the logic behind them.

For example, in our clinic model, we know we need to extract specified socioeconomic data related to the prospective client population within our particular study area (city). The data source identified for this example is the United States Census; however, because the census data contain much more information than we really need, we want to pare that down. We want to narrow the geographic extent and, via a database query, extract only those attributes we require. Graphically, this portion of the flowchart might look similar to Figure 8.2.

In this figure, we specify a logical sequence of steps but do not concern ourselves with how these steps are achieved in any particular software. It is important to have a sense of possible processing options. Once a logical flow has been developed for the entire analysis, we reach our next evaluation

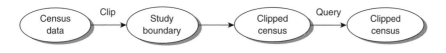

Figure 8.2   A portion of a logical data model showing the steps necessary to reduce the full United States Census data set to the appropriate spatial and attribute components necessary for our study. The logical model first indicates a clip, which is a spatial operation to cut out only the required geographic area, much like a cookie cutter. The resulting data set is then queried to obtain only those records or attributes needed in the research analysis.

point: determining the feasibility of accomplishing the necessary processing steps using available software. Just as data may be brought into the GIS analysis from a variety of software environments, it too can be analyzed and processed in a variety of environments. Sometimes you may determine that certain steps are better accomplished in a specific database program, a statistical software package, or a variety of other task-specific software. In fact, it is not at all uncommon to incorporate multiple software programs and discipline-specific models in an analysis.

Allow us a brief, related diversion: selecting the right tool for the job. Do not allow yourself to get tunnel vision when it comes to the software you incorporate into your analysis. Although many GIS software vendors purport to provide complete, out-of-the box solutions, this is rarely the case. At a minimum there will be one or more optional add-ons to your chosen GIS software that will enhance its analytical abilities. At the other extreme, you may need to develop your own custom scripts, analytical models, or other tools to supplement the built-in capabilities of a typical GIS package.

Add-ons refer to separate software components that supplement the basic GIS software and enhance its capabilities for a particular type of analysis. Such add-ons come in three primary varieties: vendor specific, third party, and user contributed. Vendor-specific add-ons are provided by the same software vendor that created your core GIS. These may be somewhat more generic in application because these companies generally are serving a wide array of practitioners across a variety of disciplines. Third-party products typically are generated by consulting firms targeted to specific disciplines. These products are often more specific to GIS tasks and data you may be using regularly. Although some of these products can be expensive, they may pay for themselves in time and effort saved on routine or repetitive analysis tasks. Finally, a wide array of user-generated add-ons exists for specific GIS software packages. These may be available through online user forums for the specific GIS package or simply located by searching the Internet. Many of these add-ons are just as good as commercial products, with the advantage of being free or inexpensive. Of course, obtaining something from an unknown individual comes with the potential downside of minimal support.

So how do you select the right GIS software to use? This can be a difficult question, but here are a few suggestions: You might wish to go with one of the more popular industry-standard GIS software solutions. There are a half dozen or so GIS vendors who dominate the market, each with their own traditional strengths. Some of the more widely recognized vendors in the GIS market include Autodesk®, ESRI®, Intergraph®, and MapInfo®. If you are going to be working with outside cooperators, use of a common, agreed-upon software package can save headaches when it comes to data compatibility. The more popular packages also tend to have strong technical support and many more third-party and user-contributed add-ons. The downside to some of the commercial packages is cost; these tend to be more expensive than some of the other options.

Second, you might go with a smaller player in the GIS software market. This can be an especially attractive solution when cost is an issue and when you have less need to collaborate with others outside your own office. As long as everyone in-house is using the same software, you may not be as concerned about the rest of the world. If you do select GIS software that is not as widely used, it is worthwhile to do some research to be sure that it will provide the tools and support you need because there may not be quite as much third-party or user-community support.

Open Source GIS

Finally, there are several open source GIS software tools. Open source software is free to download from a variety of sites on the Internet, and many of them have supportive user communities that are happy to help you out via e-mail lists. In most cases, you need to compile the program to work with your computer, and the process may require additional open source components that are downloaded independently. However, open source software can be an excellent option if you are fairly savvy with software and configurations. For most general GIS users, the time and effort spent to make a free solution work may not be worth the ease of installing a commercial solution.

Now we turn back to the topic at hand: the logical data model. The idea behind thinking through your logic, independent of the software, is to avoid one of the most common pitfalls in GIS analysis: allowing your software, or your knowledge of the software, to dictate how you analyze your data. In fact, after examining your logical data model, you might have a good basis for selecting the most appropriate GIS software and add-ons for your use. Of course, you can't change software with each new analysis, so once your organization has committed to a particular program, you need to take advantage of what it offers. A typical commercial GIS software package includes several thousand commands, more than the typical user can keep track of. So, even if you're not sure how to implement your logical model when you develop it, there is usually room to explore new options you may not have used in the past to determine the best approach to analyze your data using logic developed in this step of the abstraction process.

Physical Data Model

The final phase of model abstraction is the physical data model. At this point, we lay out the software-specific steps—the specific commands or menu options to accomplish the processing necessary for the analysis. Although many GIS programs use similar terminology for particular processes, there are variations.

Here again it can be helpful to annotate the flowchart that has been developed to this point. Where lines between data bubbles are located, the specific command for your particular software package can be indicated. Specific names of the data layers used and created at each step should be noted. Although this may sound a bit tedious, it can pay off in helping you to keep track of your data at each step along the way. The alternative, trying to keep track of everything in your head when sitting at the computer, is asking for trouble.

Even a simple GIS analysis may result in dozens of individual data layers. Developing a flowchart to help you to know what each layer is and the software options used to create each layer can help you keep track of the steps in your analysis. There is nothing worse than accidentally deleting a file you need. Equally frustrating is when you finally get the solution to your question only to realize you have no idea which steps and software options you used to get there.

Of course, we cannot give examples for specific GIS software packages because they each differ slightly in how they name commands and options. In addition to the four commercial players mentioned earlier (Autodesk®, ESRI®, Intergraph®, and MapInfo®), each offering several products, there are several dozen additional GIS software vendors serving various niche markets. For those interested in open source GIS tools, a visit to the Free GIS Web site (http://www.freegis.org/) will present you with more than 200 GIS software tools to explore.

Statistical Outputs From GIS

When considering the models you might want to develop in the GIS, it is helpful to have some sense of the information that one can easily draw from the software analysis. However, it is important to note that because GIS data tables (or data tables derived from your data via queries or other analysis tools; see Chapter 9 for more on analysis) are easily exported into standard data files, such as comma delimited text, you can typically use any statistical analysis package you prefer in conjunction with your GIS.

In most cases, a basic GIS package will provide summary statistics for your data or subsets of data. Summary statistics include basic information, such as counts (frequency), minimum and maximum values, mean (average), and standard deviation. Most GIS software packages also provide a variety of tools for interpolation of values from a set of sample points.

Depending on your particular GIS software or add-on components, additional statistical analysis options may be available from directly within the GIS software. Several of the more popular statistical analysis packages provide tools to allow direct communication with the GIS software.

In many cases, you will need to rely on an external statistics package to carry out analyses such as multivariate regressions or statistical tests for significance. In other words, because GIS data are readily summarized and exported from the software, you should not limit your statistical analysis based on the specific GIS software selected. Instead, you should determine which statistical analysis is most appropriate to your question and select the appropriate statistical software to carry it out. In addition to a wide variety of commercially available statistics packages, many common analyses can be carried out using software you may already have. For example, Microsoft Excel® has a good suite of statistics tools you can use. Free open source options also exist; in particular, the R statistical package offers a high-end analysis suite, albeit with a relatively steep learning curve. In addition to most of the standard statistics you may desire, R offers a variety of tools for spatial statistics (geostatistics; map, area, and pattern statistics; as well as some GIS connectivity tools).

Relevant Web Sites

Federal Geographic Data Committee: This is the main site for U.S. Federal standards and information related to metadata, content standards for metadata, and the National Spatial Data Infrastructure. http://www.fgdc.gov

FreeGIS.org: This site is a clearinghouse for a wide variety of free, open source GIS tools. http://www.freegis.org

The R Project: This is the starting point for the R statistical analysis environment. Note links from the main page to R spatial projects of particular interest to those doing spatial analysis with data from GIS. http://www.r-project.org

The following links are for several of the most popular commercial GIS software packages:

Autodesk: http://www.autodesk.com

Environmental Systems Research Institute (ESRI): http://www.esri.com

Intergraph: http://www.intergraph.com

MapInfo: http://www.mapinfo.com

9 Analysis, Interpretation, and Application

Chapter Description

The focus of this chapter is the analysis of social science data using GIS, including appropriate computer programs and the level of analysis. Approaches to carrying out the GIS analysis, and techniques for doing so, are included, using realistic examples that benefit via the addition of a spatial component. Examples are provided showing how researchers might enhance their view of data as having a valuable geographic element. We introduce numerous forms of analysis, including those that most commonly apply to the analysis situations you're most likely to encounter as you begin to use GIS technology. Major topics include buffers, overlays, networks, map algebra, and raster analysis as well as interpolation, simulation, and modeling. The chapter concludes with a discussion of some common pitfalls to be aware of in your analysis and interpretation of results.

Chapter Objectives

- Introduce a conceptual approach to data analysis.
- Provide an overview and examples of several of the most commonly used data analysis techniques for spatial data in GIS.
- Present the concept of modeling and probability as additional techniques for data analysis.
- Emphasize appropriate and careful design and implementation of the research approach and reporting of results.

After reading this chapter, you should be able to perform the following tasks:

- Give an overview and example of how each of the analysis techniques discussed in the chapter might be applied in a social science research application of interest to you.

> - Explain how a GIS can be used as a tool for modeling options and accounting for both measurement and spatial uncertainty in your data.
> - Describe some of the common pitfalls encountered in a GIS analysis and ways you can minimize them in your work.

Analysis Techniques

Analysis in GIS includes a vast array of possibilities. In the last chapter, we discussed the conceptualization of your analysis. Moving from the conceptual model to the logical model requires that you have some sense of what it is you want to achieve through your analysis, even if you don't know the specific commands or procedures in mind. The following sections introduce several of the most common analysis techniques used in GIS. In each case, we present the logic and application behind the technique. Any of these may be used individually or in combination with others, and in some cases more than one approach may lead you to a similar end result.

One of the important and powerful aspects of GIS is that there is not always one single correct approach to answering a question with GIS. In fact, when a classroom of GIS students is provided a set of data and an analytical question, each student approaches the analysis with a somewhat different tack, but all of the students may be perfectly correct. This shouldn't be too surprising using a very simple example.

Consider the following basic arithmetic problem. As you solve it, pay attention to your solution process.

$$5 + 3 - 12 + 8 + 4 + 7 - 6 - 2 = ?$$

Individual approaches will vary. Some people will simply run through the list in the order it is presented. Others may do all of the addition first and then do the subtraction, perhaps to avoid dealing with negative numbers. Still others may work the solution by canceling out positives and negatives; for example, the $+ 8$ cancels the $-6 -2$, and $5 + 3 + 4$ cancels the -12, leaving the $+ 7$. However you approach the solution, so long as you use valid logic your process will result in the same answer. Similarly in GIS, there are a variety of approaches that might be used in solving a problem, some in fewer steps and others in more. So long as the logic is correct, the specific approach may not be as important. Of course, if you are going to be running an analysis often, taking extra time up front to develop a streamlined approach to the analysis may be worthwhile.

With this backdrop, we examine some specific techniques for your consideration. Each of these techniques should be available in most GIS packages you encounter, although the exact names may vary. If a particular approach is not available but is necessary for your analysis, this is a good indication you'll need to look for add-on tools or possibly even a different software package that provides the tools you require to complete your analysis.

Although finding the proper add-on tools may sound intimidating, it is actually quite easy. There are Web sites and even user groups for the major software packages that will point you to both free and commercial add-ons and to forums where fellow users answer questions. In most cases, there is an add-on component or user who can assist you in accomplishing almost anything you can imagine needing in an analysis.

Cartographic Classification

One of the most simple, yet quite powerful, analytical tools is based on data classification. When mapping data, the categories used can make a huge difference in how the output appears, both visually and statistically. The same data set can communicate very different information depending on how it is categorized. For example, if you analyze the retired population in a particular region of the country, you will get very different results based on how you choose to classify retirement age. If you use the United States' Social Security definition of age 65, there will be a significantly smaller number of people in the category when compared to the same data using the American Association of Retired Persons (AARP) age of 50. Of course, there are benefits to using a higher age if you are the Social Security office: Fewer people will receive benefits, and the money lasts longer. This also explains the logic of increasing the age to 67 in the future. The AARP, on the other hand, garners much more political clout by including a large number of people in lower age groups.

If we were to put this population data on a map of the United States (Figure 9.1), we would expect to see a visibly denser map of retirement-age people when using the AARP definition, and we thus might feel a greater sense of urgency about issues related to senior citizens. If we were to combine these maps with the population under the retirement age (those paying into the system), the picture may appear even more dramatic. Such combinations might be accomplished via a variety of categorization tools offered by the software.

These examples have little to do with true analysis; they simply require a bit of manipulation of category definitions or statistics underlying the map. However, many data collection processes impose classification categories up front. For example, we typically collect items such as age or income in fairly broad categories:

Less than $20,000	$60,000–79,999
$20,000–44,999	$80,000–100,000
$45,000–59,000	More than $100,000

Number of Senior Citizens in the United States

Seniors 65 and older (Social Security definition)

Number of Senior Citizens

☐ 0 – 1000000
1000001 – 2000000
2000001 – 3000000
3000001 – 4000000
4000001 – 5000000
5000001 – 6000000
6000001 – 7000000

Seniors 50 and older (AARP definition)

Figure 9.1   A comparison of maps showing the number of senior citizens in the lower 48 United States according to the Social Security definition (top) and the AARP definition (bottom). These maps are based on the raw number of individuals in 1990 census data. However, variations might be used to further emphasize certain aspects of the data.

When the data are precategorized in this way, you lose the opportunity to reassign or break down the categories. For example, you could not determine how many families have incomes between $30,000 and $50,000 from data collected using the categories in the previous list. If you have an option to collect and retain actual values for each respondent, the GIS allows you to categorize the data in whatever way your study requires. In this sense, there are clear analytical advantages to collecting more detailed data, such as the ability to redefine breaks in categories as the specific requirements of the analysis change.

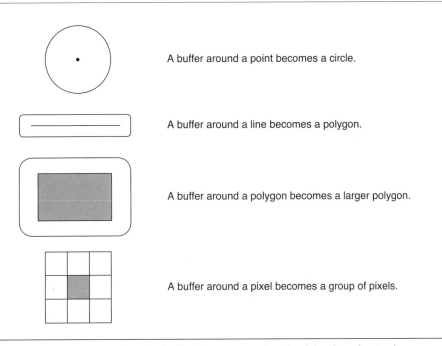

A buffer around a point becomes a circle.

A buffer around a line becomes a polygon.

A buffer around a polygon becomes a larger polygon.

A buffer around a pixel becomes a group of pixels.

Figure 9.2   Graphic examples of a buffer drawn around each of the three basic elements of a vector GIS (point, line, and polygon) that would result in a raster GIS (around a pixel). In each case, the result is represented by the white zone, an area defined around the original feature. Buffers are useful in a variety of distance-dependent analysis questions.

Buffer and Overlay

Two of the most commonly used tools in GIS fall into the categories of buffer and overlay. Although it would be impossible to assign a precise value, it would be reasonable to estimate that 50% to 75% of GIS analyses are achieved using variations of these two concepts alone.

Buffer

Buffering refers to a process of delineating an area around an object most often defined as a simple Euclidian distance (a straight line distance "as the crow flies"). Essentially, all mapped features in both the vector and raster GIS environments may be buffered, as shown in Figure 9.2.

Why are buffers popular as an analytical tool? Buffers provide a simple, yet effective method for analyzing a variety of spatial questions. Many GIS questions involve spatial concepts of proximity. You might find yourself using the following common phrases as you conceptualize your own research questions:

- Close by . . .
- Within a distance of . . .

- Next to . . .
- Less than ___ distance away . . .
- Influenced by . . .
- At least ___ distance away . . .
- Further than . . .

If you do find yourself phrasing questions in this manner, there is a good chance that a buffer will be a useful component of your GIS analysis. For example, if you are a city planner interested in determining a good location for a new community park, you might want to be sure that the location selected is within reasonable walking or biking distance of currently underserved residential areas. This simple question involves two proximity issues:

1. Determination of desirable proximity (being close to underserved residential areas).

2. Determination of undesirable proximity (to determine underserved neighborhoods, you need to know which neighborhoods are currently too far from existing parks).

Using the concept of a buffer, such an analysis can be easily achieved. However, we are getting ahead of ourselves; a second technique, overlay, must also be considered, which we explore in the next section.

Use of buffers does not necessarily require that the lines representing the buffer distance be generated on the map or computer screen. In many GIS software, these spatial calculations can be achieved in the computers' memory, without you, the analyst, ever seeing the circle drawn around the point on the screen. This is important for two reasons. First, having all of your analytical buffers visible on the map or screen can lead to excess clutter, making it hard to visualize your results, so alternatively some GIS software will simply highlight the features that fall inside the defined buffer. Second, if you need to know where the lines of the buffers fall, you may need to specify that you want the resulting data saved into a new data layer. This is essential if your analysis requires that you use the buffers in a subsequent step of the analysis.

It is worthwhile to mention a few additional aspects of buffering in GIS. Buffers need not be a fixed distance. In some analysis situations, it may be appropriate to buffer only to one side of an object or to buffer at different distances around objects based on characteristics of the feature being analyzed (Figure 9.3). For example, consider a buffer used to represent pollutants coming out of a smokestack. Although it might be a reasonable abstraction to assume that the pollutants will affect residents surrounding the facility, using a fixed (circular) buffer around the smokestack location is probably not quite realistic. Most could reasonably assume pollutants will be carried farther in the direction of the prevailing winds.

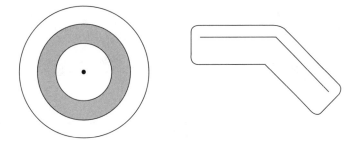

Figure 9.3   An example of doughnut buffer and a non-Euclidian or variable buffer. The doughnut buffer (left) contains area of interest located no closer and no farther than a specific distance from the given location. The area meeting these criteria is represented by the grey ring. Areas too close or too far are represented by the white rings. The variable buffer (right) is an example of a non-Euclidian buffer, in which the feature being buffered is a line. The buffer distances to one side of the line are three times greater than the buffer distances defined on the other side of the line.

Another variation on a buffer is the doughnut buffer. These buffers are concentric rings around an object and may be used to represent places that are considered desirable in the analysis when the goal is to be close, but not too close. For example, if you are locating a new factory to provide jobs in a community, there is a balance to be found. The factory should be close enough to be convenient for employees to get to but at the same time not so close as to be located in the middle of a residential area.

Finally, non-Euclidian buffers may use characteristics other than distance, such as time, as the metric for the buffer. If you are planning for the location of a new fire station, the goal may be to place the station no more than 5 min driving time from the homes and businesses that are in its designated service area. Of course, drive time is affected by numerous variables, perhaps the type of road (major artery or freeway vs. neighborhood or city street), the number of intersections that must be crossed en route, and the average traffic congestion on the roads. In situations where buffer size varies based on other criteria, a look-up table of values for various criteria or a formula to calculate the buffer distance may be substituted in place of a fixed value.

Overlay

Overlays are another powerful analysis tool used to address the concept of spatial correspondence, or things that occur together in space. Conversely, we can use overlays to look at the negative occurrence, or noncorrespondence. Overlays are most easily conceptualized by using common Venn diagrams of overlapping circles, as shown in Figure 9.4.

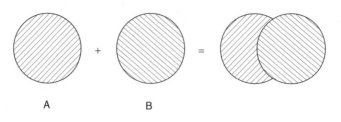

Figure 9.4   A Venn diagram showing two separate data layers (A) and (B) that are combined while retaining their appropriate spatial position. In a GIS context, the spatial position would most commonly be the mapped location on the ground. Some portions of polygon A overlap with polygon B, whereas other portions do not. Similarly, some portions of polygon B overlap with polygon A, whereas other portions do not.

If you have two sets of data, A and B, that overlap as shown in Figure 9.5, there are four basic questions that can be asked about the spatial relationships between them. Each is presented visually in Figure 9.5. First, we can ask where A and B occur together. That is, where do these data sets overlap in space (in GIS jargon this is the intersection of the data)? Second, we can ask where either A or B occurs in space (in GIS jargon this is also called a union). Third, we can ask what occurs within the area contained by A, including those portions of B that fall inside of A (in GIS jargon this is sometimes called an identity). Finally, we can ask where A or B, but not both, occurs (in GIS jargon this is referred to as a complement or an exclusive). Examples of the resulting output for each of these overlay concepts (assuming polygon area type data) are illustrated in Figure 9.5.

We can extend most of these overlay concepts to include the other vector data types, points, and lines. When considering points or lines, we typically take one of two approaches. By creating a buffer around a point or line, you can generate a polygon for use in an overlay as described previously. Alternatively, you can examine the interaction between a polygon and either a point or a line. You can also examine interactions between sets of lines or between points and lines (Figure 9.6). For example, a point or line may be inside the polygon (contained by) or outside the polygon (not contained). Lines may intersect (e.g., a road intersection).

In the raster GIS realm, the overlay process works very differently, using a process commonly referred to as map algebra. We discuss raster approaches in detail in the modeling section later in this chapter.

Proximity Polygons and Nearest Neighbors

When we assess how close things are to one another, there are two general approaches we use. The first of these, proximity polygons, examines each location of interest and delineates a polygon surrounding these locations

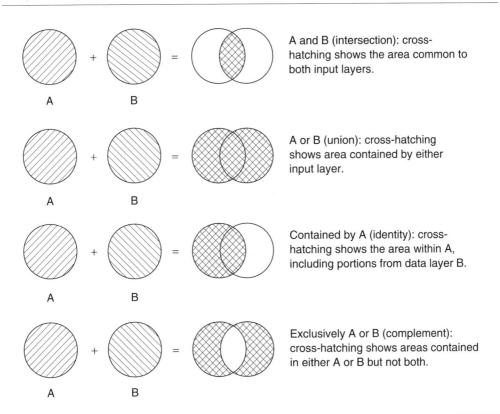

A and B (intersection): cross-hatching shows the area common to both input layers.

A or B (union): cross-hatching shows area contained by either input layer.

Contained by A (identity): cross-hatching shows the area within A, including portions from data layer B.

Exclusively A or B (complement): cross-hatching shows areas contained in either A or B but not both.

Figure 9.5   Examples of each of the four polygon overlay types (intersection, union, identity, and complement) and their associated results.

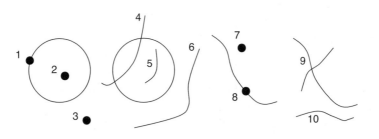

Figure 9.6   The results of overlays of vector feature types. Combining point locations with a polygon feature gives three possible results: (1) The point falls on the boundary, (2) the point falls inside the polygon (containment), and (3) the point falls outside the polygon. Combining lines and polygons provides possibilities including (4) the line passes through (intersects) the polygon, (5) the line is entirely inside the polygon, or (6) the line is entirely outside the polygon. Combining lines and points, you may get results including (7) the point falls off the line and (8) the point falls on the line. Finally, lines can either (9) intersect or cross or (10) not intersect or cross.

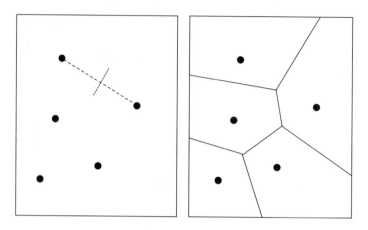

Figure 9.7   The construction of a Voronoi diagram. Assume you are starting with the map on the left showing five point locations (perhaps representing fire stations). To delineate polygons that include the areas closest to each point we use a simple fact. Any location just less than halfway between points must be closer to one particular point than to another. In geometry, this is defined by the perpendicular bisector of a line connecting any pair of points on the map (in the figure, the dashed connecting line is bisected at the midpoint by the dotted line). If you do this for every point pair, the bisectors will converge and create polygons around each point on the map, as shown on the right. These represent the proximity polygons for each point on the map.

representing the area closer to each individual location of interest than to any other. Most often the points of interest are represented in such an analysis as discreet point locations, as shown in Figure 9.7. This might be useful in delineating service areas for a fire station. Presumably, the station closest to the emergency would respond first.

Nearest neighbor analysis does not delineate areas but instead determines the closest location to a point of interest or the closest location to any other location on the map. For example, a nearest neighbor analysis might be useful if you wanted to determine how far it is from your home to the closest playground (Figure 9.8). Similarly, you can obtain nearest neighbor statistics for entire combinations of data layers, for example, the minimum, maximum, and average nearest neighbor distance between homes and playgrounds.

Social Networks and Network Analysis

GIS can play an important role in analyzing concepts that are less evidently spatial. For example, consider the concept of social networks within a community. Social networks are important to a community because they represent the degree of social cohesion and communication within a community.

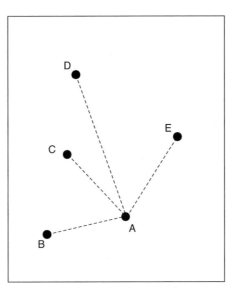

Figure 9.8   In a nearest neighbor analysis of points, the GIS determines a distance measure between point pairs (shown for point A in the figure) and the nearest point. In this case, point B is closest to point A. If we had two sets of data—for example, a set of points representing neighborhoods and another representing playgrounds—we could take the nearest neighbor distance between each neighborhood and each park to get an average nearest neighbor distance for all combinations of the data, rather than for a single point.

Examining social networks in a community could be useful in planning for community development. An understanding of the link between individuals and groups in a community is useful when seeking to organize local groups to accomplish community-oriented goals.

These social networks can be studied using GIS to map geographic distances and locations between the members of a particular group or community. For instance, you might expect to find that social networks are related to the geographic proximity of individuals relative to the center of town. In Figure 9.9, we present a simplified example of such a map.

A study that identifies the different types of social networks—in essence, the connections between groups and individuals—can aid communication and response to any crisis or situation. A GIS would allow for mapping differing degrees and levels of social cohesiveness and acquaintanceship networks, which could be key to responding to any disaster. Using GIS to catalog and geographically locate where local skills reside and who possesses which skills and resources could be very instrumental for emergency management and crisis response, be it environmental or social. Additionally, an understanding of these social networks is great for promoting community projects and increasing community strengths. That way, when the community faces a need or an emergency, there could already be a plan in place based on the GIS data of mapped skill sets and patterns of social interaction.

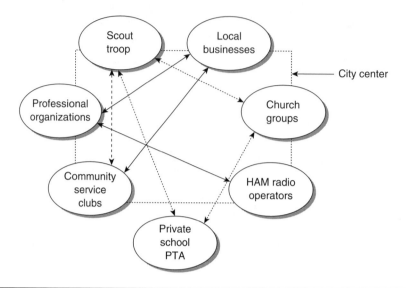

Figure 9.9   Social network connectivity of community groups and their geographic positions relative to the city center. The city center is represented by a rectangular area near the center. Each group in and around the community is represented by a circle. These circles may represent the actual geographic position or perhaps a representative location based on the percentage of that group inside or outside the city center. Finally, the ties between and among these groups are represented by the arrows. How the groups are defined (variables or entities) and the relevant attributes that are collected about the groups would be determined by the researcher and then stored in a data table associated with the map shown in the figure. Any type of data could be collected on the groups.

Key information and local social mobilization could be quickly initiated using a GIS-based alert system. Similarly, a GIS could be very useful in visualization, planning, and disaster preparedness. It would allow for the visualization and response to disasters prior to their occurrence.

Network Analysis

Network analysis is most appropriate when studying connections that follow specific pathways. In GIS, these are most commonly thought of as infrastructure or transportation related, for example, a pipeline or a subway. However, networks may be equally appropriate in social science applications for exploring connections between people, social cohesion, strong and weak ties, community strength, and others. To illustrate this concept, it will first help to explain the basic structure of a GIS network.

An important location in a network is represented as a node. The node acts as the individual sample unit or measured entity in the GIS database. Connections between nodes are represented by lines. The length or other attributes of the connecting line indicate characteristics of the connection.

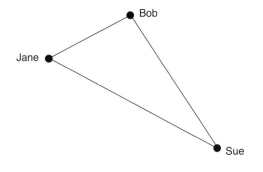

Figure 9.10   An example of a three-person social network. The black dots represent individuals (nodes) in the network, and the lines represent the connections between these individuals. The length of the line in this case is used to represent the strength of the tie between each pair of individuals: How close is the relationship between any two of these individuals?

For example, in Figure 9.10 there are three nodes representing individuals (Jane, Bob, and Sue), and the connecting lines represent the ties between these individuals.

A quick glance at Figure 9.10 shows that Bob and Jane are closer friends than Bob and Sue or Jane and Sue. It is harder to tell if Jane or Bob is a better friend of Sue's. However, one other important observation of this network is that it is fully connected; in other words, all three individuals know each other.

If we were to expand the network to include a fourth individual, George, perhaps this would no longer be the case. Perhaps both Bob and Jane are friends with George, but George and Sue have never met. Now we see that the network has a missing line (Figure 9.11).

You might be wondering if it is possible to add a significant number of nodes and still maintain the appropriate geometry, that is, to draw all of the needed connections and to place them all exactly the proper distance from all points they connect with. The answer is yes; however, it may be difficult or even impossible to visualize such complex networks graphically. Although line lengths and even directions can reasonably represent a physical network such as a pipeline, they can become cumbersome surrogates for the links that must be incorporated into a large interrelated social network. For this reason, you may need to use attributes in the database table to represent the connections and ignore the visual representation.

Fortunately, within the GIS the geography we represent does not have to exist in real space. In the case of social networks, such as described earlier, it is not the physical location or distance between individuals we are interested in. Rather, we are interested in who knows whom and how well they know each other. It is entirely possible that close friends live thousands of miles apart in real space. Network connections can be based on a variety of attributes, even attributes that may not typically be mapped in geographic

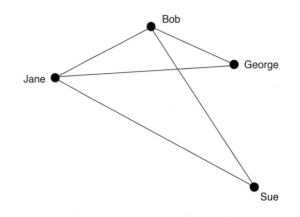

Figure 9.11   An example of a social network that is not fully connected. Four individuals are represented by nodes (black dots) in the network. However, one pair of individuals is not connected by a line (George and Sue), indicating that they do not know one another. However, an analysis of the network shows that George and Sue are indirectly connected via mutual relations, Jane and Bob.

space. Connections as represented in the previously discussed networks are close based on a defined measure of friendship.

However, connections may not always be two way or direct. For example, if we were to map relationships between these individuals based on economic rather than personal relationships, the network might change dramatically.

Consider the example presented in Figure 9.12. In this analysis, let's assume that Bob owns a small accounting firm and employs both Jane and Sue. Economic flow is one way from Bob to Jane and Sue (represented by arrows pointing from Bob to the employees he pays). George runs a small business and contracts his bookkeeping services with Bob's company, so the flow is from George to Bob, and the thicker arrow may represent that there is a larger sum transferred between them. Last, we discover that Jane is married to George; thus their finances are intermingled, and money moves both directions between them (represented by a two-way arrow).

Of course, seeing these networks on the computer screen is not really the point, and large complex networks would be difficult or impossible to visualize. However, by building these types of networks within a GIS, you can analyze the connectivity and flow within the network. Such analysis can be particularly useful when exploring how and where additional connections between individuals or organization can enhance the flow of information or the effectiveness of communication and interaction between community organizations. It would also be useful in determining which individuals or organizations are the best connected or have the most influence or other related questions.

As you can probably imagine, such networks may become quite complicated; however, so long as the attribute tables behind the network represent

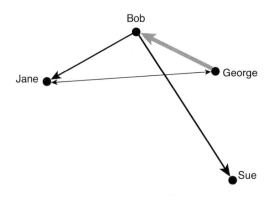

Figure 9.12   An example of a network model involving multiple individuals and variable flow between individuals. Each person in the network is represented by a node (black dots). The flow of money is represented by the arrows. Amount of money and direction of movement is represented by the thickness and directional arrows, respectively.

the magnitude and direction of the flow or connection, the GIS can be used to analyze these connections, the number of steps between individual nodes, and the stuff moving from node to node, be it real, such as dollars, or conceptual, such as good will.

One final point to introduce in the network setting is that geographic space and social network space may be very different, for example, in the case of migrant laborers. Immigrants from any ethnic group may be much more strongly connected to their immediate community of migrants, through commonalities including language, culture, and so on, than they are to the communities in which they find employment. Furthermore, their social ties to family members in other, faraway countries may be much stronger than to individuals living in the same town. Such a situation could result in community networks that are close, or even overlapping, in geographic space but that do not interconnect, as shown in Figure 9.13.

Once again, the situation can become quite complex in a hurry, but within the GIS environment analysis, such interactions in a social network are readily analyzed for connectivity and interaction.

Least Cost Path

Least cost analysis is a similar concept to the network approach. The idea of a least cost path is to find the most efficient or least expensive path through the data space. The concept of cost might be operationalized in a variety of ways in this type of analysis. For example, in a network of individuals, such as described earlier, we might be interested in the shortest social pathway between two individuals. Or in the case of community

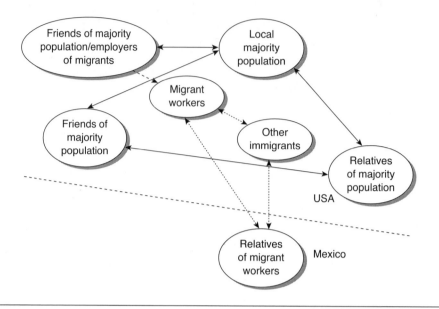

Figure 9.13   An example of mapping a social network for migrant workers in and among their work and community environments. For simplicity, in this figure, individual nodes are clustered within the ovals, each representing dozens or hundreds of individual respondents. Major connections between groups are depicted by connecting arrows.

planning we might want to know the shortest physical pathway along the road network between the fire station and a burning building. How we choose to define the cost (which could perhaps be better described as a relative measure of a particular variable) is up to us. The GIS simply needs to have those values applied to the connecting pathways in the network, as shown in Figure 9.14.

For some analysis situations, the pathways may be unrestricted; that is, you may allow for connections to occur anywhere in space. In these situations, we look for pathways through the data in an unrestricted setting, making these approaches different than network models of lines that interconnect nodes. Such situations are best implemented in a raster GIS environment. In raster GIS data, the entire study space is filled with raster cells, thus allowing for all locations to be assigned a value (Figure 9.15). These values are incorporated into the analysis, much like the lines in the network model.

Let's take the example of walking to work, as shown in Figure 9.15. In the simplest scenario, you would move from cell to cell in any direction (including diagonally) and attempt to minimize the total number of cells you must travel through (the least cost). This analysis assumes the cost, or effort, necessary to travel across all cells is identical, and, if so, the least cost path is the same as the shortest path. Try to determine which sequence of cells is best using the assumption all cells cost one move; odds are you will find

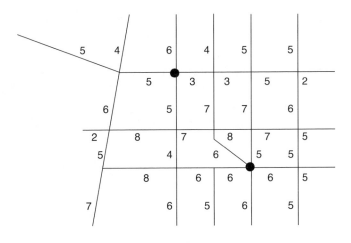

Figure 9.14   To determine the best, most efficient route between the two points represented by black dots, the GIS totals the values along all possible routes. In this example, each segment of the network is coded with a value representing the variable of interest, perhaps minutes of travel time between intersections of a road network. More complex network models may incorporate values that change based on time of day, direction of travel, or any number of additional criteria.

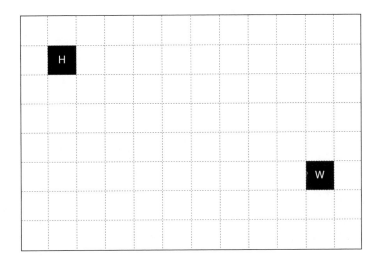

Figure 9.15   In a raster-based least cost analysis, the area under study is divided into cells. Each cell is assigned a value representing the cost associated with crossing through it. If all cells cost one move, the least cost path would be the same as the shortest physical path between the cells representing the locations for home (H) and work (W). However, if some cells cost more, the least cost path could route across a longer physical distance and still result in a lower overall cost.

multiple pathways that get you from home to work in the same minimum number of moves. Make a note of your result.

Of course, this example is not entirely realistic. Some cells may be simple to traverse, such as flat open spaces with nice sidewalks; other cells may be extremely difficult to cross because they are occupied by buildings, water bodies, or other obstructions. Cells occupied by such obstructions might be assigned a higher cost. A partial obstruction, such as a hill or a pond, may have only slightly elevated costs. Other obstructions may be total (e.g., there is an impassible obstruction that entirely prevents movement across a particular cell). If a cell is impassible, the cost assigned should be exceptionally high (e.g., equal to the total number of cells on the map) to ensure no total cost calculation including it would ever be selected.

In a least cost analysis, each cell is assigned a value based on predetermined criteria. The criteria may come from actual fieldwork or by assigning costs to an existing map based on criteria operationalized for your variables under study. For example, you might assign a value for perceived safety obtained in a survey of residents of a particular metropolitan area. Although some paths across town may be shorter, many people will choose to take a different route because they fear muggings, gang violence, or other types of perceived threats. Data for a least cost path based on perceived safety might come from Likert-scale survey questions about the safety of different areas of town.

The resulting least cost path from such an analysis will not necessarily be the shortest physical path. Instead the analysis provides the path that minimizes the sum of all cell values between two points. Thus, taking the example of walking to work, we might modify the previous example to appear as shown in Figure 9.16. Examine this figure to find the best path, again allowing for movement in any direction, including diagonally. Compare this result to the one you obtained before the additional cost information was added to this new result. You should note that the physical distance traveled (number of cells) increases to account for both the perceived safety data as well as the inclusion of a river through the center of the map.

Modifications of this approach might involve calculating the cost from a specific starting point to all destinations. In this case, the result is a cost surface that shows all possible paths rather than a specific destination. This may be useful when investigating which locations in the study area are within reach of the start location given limited resources (time, money, or calories). These analyses may be inverted to find highest cost paths, perhaps when looking for ways to burn a few extra calories on the way to the office.

Once again it is important to be creative in how you view the use of least cost paths as an analytical tool. Although cost is most commonly construed as a financial term, if you are creative in how you operationalize your variables, the concept is an excellent method for use with a variety of data attributes. In the previous example, we considered perceptions of safety as the

1	1	1	1	1	2	2	2	96	5	5	5
1	H	1	2	2	3	2	96	96	4	4	4
1	1	1	3	3	3	3	96	4	4	3	3
2	2	1	2	3	3	96	4	4	3	2	3
3	2	2	3	4	96	96	4	3	2	1	2
3	3	3	96	96	5	4	3	2	2	W	2
3	96	96	96	5	5	4	4	3	3	3	3
3	96	5	5	5	5	5	5	4	4	3	3

Figure 9.16 In this example, each cell is assigned a value representing the perceived safety of each area of the map based on a Likert scale, where 1 = *completely safe,* 2 = *safe,* 3 = *neutral,* 4 = *unsafe,* and 5 = *very unsafe.* Cells coded 96 represent a river through town and are impassible on foot except at bridges. The least cost path between the cells representing the locations for home (H) and work (W) is determined by finding the lowest possible sum of cells (19) between the starting and ending locations.

currency of interest. Time is another commonly used attribute. Perhaps the cell values represent the number of clients served in a particular location, and your goal is to accumulate the greatest number of interactions. Or values could represent the desirability of a location, and your goal is to maximize the positive effects represented by that value.

Topographic Tools

A related tool in many GIS programs is used to assess slope (and by extension drainage paths). These tools are primarily used to assess topography and how water flows across a landscape; in other words, they assess the direction of slope to determine downhill pathways. More generally, you can think of drainage as the direction of steepest change, so rather than limiting your conceptualization to the topography of the landscape you might try thinking of it in other contexts.

For example, if I have a raster layer where cell values represent the number of different ethnic groups present (ethnic diversity), the mountainous areas of the map would be the communities of greatest ethnic diversity, whereas the valley areas would represent more homogeneous communities. Rates of change would be represented by the steepness of the slopes between

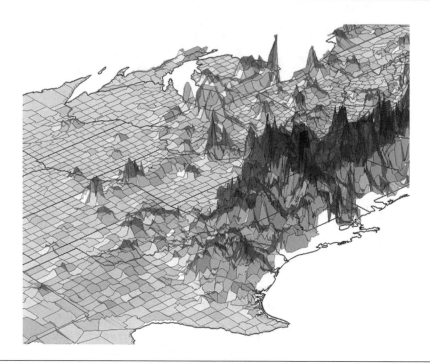

Figure 9.17   An example of the topographic visualization of social data. In this view, we are looking from the southwest side of Texas (bottom) toward the Great Lakes. This figure shows the percentage of Blacks by county. Shades of grey represent percentage categories, height and steepness of the mountains represent high values in the data, and valleys represent low values. The steepness of these slopes on the map shows the relative rate of change. It is clear from the visualization that in the southern regions of East Texas, Arkansas, Louisiana, Mississippi, Alabama, and Georgia are relatively high percentages and in some cases relatively rapid rates of change between counties. Farther north in the upper Midwest and Great Lakes states, there appear to be pockets of Blacks located in counties containing urban centers, such as St. Louis, Chicago, Detroit, Cleveland, and others. Much of the remainder of those regions shows very light colors (low percentages) and very flat terrain (low rates of change between counties). This figure was generated using ESRI ArcGIS® and ArcScene® software and 1990 U.S. Census data summarized by county.

these mountains and valleys. By visualizing any numeric raster data in this manner, you can quickly get a sense of where the peaks and valleys (high and low ethnic diversity) are located and where the areas of greatest and least change occur across the study area (Figure 9.17). This approach may be useful in operationalizing other variables, for example, economic data, teenage pregnancy, homelessness, or disease outbreaks to name a few.

Spatial Interpolation and Simulation

Spatial interpolation is another common raster analysis technique that is used to estimate values between sampled locations. A good analogy is regression in traditional statistics. There is a variety of linear and nonlinear regression techniques that can be used to fit a line to an X, Y plot of data points. Multivariate regression techniques are used in a similar fashion to estimate data for additional data dimensions. The primary difference between traditional regression and spatial interpolation is that rather than fitting data in hypothetical data space, the estimates are linked to real geographic space in some manner.

Thus, X and Y values used in spatial interpolation are typically the true X and Y positions in the coordinate system of the analysis. The estimated data value is referred to as the Z value and may represent any data variable desired. Although in traditional GIS applications Z is used to represent elevation, when working in a spatial analysis context we can interpolate for any variable in conjunction with the spatial position of X, Y, and Z. Interpolation is used in any situation where a complete census is not possible and you want to estimate data values in locations between sample points. Two underlying assumptions of a spatial interpolation are as follows:

1. Unsampled places nearby sampled locations will be more similar to the sampled location than to locations farther away (distance decay).

2. Places between sampled locations are likely to have attribute values that are in between those of the sampled locations that surround it.

For example, imagine you randomly collect and map by neighborhood square footage of 1,000 households in a large metropolitan area. It might be reasonable to conduct a spatial interpolation of this data to estimate home sizes in areas that were not covered by your sample. The assumption here, much as in a traditional regression, is that values between known, sampled points are likely to have a relationship with and fall between the sampled values. Thus, if in one part of town I measure houses at 1,200 square ft and a few blocks away I measure houses of 1,800 square ft, it might be reasonable to estimate households adjacent to these known values would be of similar size, and those located roughly in between these sampled households might be somewhere in the middle, perhaps 1,500 square ft. Granted, this may not be a valid assumption in every case or for every attribute type, but spatial interpolation is an excellent approach for many variables when you need an estimate of data values in locations where you are unable to collect them.

Box 9.1   Spatial Statistics Issues

As a brief aside at this point, we must admit that some statisticians believe that spatial statistics are invalid because of inherent nonindependence of spatial data. This stems from inherent autocorrelation in spatial samples (see Chapter 6). We would naturally expect data values

(Continued)

Box 9.1 (Continued)

geographically near a given sample location to be similar (e.g., if I sample air quality at a particular location in a city, I would expect the air quality 1 m away to be more similar than that sampled 1 mile away). There are additional issues near the boundaries of the study area and in the size selected for the study units. Suffice to say, spatial statistics are widely available and commonly used in GIS analysis. For better or worse, these tools are readily available in most GIS software packages, regardless of end-users' statistical sophistication and understanding of their appropriate use. Therefore, we leave it to individual readers to determine if these issues are concerns in their analysis situation.

The idea of spatial interpolation, simply enough, is to get more for less. We can reduce the time, effort, and cost of doing a complete census by selecting a sample of data collection sites and interpolating values for areas in between. Interpolation can also be useful to estimate values resulting from incomplete or missing data. How to best select sample locations is up to the researcher. Although it is often preferable to do random samples, sometimes it is more effective and efficient to use other sampling frames, as discussed in Chapter 7.

Spatial interpolation is done in raster GIS because the cells of the raster provide a framework to fill with interpolated values. As in any raster-based analysis, the cell size influences the detail of the result. In Figure 9.18, we see a map of the study area with sampled locations represented by the black

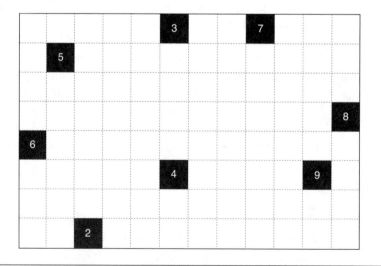

Figure 9.18   A raster map representing a study area shows values measured at randomly sampled locations (black squares). By using a spatial interpolation, estimates of data values for all unmeasured cells within the study area can be computed.

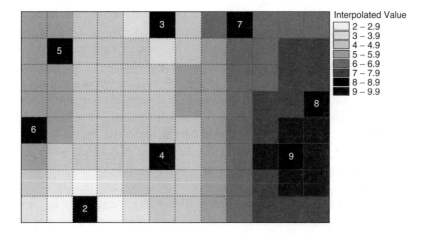

Figure 9.19   The result of a spatial interpolation of the map shown in Figure 9.18. Cell values based on an interpolation of the values at the originally sampled locations (labeled cells) are represented in various shades of grey. In this example, the interpolation technique used was inverse distance weighting (IDW). This process looks at nearby cell values and applies weights based on their distance from the cell being computed. The primary assumption of this process is that nearby cells are more similar than cells that are farther away. Available interpolators vary by the GIS software used. Selection of an appropriate interpolator is best based on the nature of the data and phenomenon being studied.

cells. The value measured at each location is labeled. Conducting a spatial interpolation in GIS, we fill in estimates of values in each of the empty white cells. The result of an interpolation of these sampled points is shown in Figure 9.19.

Note that this is only one example; variations on the interpolated map would be obtained by using different interpolation techniques. There is substantial literature on spatial interpolators and their variations. If you find interpolation to be a useful technique in your work, it would be worthwhile to further study the topic. For most day-to-day GIS analyses, a simple interpolation such as inverse distance weighting (IDW), as shown in the previous example, is probably sufficient. However, keep in mind that this is roughly analogous to a linear regression in standard statistics. Just as linear regression makes a number of assumptions about the data, so does IDW. If you have cause to believe that your data are not linear, there are additional covariates, and so forth, a more complex interpolation may be appropriate.

Of course, any given interpolation is only as good as the data it is based on. Therefore, in the earlier example we have two potential errors. There is a possibility of an error in the actual measurement made at the sample point, either due to a misreading of the measurement device or to misentering these data into the computer (measurement error). The amount of error depends on the type of data and techniques used to collect it. The other two errors are related to the (X, Y) position of the data. If you mistakenly shift data in the X or the Y direction, or both (location error), the results of the interpolation will be erroneous simply because the location, and thus the influence, of the measured point is incorrect. We can, to a reasonable degree, address both of these errors with a little more analysis.

Measurement error refers to the accuracy of the original data collection. However, in many situations we can determine the magnitude of these errors through a little checking. For example, if we stated that the measurements in Figure 9.18 were made within ± 0.05 ft, what this means is that a measurement of 3 ft could actually be anywhere between 2.95 ft and 3.05 ft. Furthermore, most errors come with a confidence (e.g., 95%), indicating that even the specified range is not 100% correct; in fact, 5% of the measurements could have errors even greater. What does all of this mean to you? Returning to our example in Figure 9.18, it is worthwhile to point out that many different realizations of this data could result. Each of the measurements on the map has a range of values that are reasonable to expect in addition to the values reported in the data. Each of these possible variations would result in a different realization, or variation, on the results.

Box 9.2 Are You a Gambler?

One approach that is sometimes used in GIS is a technique called a Monte Carlo simulation, named for the popular resort town and gambling destination in the principality of Monaco. As in gambling, the approach is based on probabilities. We generate multiple realizations of the output data based on known or likely variation in the sample data and then examine the distribution of the results. Thus, for each of the measured values shown on the map, we could randomly vary the numbers according to an appropriate distribution and within the specified range of ± 0.05. Each time we do this, we rerun the interpolation and see how it compares to the others. If you imagine running your analysis 100 times, each time varying the sample measures randomly within their specified range of error, odds are you will find that certain realizations occur more often than others. The end result of a Monte Carlo simulation is a probability that a particular result will occur at a particular location.

Fortunately, using the computer it is feasible to manage such simulations efficiently. The benefit to some analyses is that you can get a sense of the likelihood of a particular result and the range of results instead of just a single answer. For example, consider the weather reports you see on the local news every evening. The forecaster puts a map on the screen and states, "There is a 60% chance of rain tomorrow." What does that mean to you? Will you take an umbrella or a raincoat or will you chance it that the 40% chance of no rain is in your favor? Mapping in probabilities puts the onus on the end-user of the data, but it may actually be a more honest map. Of course, even if the report stated a 1% chance of rain, it could still rain. Probabilities are sometimes confusing or uncomfortable, so they do need to be used with caution and consideration of the intended audience.

A variety of interpolation techniques are available, with some variation by the specific GIS or spatial statistical software used. In general terms, these fall into the categories of exact and inexact interpolators. Exact interpolators always return the input value at the sample location. That is, if you provide a value of 5 at a sample site, the result returns a value of exactly 5 at that site. Using an exact interpolator is appropriate for data that can be measured reliably; if you are 100% certain you saw 5 people living in a particular household, there would be no reason to allow an interpolation to estimate a number other than 5. By contrast, an inexact interpolator allows the value at the sample location to vary to obtain a better overall fit of the interpolated result. This may be appropriate when you have measurement error and are less certain that the measured value is correct. In this case, allowing a measured value of 5 to be returned as 4.92 in the interpolation process might be just as valid.

If you consider these two options in a regression context, linear regression is simpler, but the line that is fit to the data in most cases does not pass through every sample value in the original scatter plot. By contrast, nonlinear regression may allow for the resulting line to pass through all of the data points, but at a cost. The resulting regression line is generally much more complex, and the equations necessary to describe such lines are similarly complex. Sometimes this complexity is desirable, but in many cases simplicity is preferred as long as the answers that result are sufficiently accurate to meet the needs of the analysis.

When we consider the issue of locational error, the same type of approach might be used, but rather than varying the measured values you might vary the coordinate location values. A global positioning system (GPS) receiver is not exact in locating where you are on the ground, and therefore the mapped location of a sample could be off in any direction by some amount. The approach is the same as described earlier. Of course, there is an added complexity that you might want to vary both the measurement and location values within their specified ranges to get an even more complete picture of the data.

So when should you use interpolation or simulation? Interpolation is appropriate when data are sampled across space and you have reason to believe that unsampled locations nearby are somewhat similar. This may not be the case with all data, so only interpolate if this assumption is valid for your data. Simulation is a powerful tool when you have some known variation in your data that you want to account for. Keep in mind also that simulation requires much more computer power because you run your analysis hundreds or even thousands of times.

Probability maps can be useful when end-users have an understanding of their meaning, but they can be confusing to a general audience. For example, it is likely most people will take an umbrella if the forecast calls for a 90% chance of rain (a 10% chance of dry weather). Strangely, these same individuals will buy tickets for the Powerball with a mere 0.00000125% chance of winning! Many people don't understand probability values in a rational or logical sense. If they did, all those Powerball players would feel completely content walking around with no umbrella, even when the forecast called for a 90% chance of rain (a 1 in 10 chance of staying dry vs. a 1 in 80,089,128 chance for a Powerball win).

Modeling

Earlier in this chapter, we discussed the four levels of abstraction as we prepare to model a portion of reality in a GIS context. In general, when we talk about modeling in GIS, we are referring to the development of a series of analysis steps that are designed for a particular analytical situation. Models are based on a combination of theory, research, expert knowledge, and individual creativity from relevant disciplines. In most cases, you will develop and implement your own models in GIS. In analysis situations that are more common, there may be existing models built by a third party with a user-friendly interface within the GIS. The saying "why reinvent the wheel" comes to mind here. If there is already a GIS approach that works for your situation, be it one that is freely available or one you purchase, it may be worthwhile to stick to these known and tested solutions, especially when your application is oriented to problem solving as opposed to basic research.

The advantage of using models developed by others comes in the development and testing based on research and knowledge that may be out of reach of the average GIS end-user. Preexisting models are readily available for a variety of natural resource applications but are more recently starting to appear in social science applications, such as crime analysis, community planning, and public health. It is important to note that many of these GIS models are simply presented in research journals or conference proceedings and are not available as ready-to-install software for your computer. Instead, such models provide you with a framework (a logical or physical model) that you can implement in your own GIS environment.

Some models are available as installable software that stands alone or in conjunction with a GIS software package. A caution when using such pre-programmed models is to be aware of the assumptions used. Not all models perform equally well in all situations; thus it is essential that as the end-user you understand these assumptions and, when appropriate, understand how to modify them for your particular situation.

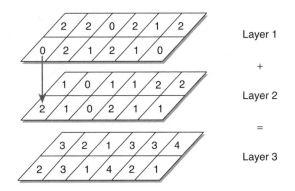

Figure 9.20   An example of map algebra used to add two map data sets (Layer 1 + Layer 2) resulting in a new, third data set (Layer 3). Cells are added based on their spatial overlap; thus, when the cell in the lower left corner of Layer 1 (0) is added to the cell in the same position in Layer 2 (2), result is 2 in the output (Layer 3). Map algebra can be based on any mathematical function: addition, subtraction, multiplication, division, logs, powers, and so forth.

Raster Modeling

Of course, it is not unusual to find that the model you need does not exist in an easy-to-use, canned format. This may be hard to believe given that Web searches turn up over one million hits when searching for "GIS modeling." But assuming you cannot find the perfect model, you may need to develop your own. Earlier we suggested that modeling in raster using map algebra is a powerful approach for developing your own models. Put simply, map algebra is the mathematical combination of data layers in GIS as introduced in Chapter 2.

In Figure 9.20, we show a simple addition of two map layers using map algebra. In your GIS software, this is achieved by using a tool to organize the mathematical combination, or by simply writing the formula directly using the names of the map layers involved. The actual software processes are relatively simple; the more difficult question is, what mathematical combination of layers should you use? There are two options that come to mind in answer to that question.

First, you could go through the process of abstraction described earlier in the chapter. In doing so, you would determine which data you want to include, how the data will be collected and coded and at what spatial scale (cell size), and how that data will ultimately be combined. Such a process requires that you determine how to combine the layers using a meaningful mathematical approach. For example, if you were conducting a study of criminal activity in a particular city, you could assign a value to each cell location representing the number of crimes at that location. Individual data layers might be used to represent individual months. By simply adding together various groupings, you could accomplish several outcomes. Adding all 12 months of data would aggregate crime rates on an annual basis. However, if we wanted to determine whether certain seasons show higher crime rates than others, we could add together only the layers representing the warm months, the holidays, or any other combinations of interest. Similarity, if we had crimes broken out by type (burglary, murder, rape, etc.), we might find that certain types of crimes occur more at certain times of year. Of course, this is a very simplistic example and doesn't incorporate socioeconomic or environmental factors that would also be appropriate to consider.

Alternatively, there might be a mathematical model that has already been developed in answer to your question or that can be modified slightly from a similar question. Mathematical models are common in the social sciences, and in many cases these models can be extended into a spatial context by implementing the equation in your GIS software. For example, a multivariate regression model could be implemented by developing a raster data layer for each variable in the regression equation. If the necessary data for the selected model can be found or collected in a spatial context, map algebra can be used to combine those data in geographic space, thus generating a spatial data set as the result of carrying out the regression for each cell position in the input data layers.

Keep in mind that to accomplish this, it is not unusual to collect samples across the study area for one or more of the necessary layers and then to interpolate a complete data layer from the samples. In doing this, there is an added level of uncertainty introduced by the interpolation process, uncertainty not typically accounted for in the original mathematical model unless it was designed explicitly as a spatial model.

Although it can be perfectly reasonable to extend nonspatial models into the spatial realm, it is worthwhile to do some pilot testing and assessment of the results before moving forward with a large analysis. However, with care and a little critical thinking, it is perfectly reasonable to implement mathematical models in GIS to determine how they vary in space. Ultimately, GIS modeling is a process of working through the steps of the abstraction process in sequence:

1. Examine the reality you are attempting to model.

2. Conceptualize it into terms that can be put into a GIS (data layers and relationships).

3. Work through the logical relationships of these component parts to develop a model that makes sense (and, if possible, is based on a previously developed model of the system in question).

4. Develop an approach to implement this logic in either a vector- or raster-based analytical process given the capabilities of available software and resources.

When to Use GIS as a Problem-Solving Tool

Ultimately, the use of GIS and the particular tools and approaches selected depend on the analysis you want to make. A GIS can be used as a tool to analyze almost any type of data and in many cases is very effective. However, this does not mean a GIS is a panacea; it may not be the best solution to every problem, regardless of what the software's marketing brochure suggests.

So when is GIS appropriate? We reiterate a few indicators here for your consideration:

1. Your question has a clear spatial component, and GIS is excellent for creating, storing, updating, and analyzing your spatial data.

2. Your question will benefit from the spatial analysis capabilities of GIS (questions that include phrases such as *near, next to, in conjunction with, related to,* etc.).

3. Your analysis is one that can benefit from existing base data sets or will build on them, or both.

4. Your study will be revisited. In such situations, the up-front investment in GIS and data development will pay off over the longer term.

5. The visualization capabilities will assist in data exploration or map and data output appropriate to your study, final reports, or other uses.

Potential Pitfalls

The greatest risk in using a GIS as an analysis tool comes through its unintentional misuse. To help you to avoid some common problems, we review them here. Several of these have already been discussed in greater detail elsewhere in the book and are presented again for the purpose of review; others are discussed in detail in the sections that follow.

Given the complexity of a typical GIS software program, there are numerous points in an analytical process where you can make mistakes. Most of the errors related to the use of your GIS software can be eliminated by reviewing the function of each command or process in the software documentation and understanding how it works and what it does. Because there is no risk of permanent damage to your data as long as you keep a backup, the best way to understand what a particular command does is to try it.

Although this may seem obvious, a surprising number of individuals new to GIS are fearful of exploring a tool or command they have not used before. Experiment! Just do so after you have made sure your data are safely backed up so that if you are not happy with the results you can go back to your original data to try something else. There is no harm in experimenting in GIS, and in many cases it is the best way to discover new and useful possibilities. No single book on the topic of GIS covers everything that is possible; in fact, much of what is possible in a GIS analysis has not yet been done because every new analysis or question presents new possibilities.

Most important, before you even begin an analysis in GIS, you should make sure that you have a clear understanding of your project goals. Knowing what it is you are studying, what data you require, and how you will collect and measure that data are all essential issues that may be influenced by the GIS but should not be dictated by it. Remember, you should determine how you want to carry out the analysis as opposed to allowing the software dictate what you do.

Other considerations in carrying out your analysis relate to the choice of scale, projection, coordinate system, and datum for each data layer as discussed earlier in the book. A good rule of thumb is to minimize the number of different combinations used as much as possible. The more consistent your source data is, the less room for error in any conversions or processing done within the GIS software. It is especially important to avoid using drastically different scales of data (e.g., orders of magnitude) because scale-related errors cannot be addressed effectively by the GIS software. Projection, coordinate, and datum conversions can, for the most part, be converted with minimal error.

Of greater concern are the issues that fall outside the GIS software, those being the issues that you, the analyst, decide through the abstraction process. Looking at reality seems easy enough; the problem comes when you begin to simplify into terms that will work in the GIS. For physical features, the abstraction process is somewhat more straightforward; you can measure the location of a road, river, or town. However, much of the data relevant to the social science is qualitative or conceptual, making it harder to link to discrete mapped locations and categories. This is not to say you cannot work with data of these types but rather that you need to be conscientious about how you make these linkages.

Revisiting the Accessibility Example

Let's refer back to the example of accessibility presented in Chapter 8. In this example, we considered a variety of criteria that might help to define a woman's access to prenatal care at a public health clinic. Issues such as location along public transportation, available day care, ability to miss work, hours of clinic operation, and so forth were suggested as variables that could be used to create an index of accessibility. The problem is that we may not understand and include all of the actual components that truly define the concept of accessibility. Thus errors in our analysis may arise in the original conceptualization of the problem.

Furthermore, even if we assume for a moment that we reliably identify all of the appropriate components, we may not know how to appropriately weight them into an index of accessibility that can be applied to the GIS data layer. For example, are all of the variables of equal importance or are some more important than others? If the latter, we need to incorporate weighting values into the model. Is there a variable in the analysis that is mandatory? In other words, even if all of the variables are positive, thus allowing a woman to get to the clinic, would just one negative criterion, perhaps language, have the ability to counteract everything else in the model? Finally, even if we assume a valid index for the accessibility layer, we may not properly understand how that layer should interact with the other layers in the GIS. Accessibility may be one of several data layers incorporated into the final analysis.

So how can you possibly address all of these issues? It is unlikely you can or even need to. But to avoid the pitfalls that come with the abstraction process, what you should do is carefully consider each step in the process. Consider the input and opinions of other professionals in the discipline, others who use GIS, and the published literature. Working in a vacuum is a sure-fire way to overlook something that should be included in your model.

Test It

Test your models before assuming everything is working appropriately. When you arrive at the physical implementation phase, run a small sample data set to pilot test the effectiveness of your analysis and to determine if you are getting results that make sense. One of the common pitfalls in using computers for analysis is that we can run very large data sets efficiently; however, these large data sets can mask errors that might be obvious in smaller data sets. This is especially true if you have the ability to get out on the ground to see, in person, if your results make sense. There is no better way to know your model is doing a good job at representing reality than to ground truth it against reality. If there is a difference, you have a much better chance of identifying the cause of the error in a small data set, for example, a single neighborhood as opposed to a large metropolitan area. Sometimes it is even useful to check your model with artificial data so that you can determine the correct result in advance and see if your GIS analysis provides the expected results.

Virtual Reality: Still Not Reality

Another pitfall in GIS-based analysis is that of being so engrossed by the technology itself that you blindly trust the output. Remember that what you do with the GIS is always a simplification of reality, and the results are based on that simplification, not on the reality behind it. The GIS is most effective as a tool to filter large amounts of data in a spatial analysis to efficiently identify locations that meet a set of criteria, show a relationship, and so forth. Computers do exactly what we tell them to do, but if we tell them the wrong thing, they will, very precisely, do the wrong thing. We can analyze spatial data in a GIS far faster and easier than we ever could with paper maps, rulers, and markers, but sometimes that just means a faster, more efficient way to make a bad map.

Good data, thoughtful conceptualization of your analysis, and at least occasional checks on the ground (or with a reliable surrogate) are essential before making a final decision based on a computer model. A very public example of blindly trusting the map was the erroneous bombing of the Chinese Embassy in Belgrade, Yugoslavia, in 1999. The CIA later attributed the error to a mistake on the map that was used in planning the attack intended to destroy a Yugoslavian arms agency. If you start with bad data, you'll get a bad result no matter how precise the GIS is in telling you the location of that result.

Finally, we state a more general caution but one that all too often leads to unpleasant GIS experiences: expecting too much from your GIS. As mentioned earlier in this text, it can take a great deal of time and effort to prepare data for use in GIS analysis. It is rarely if ever the case that all of the data you require for an analysis will exist in the appropriate format and be ready to go. Although GIS analysis can be done rapidly once everything is in place, it may take months or even years to get to that point. GIS can take a little getting used to at first, as can getting all of the appropriate data for your common analysis tasks. Once you have those things in place, a GIS is a fantastic tool with immense potential. But just as installing a word processor on your computer won't have you writing Shakespeare overnight, installing GIS software is only the beginning of doing meaningful spatial analysis. With a little patience, time, and practice, it will happen!

A GIS, when used with care and consideration, can be a wonderful tool for social science research. Although as a tool GIS was originally developed for natural resource management and has a longer history in those disciplines, the possibilities for spatial analysis of social science data with GIS are only recently being explored. There are untold possibilities for the application of GIS to questions yet to be asked and, no doubt, important and meaningful surprises in the answers that it will provide in the future.

Relevant Web Sites

The Geographer's Craft: This site provides a chapter on cartographic communication. http://www.colorado.edu/geography/gcraft/notes/cartocom/cartocom_f.html

The GIS Primer, Data Analysis: This publication, by David J. Buckley of Pacific Meridian Resources, Inc., provides a good overview of many of the analysis approaches described in this chapter. http://www.innovativegis.com/basis/primer/analysis.html

Grass GIS: GRASS is a raster-based GIS package that is freely available and runs on most computer platforms. http://grass.baylor.edu

"Network Analysis—Network Versus Vector—A Comparison Study": This article, by Jan Husdal, University of Leicester, provides an excellent comparison of the application of routed network analysis in both vector and raster GIS systems. http://www.husdal.com/mscgis/network.htm)

"Raster GIS Packages Finally Receive Well-Deserved Recognition": This is an article by W. Fredrick Limp, director of the Center for Advanced Spatial Technologies at the University of Arkansas, Fayetteville. http://www.geoplace.com/gw/2000/0500/0500re.asp

10 Future Opportunities for Social Research and GIS

Chapter Description

This chapter explores the important role that GIS can play in the toolbox of the social scientist. As a research tool in the social sciences, GIS have not been explored and applied to nearly the same depth relative to applications in the natural resource sciences, where GIS have a longer history. Current and future opportunities for the application of GIS in the social sciences are tremendous; the surface has just been scratched. As a means to analyze societal structure and change, a GIS provides an additional and often unconsidered geographic variable in the mix of applied social science research. GIS have an extremely valuable role to play in assisting social science researchers in their quest to study issues such as inequality, social capital, crime, social services, and historic change as well as many other issues in our society. GIS also have great potential to incorporate and visualize the concerns, goals, and ideas of various stakeholder groups. This chapter presents opportunities for government agencies, service organizations, and community groups to incorporate a GIS as a tool to examine and plan for their community's needs and to improve their effectiveness in managing information. Finally, we present a brief discussion of some of the future directions of GIS, including a move toward common, open standards for spatial data and availability of open source software tools.

Chapter Objectives

- Review the integration of GIS with social science research.
- Provide an example research application.
- Offer suggestions for the future incorporation of GIS in the social sciences.
- Provide suggestions for developing analyses in GIS.

After reading this chapter, you should be able to perform the following tasks:

- Explain how GIS and social science research can be effectively integrated.
- Review an example analysis and develop your own suggestions for operationalizing and carrying it out.
- Develop your own ideas for a GIS-based analysis in an area of the social sciences of particular interest to you.

Linking GIS and the Social Sciences

When one considers how common it is to see maps incorporated into social science research—going back at least 150 years—it may come as a surprise that research with GIS is still considered a relatively new idea in many disciplines within the social sciences. A variety of reasons might be suggested as to why social scientists did not become more closely involved early in the development of GIS (the U.S. Census Bureau being a notable exception, entering the field in 1967). If you are a social scientist and are beginning to use GIS, you may find that you are in a group of early adopters. The good news is that as you incorporate GIS into your own work you will be one of the people whom others go to for suggestions and ideas.

If you work in a public agency, find out who else is using GIS. It may be colleagues down the hall in departments focused on infrastructure, parks, or other natural resources. If you are in academia, you may find GIS people in one of several different departments on campus. If there is a forestry or natural resources department, odds are there are people there you can talk to. Computer science is another place you might find people with insight into GIS. Geography departments are certainly likely sources of expertise, and individuals in those departments may have a better understanding of the types of analyses you are interested in. In the private sector, many consultants are using GIS to some degree as are a variety of nongovernmental organizations.

Of course, being at the leading edge of users of any new technology also means you will need to be creative in approaching these tools. It may not be immediately obvious how you can translate a GIS study of wildlife habitats to a social science analysis situation, but try to be imaginative. Of course, the reasons that an animal in the wild chooses to live where it does may be far more similar to how people select and develop their communities than is at first apparent. Both have a set of needs they are attempting to meet, such as being close to resources, having a safe place to live away from noise and congestion, and so on.

We can't emphasize enough that using a GIS as an analytical tool is as much an art as it is a science. The art is in conceptualizing your analysis and implementing it logically in the GIS. Of course, the actual processing, map analysis, and statistical results are the science behind the GIS. As we pointed out earlier, a GIS is an integrative technology that allows you to bring together data from a variety of sources and disciplines. Being creative in how you apply these tools is one of the most important components of successful GIS analysis, particularly when applying it in new situations. Of course, once you work out a reliable process, you'll probably want to stick with it.

Although GIS have existed for more than four decades, it is just beginning to come into its own in terms of its application within the social sciences. With the exception of some large government agencies, most social science researchers did not start to rediscover their spatial roots until only recently. Whatever your specific discipline within the social sciences, odds are that if you go back to the roots of your discipline you will find that maps were integral to the analytical process in some capacity. Over time, many social science disciplines got away from these roots, looking to new and different approaches. Even the geographers largely ignored GIS in its early years of development. Nonetheless, GIS continued to develop within other disciplines, primarily in the natural resource sciences, during those intervening years, largely unnoticed by social scientists.

Now with a variety of easier-to-use and more accessible GIS software, social scientists are once again beginning to realize the value of a spatial perspective and are exploring applications of GIS in their disciplines. What was old is new again! There are countless agencies, private companies, community organizations, and nongovernmental organizations that can better achieve their goals by incorporating GIS approaches into their work. Of course, GIS are not without fault. Most important, one cannot rely on developing a technology without also developing an equal consideration for the people who will use the technology (the social side of GIS).

Using GIS to Study Society and Change

Many social scientists deal with the concepts of change over time. This is especially true for researchers interested in social policy and social structure. Social structures are defined as the recurrent patterns of social relationships (Brinkerhoff, White, Ortega, & Weitz, 2005). Individuals' behaviors can, in part, be understood and predicted based on the various social structures in which they operate. For instance, every social group has certain expectations, or norms, regarding behavior. In modern American society, children are expected to go to school, and adults are expected to go to work.

The social scientist is often interested in changes that influence society and might ask questions such as the following: What social changes are affecting society today? What type of a society does one live in? What political or environmental changes are influencing society today? Is a type of inequality occurring? (Social scientists try to give different types of inequality different names, such as ageism, sexism, or racism.)

Essentially, any of these questions might benefit by considering the spatial context. For example, where are different types of inequality occurring? Because environmental and social resources that support certain societies and social structures throughout the world are dwindling, questions of geographic location and inequality are gaining increasing importance. Increasingly, as information sharing continues, the question of where these different types of inequality are occurring will become increasingly predominant. There are even terms to refer to such concepts, such as environmental justice.

Identifying Social Inequality

Social inequality can exist at any level, be it an organization, a community, a neighborhood, a state, or a nation. In the world that we live in today, the gap continues to widen between the haves and the have-nots. A GIS is an important tool that can be used to help document and analyze where and what types of social inequality are occurring throughout the world. Additionally, by exploring the social structure of the locations where inequality occurs, we might gain a better understanding of the causes and potential solutions.

This is valuable information because it can provide a faster response time for dealing with a variety of social, economic, medical, environmental, and political issues that arise around the world. Solutions based on GIS analysis allow for a geographic perspective to be considered. The solution might be as simple as determining access to clean drinking water by using a GIS to explore the distance to water supplies in a community suffering from high levels of waterborne disease. Perhaps drilling a new water well in a location convenient to the community would solve the problem. Both analyses of where people get their water and where a new well should be located would be well served by a GIS analysis. This process of determining factors or variables causing the problem and pointing to an appropriate solution is an example of applied social change in a very concrete and real sense.

Finding remedies to different types of social inequality involves finding ways to improve society, improve the world, solve existing problems, and right existent wrongs and inequalities in a society, a community, or an organization. Each of these goals can be assisted through the use of a GIS. The applied or practical view of social change encourages people to work out the steps that must be taken to right the wrongs and to concretely determine the steps necessary to fix a specific social problem. Examples of such applications may involve establishing greater equality for groups that have previously experienced unfair or unequal treatment.

GIS City Case Example

Let's say that you are a researcher who works for the city government, and you recently received a grant to improve overall community well-being for three different neighborhoods in your city: North Town, East Side, and South Town (Figure 10.1). The reason that the city has decided to conduct such a study is because some communities claim that they are not provided with the equal health and well-being opportunities afforded to individuals in other, perhaps wealthier neighborhoods and communities. They feel that their general communities are suffering because of perceived inequality in facilities. As a result, the city has decided to take action to assess the overall health and well-being of three specific communities that represent different socioeconomic strata in light of the communities' claims.

Having worked in city government for the past several years, you are well aware that there are discrepancies in terms of availability and access to different facilities that contribute to generating and maintaining general community well-being. Community well-being is tied to a person's general health, physical activity, and mental/emotional stability, including a person's perception of community safety and nutrition. You have recently become acquainted with GIS and feel that it could be an important part of your research project.

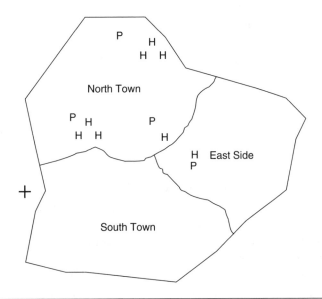

Figure 10.1   Using a base map of the three communities in the study, we can examine a variety of spatial relationships both within and between these communities. Depending on the form of the analysis you choose, it might also be important to include resources that lie just outside the study region; for example, a park lying just to the west of North Town would be an amenity for that community that would not otherwise appear if only looking at information contained inside the boundary shown in the figure.

Developing Community Profiles

A GIS database can be created for each for each of the three communities under study and linked to an appropriate base map (Figure 10.1). Brief community profiles are provided in this section for each of the neighborhoods being assessed.

North Town

North Town is a wealthier community in the city, characterized by high-rise apartments and community recreation centers that include indoor gym facilities and outdoor tennis courts. Grocery stores are located on the ground floors of some of the high-rise apartments. Three police stations employ officers that regularly patrol the area, and there is ample access to medical facilities.

East Side

East Side is characterized by smaller townhouses and apartments; a few outside recreation facilities such as basketball courts, tennis courts, and a park with a jogging trail; limited grocery store facilities; one medical facility—a hospital, not private practice doctors; and one police station to provide officers to regularly patrol the area. Crimes that occur in East Side are mostly muggings and robberies.

South Town

South Town is quite different from the other areas of the city. Residents of South Town constantly live in fear for their lives under a barrage of weekly drive-by shootings and murders, and there is no police station in the neighborhood. In South Town, police presence is minimal to none, which has been a complaint of South Town residents for years. South Town has a few old, dilapidated outdoor basketball courts and no indoor recreation facilities. There are no big grocery stores in this part of town, just a small convenience store that carries mostly liquor and charges high prices for unhealthy snack foods. Fresh fruits and vegetables are at a minimum in South Town. There are no artistic venues in South Town except for the local high school, which has a gym where the school puts on plays and community-oriented cultural events.

In Chapter 7, we suggested a series of guiding questions to assist researchers in determining the GIS variables for a particular study. We revisit and address each of those questions now in light of the City Case Study example.

Factors Affecting Choice of GIS Variables

1. What is the main goal of your study? Is it predictive, comparative, or descriptive?

2. Does your study involve a variety of variables? Does their location matter?

3. What kinds of data exist for your study location and variables?

4. Does your study involve comparison of different locations?

5. Does distance play a role in your study?

6. What are your project resources?

Question 1: What is the main goal of your study? Is it predictive, comparative, or descriptive?

The main goal of the study is to identify the discrepancies in availability of facilities that contribute to general community well-being. It is comparative in nature because you will be seeking to identify access to specific facilities in combination with a variety of sociospatial traits for each of the three different communities under study: North Town, East Side, and South Town.

Question 2: Does your study involve a variety of variables? Does their location matter?

In answer to this question, yes, the study does involve a variety of variables. The primary dependent variable is community well-being. Variables that might be of interest in a community well-being study include indoor and outdoor recreation centers, mental health providers, medical doctors, larger grocery stores that sell a variety of affordable healthy foods, police stations, and cultural arts venues. Conducting such a study involves integrating a variety of geographic and social variables. The study needs to assess the presence or absence of these facilities and their locations using a GIS.

Question 3: What kinds of data exist for your study location and variables?

The researcher who is going to tackle this problem would benefit from talking to personnel at the city planning department and seeing if he or she can get access to a GIS data layer that indicates all of the local roads and community boundaries. Of course, it would be very desirable if some of the other facilities of interest were also available in a GIS data layer or even on an existing paper map, but this may not be a realistic expectation.

The next step would be to validate and, if necessary, ground truth the data that you have available for your communities. If you are fortunate, the data are up to date and will not require much additional work. If the data are older and changes are likely, either new facilities or facilities that are no longer in service, you may need to physically go out and check the locations of these facilities on the map to make sure that these places exist at the recorded location. Often when you get access to existing data, portions of it may be out of date and need to be updated. The agency or organization that provides you the data would be happy to benefit from your ground truthing efforts. In fact, that might be one of the things that you offer in return for use of their data. You could provide them with an updated copy of the GIS data layers once you are done with your study.

Question 4: Does your study involve comparison of different locations?

Yes, it does. You will compare data for the three different communities: North Town, East Side, and South Town.

Question 5: Does distance play a role in your study?

Yes, in this study you will investigate how far individuals have to travel, and potentially by what means (personal vehicle, public transportation, or on foot), to reach the facilities identified as relating to community well-being. We are hypothesizing that the individuals who live in South Town (the poorest community) probably have to travel the farthest to reach such facilities.

Question 6: What are your project resources?

The project has sufficient funds from the federal government to promote urban community development in the United States. We have the ability to do all of the necessary data development and ground truthing by whatever methodology is most appropriate. (Perhaps this is unlikely in real life, but we'll pretend!)

Now that we have covered the questions regarding the inclusion of GIS in the study, let's turn to following the 10 specific steps from Chapter 4 concerning deductive sociospatial research. Once again, remember that a deductive approach means that you are beginning the research process with a hypothesis or general idea about the kinds of relationships you expect to find in your study. In this section, we go through each of the 10 steps for the given example.

Stages of Sociospatial Research for Deductive Research

The following 10 research steps are discussed in detail in this section:

1. Choose a topic.

2. Define the problem.

3. Conduct a literature review.

4. Develop a hypothesis.

5. Develop a conceptual framework.

6. Choose research methods.

7. Collect and prepare data.

8. Verify the data (ground truth).

9. Analyze the data.

10. Share results.

Step 1. Choose a topic: The topic for your study involves an urban community's social inequality.

Step 2. Define the problem: Your definition of the problem stems from your knowledge of local communities' complaints. Some communities feel they are not receiving access to the same quality of facilities and opportunities that others experience.

Step 3. Conduct a literature review: As a researcher, you need to conduct a review of the literature related to urban community development and community well-being. You should seek out journals, books, and Web sites that relate to urban planning, the environment, and health and human services.

Step 4. Develop a hypothesis: Your working hypothesis going into the study is that poor communities have less access to resources/facilities necessary to promoting community well-being and as a result have lower community well-being than those with greater access to these facilities.

Step 5. Develop a conceptual framework: Figure 10.2 illustrates the relationships among the main variables in our study. The dependent variable is community well-being. Our study illustrates that there are many factors that can affect general community well-being, including a series of geographic variables (proximity to medical/mental health care, grocery stores, good jobs, community center/exercise facility) that influences general community well-being. Our hypothesis is that community members who are located farther from the variables' locations have less community well-being; those located closer to the variables' locations have greater community well-being.

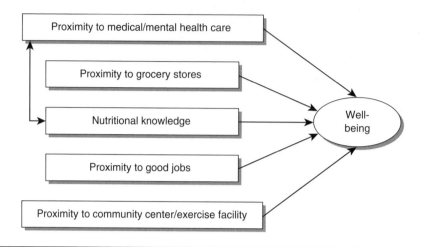

Figure 10.2   A partial conceptual framework for community well-being consisting of five variables believed important in assessing community well-being. Additional variables would be added to capture the other components discussed earlier. The four proximity variables shown here would be mapped in their true, geographic locations as would the locations of individual respondents in the community survey.

Step 6. Choose research methods: The research methods that will be used as part of this study include secondary information, surveys, focus groups, and GIS.

Step 7. Collect or locate data: There are a variety of approaches that can be applied to data acquisition in this project. Some data may already exist in useable form, whereas other data may need to be collected from scratch. The following sections provide examples of data acquisition that might apply here.

Finding Sociodemographic Data

Because a focus of this study is social inequality, you should first establish an understanding of the sociodemographic characteristics of each community. There are several ways to accomplish this. First, you could look at census block data from the most recent U.S. Census for each area. These data are available on the Internet (http://www.census.gov/geo/www/census2k.html/). If there are any nonprofit agencies already in these communities, they may also have data concerning social composition of the communities that would be useful to your research. If these agencies do not have specific data, you can simply conduct some key-informant interviews with members of these agencies to gain an understanding of some of the issues that face the local population and gather information about the sociodemographic background of the local community: Is it a diverse community?

Does it consist primarily of low-income or upper-class people? Is there a variety of job opportunities for local people here?

Surveys

In addition to relying entirely on preexisting or secondary data, you could implement a survey. Surveys are a great way to cast a wide net to gather information on a particular topic. For more detail on how to prepare a survey, see *Mail and Internet Surveys: The Tailored Design Method* (Dillman, 1999). To gain a sample that is truly representative of your population, you could randomly select individuals from each of the three local communities. The key to conducting a random sample is to obtain a sampling frame or list that provides every individual who lives in the area with the same chance of being on the list. You might be able to find such a list from the local tax assessor, voter registration or driver's license registration lists, or other similar sources of public record. To protect the identity of individuals, these agencies might restrict your access to a list of addresses without names. This is an advantage because it helps to preserve the anonymity of those whom you are surveying.

An important requirement of your survey is for each respondent in the three communities to geographically identify the specific neighborhoods and blocks they live in; this could be accomplished by geocoding addresses to their respective blocks and coding them accordingly. In the survey, you should identify what residents perceive as the primary issues and problems for their community. By gathering this information, you are able to then compare responses both between and within each of these three communities. Sociodemographic information, such as age, income, education, ethnicity, and length of residence, is also gathered in the survey.

Gathering social data that have a geographic component allows for a richer, greater comparison of the different issues faced by residents in these communities. Important results of this study are to identify key neighborhood needs; to identify who requires these needs (e.g., by gender, age, ethnicity, or other population characteristics); and to identify where specifically these need are located. This would be especially important in developing geographically based solutions to some of these problems. Such information could assist in implementing social policy and the allocation of resources and future facilities related to health and well-being. You should ask some of the key questions on the survey in the focus group as well. This provides the opportunity for a validity check of questions asked.

Some potential survey questions include the following:

a. What facilities are currently available in your neighborhood? Where are they?

b. What facilities do you wish were available in your neighborhood? Where should they be located?

c. Is your neighborhood safe? If yes, why? If not, why not?

d. What are the three top issues for residents in your neighborhood?

e. Are there certain ethnic groups, celebrations, or issues of cultural sensitivity that should be considered in the city planning efforts (e.g., special cultural events that might require access to a community center facility, such as Cinco de Mayo or Chinese New Year)? Are some of these events more marginalized than others regarding access to city facilities?

f. Are there any churches, synagogues, mosques, or other places of worship in your community? (The reason to ask this question is to determine the level of spiritual support and to identify some locations where local cultural events could occur.)

g. What grocery stores are currently available to you?

h. Where do you go to the doctor? Do you have to travel far?

i. What sorts of public transportation do people use in your community?

j. In what year were you born?

k. What is your gender?

l. What is your household income?

m. How long have you lived in the area?

n. What is the highest level of education that you have completed? (select one)
Less than high school
High school
Some college
College graduate
Some graduate classes
Master's degree or higher

Focus Groups

In addition to surveys, you can approach your study by conducting a series of focus groups in each community. Focus groups can be defined as a qualitative method of data collection that involves holding "a semi-structured group discussion, moderated by a group leader, held in an informal setting with the purpose of collecting information on a designated topic" (Carey, 1994, p. 226). The idea of the focus group is to help the researcher to understand the needs and concerns of the residents in each of these communities as they relate to community well-being. In the focus group, you should ask some of the same questions that you asked on the survey. Some questions that might be asked during the focus group session include the following:

a. What facilities are currently available in your neighborhood?

b. What facilities do you wish were available in your neighborhood?

c. Is your neighborhood safe? If yes, why? If not, why not?

d. What are the three top issues for residents in your neighborhood?

e. Are there certain ethnic groups, celebrations, or issues of cultural sensitivity that should be considered in the city planning efforts (e.g., special cultural events that might require access to a community center facility, such as Cinco de Mayo or Chinese New Year)? Are some of these events more marginalized than others regarding access to city facilities?

f. Are there any churches, synagogues, mosques, or other places of worship in your community? (The reason to ask this question is to determine the level of spiritual support and to identify some locations where local cultural events could occur.)

g. What grocery stores are currently available to you?

h. Where do you go to the doctor? Do you have to travel far?

i. What sorts of public transportation do people use in your community?

GIS is an important tool that can play a key role in ameliorating social inequality by helping people, organizations, groups, and companies to identify where such social inequalities occur. In your focus group sessions, you could have a general map of each community. You might get input on any errors or missing information on the maps as part of your process of ground truthing. A part of the focus group session could be asking residents questions such as the following:

a. Where on the map would you identify as the heart of the community, the place where the most social interaction occurs? (You would ask this question to help determine where best to locate future recreation or art facilities or shopping centers.)

b. Where are the unsafe areas in your community and where are the safe areas? (Having residents indicate this on a map assists in determining where increased safety efforts need to occur and which types of safety efforts should be put into place; e.g., a direct phone line for 911 calls or a location for a police substation).

c. Is there a place where many young people hang out? Is this a safe place? Where is it located? (You could ask this to determine if there is a need for a place for younger people in the community to go.)

d. Currently, where do you shop? How far do you have to travel to shop? Do you walk or drive?

e. Where do most people go to receive medical attention in the community? Do they need to travel outside of the community for this? If so, how do they travel to get there?

Data Capture as a Visualization Process

If you have the GIS map in a computer and you are projecting it onto a screen, you could use these focus group sessions as a time for capturing and recording data directly into the computer. For instance, say the general community consensus is that the community needs a recreation center for younger and older people in the heart of the community. Using the GIS, you can indicate the future potential site with a dot. If multiple sites are suggested as potential locations for a community recreation center, you can enter each of the locations into the GIS. Of course, if you are limited to paper maps, you can accomplish the same thing by marking the maps with pens or stickers and capturing the data into the GIS at a later time, back at the office.

After you complete the initial stages of data collection and analysis, you might return to the community and show preliminary results to help residents visualize future developments in their communities. This allows residents to give you additional input that might further enhance your analysis and results.

Step 8. Verify the data (ground truth): To verify that the geographic data you receive are sufficiently accurate and up to date, there are a few strategies to employ. First, if you are relying on existing data, ask the people who provided the data how recently the data were collected or updated. If these people are not sure, then it will be up to you to ground truth (check the geographic reality) what is supposedly located on the map. Another procedure for ground truthing existing data is to ask local experts, people who live in the community every day, if the map is representative of the existing roads, structures, facilities and so on in their home community. One possibility we mentioned earlier would be to do this as a part of the focus group data collection process.

Step 9. Analyze the data: This project brings together a wide variety of data, including quantitative and qualitative data. Some potential sources of the quantitative data are the survey, existing data in the form of the U.S. Census, and the GIS data on location of specific facilities. Potential sources of qualitative data include some of the open-ended survey questions, information from the focus group, and some of the metadata or community-generated stories regarding community well-being specifically related to facilities and services in the community. Your analysis of the quantitative data will most likely involve use of a statistical data collection process, such as SPSS. SPSS has an export feature that is compatible with most GIS computer programs. The analysis of the qualitative data will most likely be accomplished using a qualitative data analysis program, many of which are available.

Using GIS as a part of the neighborhood study also facilitates potential solutions by asking individuals who are a part of the study what they feel they could contribute in terms of making improvements in their communities. For some individuals, it might be time that they contribute toward, let's say, constructing a school playground. For others, it could be contributions in the form of monetary donations or different skill sets that different respondents have, such as woodworking, masonry, fund raising, community organizing, and so on. Especially in communities where budgets and resources are limited, many communities are looking for ways to share the burden of community improvement with nongovernmental entities, including local residents, community groups, and other institutions.

The GIS analysis can involve both qualitative and quantitative variables. Let us explain. The information collected in answer to the open-ended survey questions and as a part of the focus groups has a geographic component. On the survey, we collect geographic information such as the town the respondent lives in, the neighborhood of residence, and the block or street address. As a result, we are able to compare and contrast survey responses within and between neighborhoods. We also collect this same information from residents who participate in the focus group. The different themes that emerge in the analysis can then be written in and attached to appropriate geographic locations. Such information provides a city planner or developer with a quick, bird's-eye summary of local concerns and interests. If a lot of individuals within a community identify an issue or concern regarding health and community well-being, this can be noted on the map.

Similarly, the overall themes generated during analysis of the focus group sessions could also be attached to a digital map of the region. One could then compare the themes that emerge from the open-ended survey questions and focus group interviews to look for similarities and differences. The primary GIS analysis tools that you will likely choose are buffer, overlay, and nearest neighbor analysis, if you are working in a vector system. If you choose to work in raster, you might develop a coding scheme and a mathematical model to use in a map algebra approach.

Identifying the geographic distribution and correlation of social inequalities with these other factors could occur through the survey process that we mentioned earlier, which included gathering information on residents' perceptions of problems and issues in their neighborhoods. Gathering individual-level data on income, education, and occupation also facilitates an understanding of the poorer communities' locations as clustered on the map and the specific issues of these communities. Different ethnic groups within these communities may also have special needs that must be addressed from a geographic standpoint. For instance, it is common in some cultures to have a gathering place, such as a plaza or park, where people go to stroll in the evening.

> Step 10. Sharing results: Whenever you do research, especially applied social research, it is always a good idea to share the results. Results can be shared with a variety of interest groups, ranging from the funding agencies and local social service agencies to local community groups who participated in the study. Applied social research is geared toward solving particular social problems. Therefore, the more you can get the word out about your study, the better. We advocate developing different forms of data diffusion, including an applied summary report for the layperson, a report that contains more advanced analysis to share with your colleagues and that might be published in a journal or presented at a professional conference, and a condensed Power Point® presentation, which could be presented to the communities and other interested groups.

Government and GIS

Government plays an important role in the production, housing, and dissemination of vast quantities of data. Some of these data exist in a GIS format, and some do not. The key is to be able to determine which types of data are available. Much of this information is accessible via U.S. governmental Web sites (see Chapters 2 and 6). Important geospatial base data may come from the U.S. Geographical Survey. The U.S. Census Bureau provides social data in GIS formats, and agencies such as the Environmental Protection Agency provide data on a variety of environmental and pollution issues by geographic location. Of course, most states as well as many county and city governments maintain their own GIS data.

Earlier chapters of this book (Chapter 2 and Chapter 6) explored how to gather and access data from the Internet. In the United States, the National Spatial Data Infrastructure serves as a starting point for local, state, and federal government agencies to provide a structure that enables effective and long-term access and location of GIS data. As was indicated earlier, we are living in an information age, where knowledge is power. Although barriers to the effective use and sharing of GIS data still exist, as the technology continues to be adopted by a wide variety of agencies and organizations geographically based information will continue to improve in both availability and quality.

Data Continuity Over Time

Governmental agencies usually house the macro data on our society. Because they contain data that pertain to the general public, these agencies are often the best sources for data on a particular topic. Although many of the governmental natural resource management agencies may have a bit of a head start in GIS, other agencies at all levels of government are catching up in their use of GIS to help portray and share the meaning of their data in space.

The mission (and mandate) of many governmental agencies is to develop policies that help alleviate social and environmental problems for the public. A major part of doing this is to develop a good baseline of information that explains the story and relates to specific issues, such as poverty, health and environmental safety, community development, and racial segregation, just to name a few. The U.S. government provides many different forms of data, ranging from paper to digital. Although much of the current data (e.g., U.S. Census data) are portrayed in a digital GIS-based form, earlier versions of this same information are not always readily available in the same format.

That data exist in many different formats sometimes necessitates that interested researchers invest a certain amount of labor and creativity to locate and assemble usable data in a form that is most beneficial for their topic or issue. (See Chapter 6 for a discussion of data collection and development.) Government institutions often possess the facilities to house data over time and the institutional structure that is necessary to facilitate this. However, government agencies don't always have the time or inclination to update data formats and translate data into forms that one might need. Although it is likely that new and future data will better meet the needs of researchers conducting spatial analyses, it is unlikely that historic, archival data will ever be converted in this manner. Therefore, this task may fall to the interested researcher.

Metadata Documentation of Your Data

You first need to establish a well-organized system for your data. An important part of this involves metadata. Whenever you create data, you should record, as accurately as possible, basic metadata—when, where, how, and in what format the data were collected. This information is extremely important for providing an understanding about what the data actually mean, and the information increases the usefulness of your data to others over time. Preferably your metadata will follow standards established by the Federal

Geographic Data Committee (FGDC) to ensure clear documentation and compatibility.

Second, an agency or organization should develop an organizational structure that will remain reliable and constant and preserve institutional knowledge over time. This means developing a structure that persists even if particular individuals come and go from the agency. It can be dangerous to have data tied too directly to a given individual or group of individuals without a clear structure for data viability. Tying data specifically to individuals in an agency creates data vulnerability.

Third, ideally an agency or organization will have a structure that encourages the open sharing of data. This means that the agency has a Web site that lists the type of data available (the types of data accessible through its Web site are clearly listed, along with the associated metadata). Finally, use and access of the system should be consistent and easy. If it is too difficult to use, then sharing information with interested parties will be impossible.

Future Directions for GIS and Social Sciences

As GIS continue to further penetrate our societal consciousness, it is inevitable that more social science issues will be viewed in a spatial context. GIS are already making their way into many people's lives via the numerous Internet Web sites that incorporate maps and mapping technology. Furthermore, a spatial perspective is regularly presented in the news, both in print form via newspapers and magazines as well as in the form of compelling three-dimensional maps or fly-through visualizations, which are often incorporated into television news broadcasts. GIS software and digital mapping technologies such as GPS are already being presented in many middle and elementary schools around the world.

With so much exposure to these tools and their numerous applications in understanding the world around us, it would be naïve to assume anything other than a growing demand for more of this sort of information and analysis from the constituencies that social scientists serve.

Visualization and GIS

A GIS is perfect for the study of social issues because it enables the user to visualize social and physical elements of a certain space over time. Therefore, this can allow for the historical examination of settlement patterns of different ethnic groups, the study of the spread of certain diseases, or the analysis of changes in the availability of environmental resources, including who has access to which resources. GIS facilitate the overall integration of different types of data, such as community stories, sociodemographic profiles, and community needs assessments. GIS allow for layering this information, which ultimately produces a picture of social issues experienced by a specific geographic area or multiple geographic areas. This gives the user the flexibility and power to understand both recent and historic trends and changes that have occurred over time.

To the researcher who is interested in history and projections into the future, GIS could be an invaluable tool. Why? Social scientists often make their predictions about future social trends, problems, and issues through a study of past social patterns. When you incorporate a GIS into the research mix, it allows for the consideration of potentially important geographic variables that had not been previously considered. It provides the researcher with the opportunity to project trends and population shifts into the future based on past data patterns. Some GIS programs allow for the researcher, city planner, or community developer to run different scenarios regarding future development issues based on population growth and available resources. By entering different numbers into the program, the individual is able to model and visualize how things would appear in the future, given a set of specified conditions.

For example, let's assume that a community just received an economic development grant to revitalize a downtown area. This revitalization includes the construction of some new buildings (to add to the downtown's existing Victorian-style building structure) and involves the installation of a new bridge. The construction of the bridge will take at least a year. During this time, various roads will be closed, and the traffic patterns will affect some new buildings in the downtown area. How and where a community decides to locate these buildings, what height the buildings will be, and how much parking is needed could all be visualized using a GIS. Of course, such visualizations require somewhat more specialized software and significantly more data and computing power than is commonly available for these purposes at the local level. However, as computers continue to become more powerful and less expensive, realistic three-dimensional visualization and simulation models of various options will become more readily available and easier to use.

On the outskirts of this realm is something even more exciting: virtual reality simulators. Such systems use three-dimensional large-screen projections, much like you might see at the movies. By wearing polarized or colored glasses, you can "walk" inside the visualization. At present, this technology is still far too complex and expensive to put into a local community resource center, but this technology isn't as far off as you might suspect and is already available in some government and university research labs.

Faster Response Time

Using a GIS to assemble information regarding communities and integrating it immediately into a database can improve analysis and save time. In the past, much of this information may have existed in diffuse form. That is, each agency may have had particular information regarding their particular issues or needs but may have been unaware of the data possessed by other agencies and organizations. The same information might have existed on a variety of maps or in files located in filing cabinets. Such data would rarely, if ever, be brought together in social issue analysis or in the planning processes. When you use a GIS to bring this multitude of different types of data together into one form, you set the stage for data sharing and a consolidation of efforts, which can then result in better data overall. Having access to better data regarding communities can be invaluable in the planning process.

Impact of Tools for the Future

GIS are already being used in a variety of social science applications at varied levels of complexity. As more social scientists become familiar with and learn how to use these tools, they will become a common part of the curriculum in university programs focused on the social sciences, just as GIS have long been a part of curricula in the natural resource sciences. The inclusion of the spatial perspective is not new to social science research; it was simply overlooked for a time and is now making a resurgence in concert with the development and availability of the computer analysis tools that facilitate spatial analysis.

Parting Thoughts

In this book, we led the reader through the salient topics that currently face users of GIS in the social sciences. Additionally, we provided a background on GIS, strategies to identify topics that benefit from this technology, and principles of research design and data collection, measurement, preparation, and analysis. It is our hope that having read this book you will have an appreciation of the opportunities that a spatial perspective can bring to your work and that a GIS can facilitate. If we have motivated you to venture forward to try to use GIS technology to meet your own needs, we have succeeded in meeting our primary goal. Oftentimes, the biggest barrier to using a new technology is taking the first step and giving it a try. As with anything new you might undertake, the more you work at it, the easier it becomes. Start off with something simple and work up to the complex. As the saying goes, you must learn to walk before you learn to run.

GIS provide a powerful tool that can be harnessed equally by social and natural scientists. As the technology continues to develop, so too will the opportunities to apply it in new and creative ways. Almost every piece of social data has a geographic element that is important to data analysis and social science policy development. Our goal in writing this book is to assist individuals like you to take the first steps toward embracing a new and perhaps foreign technology. An equally important goal is to help you to understand how this technology benefits your own data collection, analysis, and decision making in the social sciences. GIS can truly help social science researchers move closer to meeting the needs of groups of people throughout the world. GIS technology enables the social researcher or policymaker to incorporate important contextual variables into policy-making decisions. We hope that perhaps you will assist your fellow social scientists in moving forward in this direction, a direction that is simultaneously the history and the future of social science research.

As we suggested at the beginning of this text, spatial analysis techniques can be applied and can very likely provide valuable insight into a wide array of social science issues, including many that have not yet been considered. The applicability of these tools in a sociospatial context and the valuable information and analysis results they can provide are endless, limited only by the creativity of the practitioners who use them in their work. It is our hope that some of the ideas presented in this text will prompt you to begin to think creatively about GIS in your own work and to share your experiences with others via the www.socialsciencegis.org Web site for this new and growing community.

_____ Some Suggestions for Student Research Projects

As we mentioned throughout the book, any variables that have a geographic location are ripe for being included in a GIS-based study. As a starting point, we provide some suggestions that you might use directly or in modified form in developing a GIS-based social science research project in an area of your own interest.

Here are some sample hypotheses that could be investigated using a GIS:

1. Environmental justice: Poor and minority communities are more likely to be located closer to toxic waste facilities (a geographic proximity question).

2. Health: Cities that are closer to international airline connections are more likely to have higher rates of contagious diseases (a network proximity question).

3. Crime: Crime rates are higher in areas that have a higher density of teenagers (a spatial correspondence/containment question).

4. Anthropology: Rural indigenous communities that are farther from cities have a greater preservation of their culture than those communities located closer to cities (a proximity question).

5. Political science: Communities located closer to international borders tend to be more supportive of international trade agreements, such as NAFTA (North American Free Trade Agreement; a geographic proximity question).

6. Sociology: Communities that have many local service organizations have greater social networks (a spatial correspondence/containment question).

Relevant Web Sites

Environmental Protection Agency GIS Data: This site provides a wide array of GIS data related to the environment and pollution in studies of public health, social justice, and other related issues. http://www.epa.gov/epahome/gis.htm/)

First Gov: This site is a Web portal to all U.S. federal and state government sites. http://www.firstgov.gov/

Open Geospatial Consortium, Inc. (OGC): The OGC nonprofit, international, voluntary consensus standards organization that is leading the development of standards for geospatial and location-based services. http://www.opengeospatial.org

Social Science GIS: This is the Web site for this book and home to a growing community of social scientists using GIS in their own work. It is a place to share ideas, questions, and examples and to provide feedback to the authors. http://www.socialsciencegis.org

Social Statistics Briefing Room: This Whitehouse site provides links to social statistical data. http://www.whitehouse.gov/fsbr/ssbr.html

"The Story of DIME: A Progress Report": This site provides a brief history of the U.S. Census Bureau DIME model development. http://www.geog.buffalo.edu/ncgia/gishist/DIME_story.html

U.S. Census 2000 GIS Data: The U.S. Census Bureau Web site provides a variety of GIS-compatible data sets and associated information useful in social science research applications. http://www.census.gov/main/www/cen2000.html

U.S. National Institutes of Health: This site provides a variety of GIS-compatible data sets relevant to research on health. Type "GIS" in the search box as a starting point. http://www.nih.gov/

Glossary _____

Abstraction   Method of representing real-world data as an object in the GIS database, for example, the location of the city center as a point on a map or the choice of a census block as the representation of a group of individuals.

Accessibility   How easy or difficult it is to get from one location to another, for example, due to directness of routes along a road network.

Accuracy   Closeness of a measured data value to the true data value for any given measurement, often represented as a confidence interval or percentage.

Add-ons   Any software component that is not part of the standard GIS software package. When optionally installed, these components offer additional data collection, analysis, or visualization capabilities. Many add-ons are freely available on the Internet, whereas others may be available for purchase from the GIS software company or other third-party application providers.

Address matching   A process in which street addresses are located on a GIS map.

Aerial imagery   Often used in mapping and in many cases collected with cameras or sensors specifically designed for mapping to scale. Aerial imagery refers to any imagery taken from above (bird's-eye view) for the purpose of recording conditions on the ground at a particular time and is useful for characterizing both the built environment and natural features.

Aggregate   To combine multiple data elements into one for the purpose of simplifying the data set or to mask individual data elements for the purpose of confidentiality.

Animated map   A map using the video capabilities of the computer to animate in time or space a change in data or the results of an analysis.

Animation   Use of the computer to generate a changing video display of data or analysis results, especially useful in showing movement or change through time.

ASCII   Also known as American Standard Code for Information Interchange; in computing, often refers to a plain text file format that can be read by a wide variety of computer software and hardware types.

Atlas/ti®   A qualitative data analysis software package.

Attribute   Descriptive information associated with a particular object or person in the GIS database. Each entity recorded in the GIS may include one or more attributes. This is often the type of data collected as part of a survey or observation of the entities under study.

Attribute table   A data file consisting of rows and columns, where rows represent individual samples and columns represent data characteristics about those samples. *See also* table.

Base map   An initial map for your research area to which all study data will be linked. The base map typically contains the geographic boundaries of your study site as well as common reference features relevant to the study (e.g., roads, census block boundaries, political boundaries, or significant natural features).

Boundary   The geographic limits of a region of interest, which may include an entire study region or smaller areas representing units of analysis.

Buffer   A measured or representative distance around a geographic feature of interest—for example, all grocery stores within 1 mile (measured distance) of a home or within a 10-minute drive (representative distance) of that same home.

Cartogram   A map in which distance represents a unit of measure other than actual measured distance. Data are scaled to a variable or index value of interest (e.g., time, strength of social relationship, or perceived risk).

Cartographic classification   Grouping of geographic data by measurement level data type or category.

Cartographic concept   Concept related to the representation of data in design and creation of maps.

Cartographic design   Design of a map to be clearly interpreted for a particular purpose.

Categorical data   Terminology for data that exist in categories.

Categorization   Selection of the groupings of data into categories to be used in the analysis, reporting, or representation of data.

Cell   A term used to refer to the storage of information. In database terminology, this refers to the location of a single piece of data in the attribute table. In raster GIS terminology, this refers to an individual raster in a map grid.

Census block   The smallest geographic unit for which the U.S. Census Bureau tabulates 100% data. Blocks may range in size from city blocks in urban areas to many square miles in rural areas. The size designation of a census block is based on population.

Character field   A field containing any combination of letters, numbers, or symbols.

Clip   A spatial operation to cut out only the required geographic area, much like a cookie-cutter.

Coding   The process of assigning a number or symbol to represent the data. Coding is done to facilitate the process of data analysis.

Commercial data   Data packaged by a company for sale.

Community profile   Any relevant information (geographic, environmental, social, political, etc.) that pertains to a particular community.

Complement   A topological overlay operation in which the nonoverlapping areas of two overlapping polygons are retained.

CompStat   The name of a GIS-based computer analysis program for examining the geographic patterns and locations of crimes.

Concentric zone theory   An ecological/social theory that examines why and where certain groups geographically cluster.

Concept   A body of ideas taken together as a unit.

Conceptual data model   The first stage of modeling reality in a GIS, which begins by organizing analysis goals within a spatial analysis context. Key components or variables for the analysis are determined, and the appropriate data sources are identified.

Conceptual framework   A theoretical model in social science that identifies key variables, explains the links between variables, and explains the sequence and flow of relationships using arrows.

Conceptualization   Identifying and giving a name to the ideas being studied.

Conceptual map   A mental map of relationships between variables.

Connectivity   The degree of connectedness within a network. Connectivity can refer to social or physical connectedness (e.g., the density of acquaintanceship networks for a particular community or the efficiency of a telecommunications network).

Containment   A determination of a feature of interest being within a particular geographic area.

Content analysis   A social research method that involves the analysis of texts or images in an empirical manner.

Contextual level variable   A macrolevel variable related to a particular geographic area (e.g., poverty rate of a particular region or environmental pollution of a particular community).

Coordinate   A geographic location described via an (*X*, *Y*) position relative to a defined origin on the mapping surface (e.g., latitude and longitude).

Coordinate system   A means of providing a spatial reference for every location on the surface of the earth via an (*X*, *Y*) position.

Core metadata components   Essential information related to a data set as defined by the metadata standard being used. Components include who collected the data, when it was collected, and what methods were used to collect it, as well as the purpose of the data collection and information about projection, coordinate system, datum, and geographic extent of the data.

Cost surface   A raster data layer with values at all locations of the study area that provides for analysis of all possible paths through the data rather than along specific routes.

Critical thinking   The ability to analytically assess the quality, meaning, and relevance of information presented.

CSGM   Also known as Content Standard for Geospatial Metadata, CSGM refers to the specific items of information to be included in the Federal Geographic Data Committee (FGDC)-compliant geospatial metadata.

Data   The raw information collected for use in an analysis.

Data aggregation   A means of collating and simplifying data. In social science applications, this is often done to protect the privacy of individuals. The researcher may select a more general spatial level at which to view the data (e.g., averaging data collected at the household level for analysis or viewing at the neighborhood or community level).

Database   An organized collection of information designed to be easily searched, accessed, and manipulated.

Data capture   The method of collecting and recording data for an analysis.

Data compression   Reducing the amount of space required for a data file. Data compression is most commonly used to minimize the amount of storage space required and to facilitate the transfer of data via storage media or the Internet.

Data conversion   Changing the data from one format to another. Data conversion is often necessary when sharing data between different software packages.

Data degradation   A loss of information due to data detail being discarded, typically via use of a lower level of measurement (e.g., converting a person's height from a measured value in feet and inches [ratio data] to a category such as "short" [ordinal data]).

Data dictionary   A list of variable names and the description or definition of the associated meaning (e.g., the variable "tall" refers to an adult over 6 feet in height).

Data format   The structure in which a set of data is collected or obtained (e.g., printed paper maps, tape-recorded interviews, digital database files).

Data model   The computer file structure used for data storage and analysis. In GIS, we typically refer to two primary models: vector and raster.

Data overlay   An analysis process in GIS whereby two different data sets are combined in geographic space to investigate relationships between variables.

Data quality   A qualitative or quantitative assessment of a data set. Formal metadata may follow specific standards for reporting the quality of the data for characteristics such as accuracy, completeness, and currency of a data set.

Datum   A mapping term referring to the survey control grid to which the data are linked (e.g., North American Datum 1983 or World Geodetic System 1984).

dBASE   One of the earliest and most popular personal computing database programs. Although dBase is no longer the leading database package, the file structures developed for that software are commonly used by GIS and database software in use today.

Deductive research   A research process in which the researcher begins by following the scientific method, which begins with a review of literature, goes on to generation of a conceptual framework, then development of a hypothesis, and then testing of the hypothesis by gathering and analyzing relevant data.

Delimited text   A simple file structure for the export of tabular data that is readily accessible to almost any computer software program, data recorder, or field survey instrument, such as global positioning system (GPS) receivers.

Demographic data   Information related to populations, especially in statistical terms (e.g., birth rate, death rate, fertility rate).

Dependent variable   A variable whose variation is based on (depends on) fluctuations in the independent variables.

Descriptive research   Research that shows the current state of items under study. Descriptive research is determined by conducting observations in a particular geographic location at a particular time.

Descriptive statistics   Simple statistics such as frequency, mean, median, and standard deviation.

Descriptive study   A study that documents observations about what is occurring in a particular area.

Digital   Any data (text, numbers, graphics, images) stored in a computerized format as opposed to a physical format, such as paper.

Digital data   Data that exist in a computer-compatible form.

Digitize   The process of converting data from physical sources (e.g., paper maps or data sheets, photographic prints, or taped interviews) to a computer-compatible format using the appropriate computer hardware (e.g., use of a digitizing tablet to trace a paper map into a GIS).

Discreet data   Data that fall into clearly defined categories. Such data facilitate mapping in vector GIS because lines may be drawn to delineate the exact boundary between data categories.

Displacement   A cartographic technique in which one of two features that would be mapped in exactly or nearly the same location is shifted to facilitate a more readable map (e.g., a road following a river is displaced to the side to make both features clearly visible on the map).

Doughnut buffer   A special case buffer that looks much like a doughnut, with a hole in the center, and that is excluded from the area of interest.

Download   The transfer of computerized information from one source to another (e.g., placing a file from the Internet onto one's personal computer).

Dummy coding   A system of numeric coding for nonnumeric variables to allow for use of statistical analysis. Dummy coding is used to differentiate between two groups. For instance, suppose you have the variable "gender"; a 0 could be assigned to *men* and a 1 could be assigned to *women*.

Ecological fallacy   A faulty assumption that relationships existing between geographically based variables are causal.

Edge effect   Errors or variations in the results of an analysis caused by the placement of the study boundary. Each placement may provide a somewhat different result for whatever attribute or variable is being analyzed based on the selected population (or sample from this population).

Empirical   Research based on observation or experiment.

Entity   The individual items that are stored as rows in the GIS database. Entities are typically selected to be an aspect of your study that is measurable (e.g., individuals responding to a survey of city parks within your study area).

Environmental justice   The notion that all people should have access to a healthy, clean environment to live, work, and play regardless of race or class.

Ethnocentric   Using one's culture as a standard by which to judge other cultures.

Ethnography   A research method where one provides a detailed description of a situation under study rather than attempting to provide an explanation.

Euclidian distance   The straight-line distance between two points, as the crow flies. Computed as the hypotenuse of a right triangle that contains legs defined by the difference in the X and Y coordinate positions of the two points in question.

Exact interpolator   A statistical estimator that predicts values at sample locations with exactly the same value as the original sample, the underlying assumption being that the sampled values are correct, true values with no (or minimal) error.

Exclusive or   In data query, this is the equivalent of "not equal to."

Export   The process of saving data from a software application in a format that is likely to be compatible with other, different software. Sometimes referred to as "Save As" in computer applications.

Feature   An individual item on the map (e.g., road, house, neighborhood).

Feature type   The spatial data format (point, line, polygon, or raster pixel) that individual features are represented with in the GIS.

Federal Geographic Data Committee   A federal committee, also referred to as FGDC, that defines the metadata standards followed by most federal agencies when creating new data for GIS. Many state and local agencies and organizations also follow this standard.

FGDC   An acronym for the Federal Geographic Data Committee.

Field   In research methods, the social or physical environment where data are collected. In GIS, field refers to a column in the data table.

Field research   Research conducted in the social field in which the researcher spends time in a particular geographic location to collect data.

Fly-through   A process that allows users to interactively navigate through a three-dimensional landscape, giving them a feel for how things would appear if they were to actually walk, drive, or fly through the landscape.

Focus group   A qualitative method of data collection that involves holding a group discussion, moderated by a group leader, in an informal setting with the purpose of collecting people's impressions, attitudes, and feelings about a particular topic.

Free data   Data that do not have a monetary cost associated with their acquisition or use.

Fuzzy GIS   GIS that allow locations and boundaries to be less defined. Fuzzy GIS are not commonly available in commercial software but could be useful for social scientists working with data types that lack clear boundaries or scientists who want to protect the privacy of research subjects.

Geocoding   The linking of nonspatial data to a geographic base map for purposes of use and analysis in a GIS (e.g., address matching).

Geographic information system   Also known as GIS, a specialized computer database program designed for the collection, storage, manipulation, retrieval, and analysis of spatial data.

Geographic region   A defined area on the surface of the earth; in the context of GIS, the area of interest for the purpose of data collection and analysis.

GIGO   An acronym for "garbage in, garbage out." GIGO is used in computer circles to indicate the importance of having good data to draw solid conclusions.

GIS   An acronym that stands for geographic information system.

GIS database   A collection of information/data that can be used in computerized map analyses.

GIS-ready data   Data that exist in a form readily accessible for use within a GIS software package.

Global positioning system   A satellite-based navigation system, also known as GPS, that allows for the precise location of one's (X, Y) coordinate on the surface of the earth. GPS is often used during data analysis to facilitate the link of data to a GIS map.

GPS   An acronym that stands for global positioning system.

Graphical user interface   A computer interface designed for ease of use via pictorial icons and menus that are accessed with a mouse.

Ground truth   The process of checking data and maps against reality, which may involve checking the map against other data sources or traveling to the place where the data were collected.

Grounded theory   An inductive research approach characterized by first collecting data and then generating a theory to explain the data.

GUI   Acronym for graphical user interface (pronounced GOO-ey).

Hardware   The physical machines associated with data processing (e.g., a computer, monitor, scanner, printer).

Hypothesis   A prediction or best guess about relationships between variables that are to be studied.

Identity   A topological overlay operation in which the entire area of the identity polygon, including the overlapping portions of any other polygons, is retained.

Import   A process by which data from one computer program are brought into another computer program.

Independence   A statistical concept referring to the fact that knowing a particular event or data value makes it no more or less likely for a subsequent event or data value to occur (e.g., flipping a coin and getting heads has no bearing on the probability of getting heads on a second flip of a coin because the samples are independent).

Independent variable   In research, the examination of how fluctuation in this variable influences the dependent variable under study. Conceptually, it is assumed that variations in the independent variable influence the dependent variable of a study and not vice versa.

Index   A value that does not represent a true, measured variable but rather is used to represent placement on an ordinal scale.

Indicator variable   A variable that is used to substitute for the real variable of interest. For example, using level of education as an indicator of overall intellectual capital of a community.

Individual level variable   A microlevel variable. These data are related to a single entity or unit of analysis within a study.

Inductive research   Process in which researchers first collect data and then seek to develop an understanding of patterns observed. The researchers' understanding of the research topic and potential hypotheses emerge from the data.

Inexact interpolator   A statistical estimator that predicts values at sample locations that are not required to have the same value as the original sample. The underlying assumption with inexact interpolators is that the sampled values are not necessarily true values and have some error.

Information   The result of an analysis of data that provides some useful understanding of relationships observed.

International Standards Organization   An international body, also known as ISO, that sets the standards for a wide variety of disciplinary and industrial applications. In the use of GIS, the ISO defines standards for geospatial metadata much in the same manner as the FGDC in the

United States. At present the ISO has defined norms for the documentation of spatial data (ISO 19115), and many countries, including the United States, are working to harmonize their national standards with those defined by ISO 19115.

Internet   A collection of interconnected computer networks that provides public access to a wide variety of data and information using online computer technology.

Interpolation   A statistical technique used to estimate values between sampled locations.

Intersection   A topological overlay operation in which the overlapping portions of the input polygons are retained.

Interval   Continuous data grouped into ranges with a natural order. The distances between values associated with the data are meaningful and exist at set intervals. There is no absolute zero point.

ISO   Acronym for the International Standards Organization.

Key informant   An individual who is knowledgeable about the particular issue or topic under study.

Key-informant interview   An interview conducted with a key informant. Key-informant interviews are a common method of qualitative data collection in the social sciences.

Key variables   Variables perceived as being central to a research project.

Latitude   A geographic reference for the distance in degrees north or south of the equator.

Layer   An individual data set or theme in GIS. For instance, you could have a data layer of economic information that you overlay with data based on race for the same geographic region.

Least cost analysis   A process that finds the most efficient or least expensive path through the data space.

Likert scale   An ordinal scale used in the social sciences to numerically measure differences in attitudes/level of agreement or disagreement with a particular statement.

Line   In vector GIS, one of three basic data types. Line features are a one-dimensional element having length but no width and are often used to map linear features, such as roads, rivers, or connected networks.

Linear regression   A statistical analysis technique in which one seeks the best fit of a straight line to sample data points by minimizing residuals between the sample points and the line.

Locational error   An error in which a feature is placed at an incorrect (X, Y) location in the spatial data set. Small measurement errors are an expected part of any data set. The acceptable error of location is typically determined by the specifications for the project or by one or more established standards (e.g., United States National Map Accuracy Standards).

Logical data model   A model that adds specific processing steps to the conceptual data model, thus specifying the analytical procedures necessary to complete the analysis.

Longitude   A geographic reference for the distance in degrees east or west of the prime meridian.

Longitudinal study   A study that collects information about a particular phenomenon over a specified time period.

Map algebra   Data manipulation and analysis via the mathematical combination of raster GIS map layers.

Map completeness   How thorough a data set is at the time of publication, typically included as part of the metadata. Incomplete preliminary data sets often include additional information on expected date of completion or anticipated update cycle.

Masking   A means of hiding or obscuring geographic detail either to provide confidentiality or to eliminate some portion of the original data from the analysis.

Mathematical model   The use of known relationships within the data, as determined through prior research, to develop a procedure for analyzing new or different data sets in a similar context. This approach is particularly effective when using raster GIS and map algebra techniques.

MAUP   An acronym that stands for modifiable area unit problem.

Metadata   All information that relates to the data.

Modeling   Development of a series of analysis steps that are designed for a particular analytical situation.

Modifiable area unit problem   Also known as MAUP, the concept that as one alters the geographic area of the study boundary the results obtained from the analysis can change. Adjustments need to be made in the analysis or interpretation of results in recognition of these variations.

Monte Carlo simulation   An analysis approach in which multiple runs, or realizations, of the results are obtained by varying the input data using known or anticipated statistical distributions for error.

Multivariate regression   A type of statistical analysis that examines the estimated relationship between a dependent variable and multiple explanatory variables.

NAD27   Acronym for North American Datum 1927.

NAD83   Acronym for North American Datum 1983.

National coordinate system   A local coordinate system for referencing map locations. National coordinate systems are developed by many countries and used in addition to several coordinate systems commonly used on a global scale.

Nearest neighbor analysis   A process that determines the closest location to a point of interest or the closest location to any other location on the map (e.g., can be used to determine how far it is from a home to the closest hospital).

Network analysis   An analysis method for the examination of connections or flow between locations or individuals. This approach is commonly accomplished with specific software in the social sciences, although it is an integral component of most GIS software packages.

NGO   An acronym that stands for nongovernmental organization.

Node   A location of activity or interest in a network analysis, often located at the intersection of activity between two or more entities in the study. In GIS, a node also refers to a point location with the special characteristic of being at either the beginning or the end of a line.

Nominal   Data with qualitative differences that exist without hierarchy, often recorded with names. Analysis of these data is typically limited to simple counts or descriptive statistics. Sometimes for convenience nominal data are coded by assigning numbers to categories of physical or social data to indicate differences.

Nondiscreet data   Data that do not have clearly defined geographic boundaries; data that change value gradually through space, as in a temperature gradient.

Nongovernmental organization   Also known as an NGO, a good source of data for use in GIS. A number of NGOs already use GIS in their own data development and analysis.

Nonlinear regression   A form of regression analysis that uses higher order polynomials (lines that have one or more inflection points) to more accurately fit a line to the data.

Nonprobability sampling   A type of sampling that is nonrandom. Elements are selected arbitrarily from the population, meaning that individual elements have different probabilities of being included in the sample. There is no means to estimate sample variability or bias using these methods.

Nonspatial data   Data that lack a spatial element, either because spatial information was not recorded or because a spatial element is not present in the data.

Nontraditional geographies The use of traditional mapping or geographic techniques in the analyses of data not typically explored using these techniques (e.g., using mapping techniques to examine the concept of social distance between individuals in an organization).

North American Datum 1927 Also known as NAD27, one of the commonly used mapping datums in the United States, based on the 1866 Clarke ellipsoid, which estimates the size and shape of the earth.

North American Datum 1983 Also known as NAD83, one of the commonly used mapping datums in the United States based on the 1980 Geodetic Reference System ellipsoid developed from satellite-based measurements of the size and shape of the earth.

Number field A column in a database table that is set to hold integer or decimal values as opposed to letters or other characters.

NVIVO® A computer program for the analysis of qualitative data.

Observation Part of the data collection process in which the researcher is aware of or actively records data about the social or physical environment, or both.

Open source A computer software program made available with the underlying programming code to facilitate understanding, modification, and improvements to the software by anyone who uses it. Open source software is made available on the Internet free of charge.

Operationalization The process of deciding how one is going to go about measuring key concepts in a research project or study.

Oral history A qualitative research method in which a researcher gathers individuals' stories and histories associated with a particular place, event, or issue.

Ordinal A data type that has a natural ordering to the data but has no quantitative component to define the relative amount or difference between the values (e.g., a Likert scale using options such as *strongly disagree, disagree, neutral, agree, strongly agree*).

Origin In mapping, the point on the surface of the earth that is defined as the zero for both the X and the Y axis. The origin varies depending on the coordinate system selected for the map.

Output Any number of results that might come from a GIS analysis, including data, maps, statistics, charts, or other information.

Overgeneralization An inappropriate simplification of data. Overgeneralization can occur when a sample size is too small or is collected with an invalid sampling method and thus does not accurately represent the intended study population. It can also occur when the results of one study are inaccurately extended to other situations where they may not apply.

Overlay   In research analysis, the process of placing one layer of information on top of another to look for patterns, changes, or interactions in the data.

Parameter   Individual variables defined as relevant to the analysis or model.

Parameterization   The process of selecting variables for a model, typically via a statistical analysis to determine the relevance or use of each variable to the model.

Participant observation   A type of field research in which the researcher actually takes part as a member of the group or activity being studied.

Physical boundary   An actual boundary that exists or is explicitly defined (e.g., road, census block, state line).

Physical data model   The final phase of model abstraction in which one lays out the software specific steps, commands, or menu options to accomplish the processing necessary for the analysis.

Physical feature   A feature that exists in physical form on the surface of the earth and can therefore be mapped clearly and explicitly.

Pilot study   An initial test of proposed methods for a research project on a smaller scale to assess how well they work prior to conducting the main research project.

Pixel   Picture element. A pixel is commonly used to refer to the smallest unit of a digital image as on a computer monitor, digital camera, or computer scanner. The term *pixels* is also sometimes used less appropriately to refer to a raster cell in raster GIS.

Point   A nondimensional feature type in vector GIS that provides an (X, Y) location but has no inherent size. Specialized point features in GIS may also act in other capacities (as a node or vertex) to serve as a component of lines or polygons.

Polygon   A two-dimensional feature type in vector GIS that represents a contained or aerial feature (e.g., a neighborhood or city boundary or an area representing the spatial unit of analysis).

PowerPoint®   A commonly used computer program that allows for the presentation of information in graphical and text formats in slideshow form.

PPGIS   An acronym that stands for Public Participation GIS.

Primary data   Data collected by the researcher who originates the research project or issue under study.

Prime meridian   A line running along a true north–south line through Greenwich, England, which is defined as 0 degrees longitude.

Probability map   A map designed to display the likelihood of correctness as a probability, between 0% and 100%, as part of its cartographic design.

Probability sampling   Sampling that incorporates a form of random sampling such that all members of the population being sampled have an equal likelihood of selection.

Project goal   The primary outcome sought in carrying out a research project.

Projection   A process by which the spherical earth is flattened to a page or computer screen.

Proximity   A measure of closeness or nearness, either with the intent to find the single closest location or to locate a group of locations or an area with a characteristic of being nearby.

Proximity polygon   An area around a point or feature that is closer to that feature than to any other in the data set. *See also* Voronoi diagram.

Public participation GIS   Also known as PPGIS, a GIS process in which the general public is actively involved in the creation, use, and employment of a GIS.

Purposive sampling   A nonprobability sampling approach in which respondents are selected because the researcher believes they will provide an appropriate representation of the population.

Pythagorean theorem   A fundamental theorem of Euclidean geometry by which the distance between two points can be determined if one knows the length of two legs of a right triangle. In a mapping context, the lengths of the two legs are calculated as the difference between the X values and the Y values of the two points in question.

Qualitative data   Information that is primarily descriptive and nonnumeric; uses words to convey meaning and description.

Quantitative data   Information that consists of numeric data (typically interval or ratio values); uses numbers to convey meaning.

Query   A database term meaning to ask a question, typically via a specified structure known as Structured Query Language or SQL.

Quota sampling   Proportionately selecting members from a specific subgroup for sampling.

Range   The limits of the values a function can take (e.g., the values range from 0 to 1).

Raster One of the two commonly used GIS data models. Raster data are made up of a matrix of (usually) square cells of fixed size.

Ratio The highest level of measurement in which data are recorded as real numbers relative to an absolute zero. Referring to map scale, the ratio of distances on the map relative to distance on the ground (e.g., a ratio of 1:24,000 is the scale of a common USGS quadrangle).

Realization A single possible outcome of an analysis given a set of data and their associated errors. In a Monte Carlo simulation, the error values would be varied within a defined range to provide multiple or a distribution of possible outcomes for a given analysis.

Real-time analysis An analysis conducted immediately as the data are obtained (e.g., projecting the winner of an election as exit poll data are obtained throughout election day).

Recategorization The process of altering the grouping categories of data for purposes of analysis or reporting of output.

Record In a database, the data for an individual sample or entity, most often placed in an individual row of the data table.

Reliability The quality and consistency of measurement.

Respondent A person who completes a survey or interview.

Sample A selected subset of the larger population.

Scale The relative size of a map as compared to the real world. Scale can be reported in three ways on a map: visual (scale bar), verbal (e.g., 1 in. = 1 mile), or ratio (a unitless fraction, such as 1:24,000).

Scaleless Data collected without any associated scale (e.g., GPS point locations). A GIS is scaleless in that it does not impose a scale on any data entered into the system, but most source materials do have an associated scale.

Secondary data Data previously collected by someone else, perhaps with a different purpose in mind; existing data (e.g., the U.S. Census). Researchers often rely on secondary data as a part of the research process.

Simplification A process of making detailed map data less complex by removing excess detail (e.g., leaving out every bend in a map of a river channel).

Simulation An analysis using known characteristics of a process or model to experiment with real or hypothetical outcomes using the computer as opposed to implementing the experiment in reality. Simulations are often useful in comparing various options before making a decision.

Snap distance A defined distance within the GIS environment for which points closer together are assumed to be the same point and are connected and for which points farther apart are assumed to be separate and not moved or adjusted.

Snowball sampling   A type of sampling in which the researcher relies on subjects already interviewed to provide information on further potential research subjects.

Social capital   Social networks and the degree to which a community pools its social resources to work together.

Social distance   Measurable differences that exist between social science variables, such as race or class (e.g., a great deal of social distance exists between the rich and the poor).

Social justice   The concept of a fair and equal society in which there is equitable access to resources and the benefits that arise from those resources.

Socially constructed boundary   A boundary based on something social, such as a political boundary or a boundary based on social class.

Social network   Social connections between people that can be formal or informal.

Sociodemographic data   Descriptive information related to people or groups of people. Sociodemograhic data can include income, race, class, gender, or age.

Socioecological   Simultaneously social and environmental.

Sociospatial   Simultaneously social and spatial.

Sociospatial research   Research that includes both social and geographic variables.

Software   The computer programs that are used in conjunction with computer hardware to accomplish a variety of data collection, conversion, storage, analysis, and output functions.

Software package   A specific program, often from a specific vendor, that is designed to provide a complete solution to specific tasks. Software packages often include associated licenses, software support, and documentation.

Source map   The original map on which a GIS data set is based (e.g., the primary or secondary map data used in a GIS analysis).

Source scale   The scale of the original map on which a GIS data set is based, regardless of what scale the map is viewed at within the GIS software.

Spatial   Positional information or data and how the data's position positively or negatively influences the data itself or other features in the same or nearby locations.

Spatial accuracy   How closely a position is mapped relative to its true position on the surface of the earth.

Spatial analysis   Any analytical process in which the position of the data is considered to be an essential component of the analysis.

Spatial analysis technique   The specific analytical tools designed to consider the positional component of the data as a core component of the process. GIS software packages offer a variety of these tools as a major component of their suite of tools.

Spatial autocorrelation   A determination of the interrelatedness of variables in relation to the spatial position of the variable.

Spatial coding   Attaching a location (e.g., an X, Y position) to each piece of data to be incorporated in a GIS analysis.

Spatial correspondence   Things that occur together in space.

Spatial data   Data that are associated with a position in space, most often a real location on the ground (e.g., a street address). This may also refer to data associated with a conceptually defined or hypothetical position in space (e.g., the strength of interpersonal relationships).

Spatial extent   The geographic limits of a region of interest, which may include an entire study region or smaller areas representing units of analysis.

Spatial interpolation   A technique for the estimation of data at unsampled locations based on the relative position of those locations to known, sampled locations on the landscape as well as any underlying trends or processes in space.

Spatial question   A question involving something about a geographic location or the relationship between characteristics of features based on their relative positions.

Spatial relationship   Relationships based on geography or position in space.

Spatial tool   Any tool designed to account for and consider positional information as a component of the data. Spatial tools may include GIS software as well as a vast array of stand-alone or add-on software components, including software for data collection, manipulation, or analysis of spatial data.

SPC   Acronym for State Plane Coordinate.

SPSS®   An acronym that stands for Statistical Package for the Social Sciences.

Spurious correlation   An apparent correlation between data sets that is not the result of a true, statistically significant relationship between those data sets.

State Plane Coordinate A coordinate system in the United States that is derived on a state-by-state basis to provide an accurate set of local origins and control points for each individual state or portion of a state.

Static map A map designed to be unchanging; most commonly associated with printed maps, which can only be updated by manual means or by reprinting. Static map may also refer to static graphic map images on a computer.

Statistical Package for the Social Sciences® Commonly referred to as SPSS®, a popular statistical analysis program used in the social sciences.

Surrogate ground truth An alternative to actually visiting a site on the ground in person to confirm conditions. Typically, surrogate ground truthing is accomplished via the use of a second reliable data source, such as another map, an aerial image, or another data set (e.g., using archival aerial photos to determine in which year a particular subdivision was constructed).

Survey In mapping, a set of techniques and protocols for mapping locations on the surface of the earth relative to an established control grid. In the social sciences, surveying is a means of data collection via a set of predetermined questions administered either in writing or verbally.

System A set of interrelated components, including hardware, software, data, and trained individuals, used together to accomplish an objective, in the case of GIS, to conduct spatial analysis.

Table A data file consisting of rows and columns in which rows represent individual samples and columns represent data characteristics about those samples. *See also* attribute table.

Time series data Data collected at different points in time about a particular variable for a sample entity.

Topological relationships The spatial relationships and connectivity within or between data.

Trend A characteristic of data in which a general direction or tendency is present (e.g., an upward trend in the life expectancy of individuals).

Triangulation In the social sciences, studying the same phenomenon using three different research methods. Triangulation is used in mapping to describe the process of calculating a distance to a location by knowing the length of one side of a triangle and the related angles.

Union A topological overlay operation in which the entire area of both input polygons is retained.

Unit of analysis The level of measurement in which one connects data to an entity (e.g., individual, group, community, watershed, state, country). The unit of analysis can be social or geographic.

United State Geological Survey   Also known as USGS, a U.S. federal government agency with significant responsibility for mapping the nation. The USGS provides a variety of common data sets, many in GIS formats.

Universal Transverse Mercator   Also known as UTM, a global metric coordinate system to provide an accurate set of origins and (X, Y) grids for each of 60 UTM zones in the northern hemisphere and for each of 60 UTM zones in the southern hemisphere.

Unix   An operating system for what were traditionally more powerful computer workstations common to a variety of government agencies and academic institutions. With the advent of powerful personal computers, Unix and the more commonly available open source equivalent Linux have become popular options for smaller organizations and individuals.

USGS   An acronym that stands for the United States Geological Survey.

UTM   An acronym for Universal Transverse Mercator.

Validity   Congruency between the concepts to measure and the measurement techniques; in other words, does your study really measure the concept that you set out to measure?

Variability   The naturally occurring fluctuations in measurement or mapping the location of data.

Variable   A domain of attributes that relate to a particular concept.

Vector   One of two commonly used GIS data models. Vector data are made up of three basic feature types—point, line, and polygon. Vectors are especially appropriate for discreet data types.

Vertex   A point along a line or polygon boundary where the direction of the line changes, typically used for the purpose of providing shape.

Virtual reality   A simulated view or experience similar to that experienced in the real world. Virtual reality is useful in experimenting with various possible alternatives without the risk of unexpected or undesired outcomes.

Visualization   A means of presenting data in a visual form to provide an alternative means of analysis and understanding. Visualization techniques may include scatter plots, charts, maps, or virtual reality simulations.

Voronoi diagram   A map partitioned into polygons so that each polygon represents the area closest to a particular point on the map.

WGS84   Acronym for World Geodetic System 1984.

World Geodetic System 1984   Also known as WGS84, a commonly used worldwide mapping datum based on an earth-centered ellipsoid developed from satellite-based measurements of the size and shape of the earth.

ZIP file   A system that facilitates data compression to create a smaller file that takes up less space.

Web Links _____

The following link is to the Web site for this book. This site is a home to the growing community of social scientists using GIS. It is a place where scientists can share ideas, ask questions, provide examples, and give feedback.

Social Science GIS: http://www.socialsciencegis.org

The following links provide information regarding several of the most popular commercial GIS software packages:

Autodesk: http://www.autodesk.com

Environmental Systems Research Institute (ESRI): http://www.esri.com

Intergraph: http://www.intergraph.com

MapInfo: http://www.mapinfo.com

The following sites are general reference sources for your GIS-based research.

Archives of the [New York City] Mayor's Press Office, May 13, 1997: Press release from the New York City Mayor's Office about the use of CompStat in reducing crime to its lowest level in 30 years. http://www.ci.nyc.ny.us/html/om/html/97/sp268–97.html

Atlas of Canada: An example of an interactive GIS Web site. http://atlas.gc.ca/

Atlas of Sweden: An example of an interactive GIS Web site. http://www.sna.se/

Bibliography of Map Projections: A bibliography containing about 3,000 articles related to map projections from the scientific and professional literature. Although this resource goes far beyond the requirements of most GIS users, it does provide a sense of the vast array of projections and projection issues that one might consider. http://www.ilstu.edu/microcam/map_projections/Reference/Bu111856.pdf

Cartographic Communication: Part of a larger geography education Web site developed by Kenneth E. Foote and Shannon Crum of The Geographer's Craft Project, Department of Geography, The University of Colorado at Boulder. http://www.colorado.edu/geography/gcraft/notes/cartocom/cartocom_f.html

Center for Spatially Integrated Social Sciences (CSISS): An organization that recognizes the growing significance of space, spatiality, location, and place in social science research. It seeks to develop unrestricted access to tools and perspectives that will advance the spatial analytic capabilities of researchers throughout the social sciences. CSISS is funded by the National Science Foundation under its program of support for infrastructure in the social and behavioral sciences. http://www.csiss.org/

Centers for Disease Control and Prevention: An array of national databases related to public health, disease, births, and deaths. http://www.cdc.gov/

CommunityViz: This program of The Orton Family Foundation, the Vermont-based, nonprofit operating foundation, is dedicated to helping communities make better, more responsible land use planning decisions. http://www.communityviz.com/

"CompStat: From Humble Beginnings": An article on the history and development of Compstat as a spatial analysis tool for crime. http://www.baselinemag.com/article2/0,1397,538007,00.asp

"Demystifying the Persistent Ambiguity of GIS as 'Tool' Versus 'Science'": This site provides an article by Dawn Wright, Michael Goodchild, and James Proctor. http://dusk.geo.orst.edu/annals.html

Federal Geographic Data Committee: The focal point for U.S. federal standards and information related to metadata, content standards for metadata, and the National Spatial Data Infrastructure. http://www.fgdc.gov

FirstGov: Web portal to all U.S. federal and state government Web sites. http://www.firstgov.gov/

FreeGIS.org: A clearinghouse for a wide variety of free, open source GIS tools. http://www.freegis.org

The Geographer's Craft: This site provides coverage of most key geographic mapping concepts as well as references and additional links. http://www.colorado.edu/geography/gcraft/contents.html

"The Geographer's Craft": Chapter on cartographic communication. http://www.colorado.edu/geography/gcraft/notes/cartocom/cartocom_f.html

The Geographer's Craft (Map Projections Overview): This is a direct link to the section on map projections. http://www.colorado.edu/geography/gcraft/notes/mapproj/mapproj_f.html

GIS.com: A general GIS portal managed by the Environmental Systems Research Institute (ESRI)®, one of the major GIS software providers. It offers a variety of general information and resources relevant to getting started with GIS technology. http://www.gis.com/

The GIS Lounge: A general GIS portal offering a variety of general information and links related to GIS technology, software, data, and other related resources. http://gislounge.com/

"The GIS Primer, Data Analysis": A good overview of many of the analysis approaches, by David J. Buckley, Corporate GIS Solutions Manager, Pacific Meridian Resources, Inc. http://www.innovativegis.com/basis/primer/analysis.html

GRASS GIS: GRASS is a raster-based GIS package that is freely available and runs on most computer platforms. http://grass.baylor.edu

"Grounded Theory: A Thumbnail Sketch": This site, from the Resource Papers in Action Research Web site, is a nice overview of grounded theory. www.scu.edu.au/schools/gcm/ar/arp/grounded.html

The Grounded Theory Institute: This entire site is devoted to the methodology of grounded theory. www.groundedtheory.com

Housing Patterns: U.S. Census Bureau site regarding choice of units of analysis for census data analysis. http://www.census.gov/hhes/www/housing/resseg/unitofanalysis.html

"The Influence of Data Aggregation on the Stability of Location Model Solutions": This article explores the influence of data aggregation on census block group data. www.ncgia.ucsb.edu/~jgotts/murray/murray.html

Map Projections: A good overview of projections as well as references and software tools related to map projections and conversions. http://www.geography.hunter.cuny.edu/mp/

National Aeronautics and Space Administration: This site provides a variety of imagery and monitoring data for the world or portions thereof. http://www.nasa.gov

National Atlas of the United States: http://nationalatlas.gov/

National Map of the United States: http://nationalmap.usgs.gov/

Natural Resources Canada: A variety of national data sets, including aerial images, geographic places, maps, and topographic information. http://www.nrcan-rncan.gc.ca/inter/index_e.html

Natural Resources Canada: Multivariate statistics and spatial autocorrelation. http://www.pfc.forestry.ca/profiles/wulder/mvstats/spatial_e.html

"Network Analysis—Network Versus Vector—A Comparison Study": An article by Jan Husdal, University of Leicester, UK. http://www. husdal.com/mscgis/network.htm

New York City Police Department, CompStat Process: A description of how Compstat is incorporated into the processes of community-level crime analysis, planning, and prevention. http://www.nyc.gov/html/nypd/html/ chfdept/compstat-process.html

"Notes Regarding the Principles of Cartographic Design": From an online discussion list of the Cartographic Society. http://www.shef.ac.uk/ uni/projects/ sc/cartosoc/1999/Nov/msg00044.html

NYU Information Technology Services: Focus on GIS: A listing of GIS links. http://www.nyu.edu/its/socsci/GIS/

Open Geospatial Consortium, Inc. (OGC): A nonprofit, international, voluntary consensus standards organization leading the development of standards for geospatial and location based services. http://www. opengeospatial.org

Oral History Association: This organization, established in 1966, seeks to bring together all persons interested in oral history as a way of collecting human memories. http://omega.dickinson.edu/organizations/oha/

Oral History Society: This national and international organization is dedicated to the collection and preservation of oral history. http://www. oralhistory.org.uk/

PPgis.net: This electronic forum focuses on participatory use of geospatial information systems and technologies. http://ppgis.iapad.org/

Primary Data Collection Methods: From the Thames Valley University dissertation guide Web site. http://brent.tvu.ac.uk/dissguide/hm1u3/hm1u3text3. htm

"Public Participation GIS (PPGIS) Guiding Principles": This article is by Doug Aberley and Renee Sieber. http://www.urisa.org/PPGIS/2003/papers/ PPGIS%20Principles2.pdf

"Raster GIS Packages Finally Receive Well-Deserved Recognition": Article by W. Fredrick Limp, Director, Center for Advanced Spatial Technologies, University of Arkansas, Fayetteville. http://www.geoplace. com/gw/2000/0500/0500re.asp

The R Project: The starting point for the R statistical analysis environment. Note links from the homepage to R spatial projects of particular interest to those doing spatial analysis with data from GIS. http://www.r-project.org

"Social Sciences: Interest in GIS Grows": This article was written by Michael F. Goodchild of the Center for Spatially Integrated Social Science,

University of California, Santa Barbara. http://www.esri.com/news/arcnews/ spring04articles/social-sciences.html

Social Statistics Briefing Room: Whitehouse site links to social statistical data. http://www.whitehouse.gov/fsbr/ssbr.html

StatSoft, Inc. (2004): A complete introductory statistics textbook online, including sections on measurement scales, sampling, and analysis. http:// www.statsoft.com/textbook/stathome.html

U.S. Census Bureau: This is the official site of the U.S. Census and includes demographic data, TIGER files, and other related data. http://www. census.gov

U.S. Census 2000 GIS Data: http://www.census.gov/geo/www/census2k. html/

U.S. Department of Labor, Bureau of Labor Statistics: Occupational Outlook Handbook: This is the link to the handbook's entry on social scientists. http://stats.bls.gov/oco/ocos054.htm

U.S. Environmental Protection Agency: A variety of national databases related to environmental quality. http://www.epa.gov

U.S. Geological Survey: This site provides a variety of national data sets, including aerial images, geographic places, maps, and topographic information. http://www.usgs.gov

USGS Map Projection Decision Support System: An interactive Web interface to assist in determining an appropriate map projection for any portion of the globe. http://helios.er.usgs.gov/research/DSSMain/DSSApplet. html

U.S. National Institute of Health: http://www.nih.gov/

References _____

Addams, J. (1895). *Hull-House maps and papers, by residents of hull-house, a social settlement, a presentation of nationalities and wages in a congested district of Chicago, together with comments and essays on problems growing out of the social conditions.* New York: Crowell Publishers.

Arlinghaus, S. L., Goodman, F. L., & Jacobs, D. (2004). *Buffers and duality.* Retrieved March 21, 2005, from http://www.personal.umich.edu/~sarhaus/image/solstice/win97/solsb297.html

Babbie, E. (2003). *The practice of social research* (10th ed.). Belmont, CA: Wadsworth/Thompson Publishing.

Bernard, R. H. (2000). *Social research methods: Qualitative and quantitative approaches.* Thousand Oaks, CA: Sage.

Brinkerhoff, D. B., White, L. K., Ortega, S. T., & Weitz, R. (2005). *Essentials of sociology* (6th ed.). Belmont, CA: Wadsworth.

Brown, N. (2004). *Florence Kelly: Slums of the great cities survey maps, 1893.* Retrieved March 21, 2005, from http://www.csiss.org/classics/content/35

Carey, M. A. (1994). The group effect in focus groups: Planning, implementing and interpreting focus group research. In J. M. Morse (Ed.), *Critical issues in qualitative research methods* (pp. 225–241). Thousand Oaks, CA: Sage.

Corbett, J. (2004). *Mark Jefferson: Civilizing rails, 1928.* Retrieved March 21, 2005, from http://www.csiss.org/classics/content/12

Dey, I. (1999). *Grounding grounded theory: Guidelines for qualitative inquiry.* San Diego, CA: Academic Press.

Dillman, D. (1999). *Mail and Internet surveys: The tailored design method.* New York: John Wiley and Sons.

Federal Geographic Data Committee. (2000). *Content Standard for Digital Geospatial Metadata workbook.* Reston, VA: Author.

Glaser, B. G. (1978). *Advances in the methodology of grounded theory: Theoretical sensitivity.* San Francisco: University of San Francisco Press.

Glaser, B. G., & Strauss, A. L. (1967). *The discovery of grounded theory: Strategies for qualitative research.* Chicago: Aldine Publishing Company.

Goodchild, M. (2003). Foreword. In Z. R. Peng & M. H. Tsou (Eds.), *Internet GIS: Distributed geographic information services for the Internet and wireless networks* (p. iv). Hoboken, NJ: John Wiley and Sons.

Henslin, J. M. (2003). *Down to earth sociology: Introductory readings.* New York: The Free Press.

Jefferson, M. (1928). The civilizing rails. *Economic Geography, 4,* 217–231.

Openshaw, S., & Taylor, P. J. (1979). A million or so correlation coefficients: Three experiments on the modifiable real unit problem. In N. Wrigley (Ed.), *Statistical applications in the spatial sciences* (pp. 127–144). London: Pion.

Park, R., Burgess, E. W., & McKenzie, R. D. (1925). *The city.* Chicago: The University of Chicago Press.

Schaefer, R. T. (2004). *Sociology* (9th ed.). New York: McGraw Hill.

Snow, J. (1855). *On the mode of communication of cholera.* London: John Churchill.

Strauss, A., & Corbin, J. (1998). *Basics of qualitative research: Techniques and procedures for developing grounded theory* (2nd ed.). Thousand Oaks, CA: Sage.

U.S. Census Bureau. (1990). *TIGER/Line data.* Washington, DC: Author.

U.S. Census Bureau. (2000). *QT-H1. General housing characteristics: 2000. Census summary file 1 100 percent data. Gabbs City, Nevada.* Retrieved April 15, 2005, from http://factfinder.census.gov/servlet/BasicFactsServlet

Index _____

About the Authors _____

Steven J. Steinberg is an associate professor of environmental and natural resource sciences at Humboldt State University, Arcata, California. He received his bachelor's degree from Kent State University, Ohio; his master's from The University of Michigan, Ann Arbor; and his doctorate from The University of Minnesota, Twin Cities. He has been involved extensively in the development and teaching of geographic information systems (GIS) and remote sensing courses in both the university and professional development arenas. Since coming to Humboldt State University, Dr. Steinberg has taught and developed a variety of courses in the area of GIS, remote sensing, and spatial data analysis, with an emphasis on human interactions with social and environmental surroundings. His recent research interests include the development of simple, Web-based spatial analysis tools. He also has interests in the interactions between people and their surroundings through the use of spatial analysis techniques. As cofounder and director of Humboldt State University's Advanced Spatial Analysis Facility, Dr. Steinberg has overseen a variety of GIS and spatial analysis projects and research with organizations and government agencies in northern California and elsewhere. He was selected as a Fulbright Scholar for 2004–2005, serving as distinguished chair in airborne remote sensing with the Centre for Scientific Computing at Simon Fraser University, Burnaby, British Columbia, Canada. During 2005–2007, he is participating as part of an interdisciplinary team of scientists at Humboldt State University on a National Science Foundation project extending research experience to undergraduate students in a cross-disciplinary computing modeling and applications environment.

Sheila L. Steinberg is associate professor of sociology at Humboldt State University, Arcata, California. She completed her bachelor's at the University of California, Santa Barbara; her master's at the University of California, Berkeley; and her doctorate at The Pennsylvania State University. Her research interests include sociospatial research, applied sociology, community development, and environmental sociology. She has conducted field research in Nepal, Guatemala, New Mexico, Pennsylvania, and northern

California. The theme throughout this research has been the examination of people and their relationship to space and place. Her current research examines social and human capital for rural communities that have experienced an altered physical and social environment. In 2000, she joined Humboldt State University, where she now teaches courses on human interactions with the physical environment at the local, national, and global levels.